THE COURT-MARTIAL
OF GENERAL GEORGE ARMSTRONG CUSTER

Lawrence A. Frost

THE
COURT-MARTIAL
OF GENERAL
GEORGE
ARMSTRONG
CUSTER

by Lawrence A. Frost

University of Oklahoma Press : Norman

By Lawrence A. Frost

The Custer Album (Seattle, 1964)
The U. S. Grant Album (Seattle, 1966)
The Court-Martial of General George Armstrong Custer (Norman, 1968)

The paper on which this book is printed bears the watermark of the University of Oklahoma Press and has an effective life of at least three hundred years.

Library of Congress Catalog Card Number: 67–24614

Copyright 1968 by the University of Oklahoma Press, Publishing Division of the University. Composed and printed at Norman, Oklahoma, U.S.A., by the University of Oklahoma Press. First edition.

To my wife, Ethel, and to my daughter, Jill

FOREWORD

NEVER TO MY KNOWLEDGE, has the complete story been told of the court-martial of General Custer. Dr. Frost has spent many years searching for little-known source material relating to this interesting event in the career of my great-uncle.

The court-martial was an obvious attempt by high officials to white-wash the disastrous Hancock expedition in answer to the public's cry for a victim. It was this Hancock expedition that provided Uncle Autie with the Indian experience that motivated Generals Sherman, Sheridan, and Sully to ask for his early reinstatement to lead them to victory over the depredating Indians.

To Dr. Frost, one of the country's foremost authorities on the General's army career, the entire Custer family is indeed grateful for this clear, authentic presentation of a most important chapter in the life of the General.

Colonel BRICE C. W. CUSTER, U.S.A. (*Retired*)

PREFACE

THE YEAR 1867 marks the period in the life of George Armstrong Custer in which he became "Indian-wise," if that can be said of any white man. He had an enviable Civil War reputation and record, but he had yet to experience the tactics of the wily red man. It was a type of warfare to which he was unaccustomed but to which he readily adapted himself.

Anxious to understand the Indian mind and methods of warfare, he used every opportunity to obtain information from his guides and interpreters. On numerous occasions councils were held with the Indians in attempts to obtain information and to study them further.

Although Custer was in command of the cavalry, the officer commanding the expedition was Major General Winfield S. Hancock. Hancock, too, had a fine Civil War record but, like Custer, knew nothing about fighting Indian-style. He now had a foe who would not stand up and fight but who, on attack, would disappear in a fashion that made it impossible to follow.

That the summer campaign was a series of disappointments and disillusionments was clearly evidenced by the clamor of Congress and the press.

When a ranking officer in the disastrous campaign made the wrong move it was the subject of a diversionary court action that relieved some of the pressure. The resulting court-martial was the headline news of the day. Momentarily, Custer's luck had deserted him.

Few civilians and relatively few military personnel have had the opportunity of observing a court-martial.

The verbatim proceedings of the Custer court-martial of 1867 included herein have been transcribed from a microfilm of the original. No attempt has been made to alter the text or spelling, although repetitious legal formality has been eliminated where it does not affect the continuity or meaning.

The original transcript consists of 350 pages of longhand. Its publication has been made possible through the kindness of the Judge Advocate General, Department of the Army, through the kind intercession of Richard O. Wood, War Records Branch of the General Services Administration.

I am most grateful to Edward M. Beougher of Grinnell, Kansas, for supplying valuable material, assistance and legal opinions. His knowledge of the Smoky Hill Trail exceeds that of any other living person. To travel over it with him in stagecoach and army ambulance (he did it on horseback) is an experience never to be forgotten.

There are many to whom I am indebted. My good friend Colonel Brice C. W. Custer, U.S.A., (retired) gave the manuscript a critical reading and supplied much useful information. His brother, Colonel Charles Custer, U.S.A., (retired) and his son, Lieutenant Colonel George A. Custer, III, also were valuable informants. The late Major Edward S. Luce loaned me valuable source material. The Devin-Adair Company graciously granted permission to quote from Merington's *The Custer Story*. Attorney Corwin C. Spencer of Oakley, Kansas, Edgar Langsdorf and Nyle H. Miller of the Kansas Historical Society, Emma Sihler of the Adrian Public Library, Mrs. Elleine H. Stones of the Burton Historical Collection, Ruth Abrams of Grand Rapids Public Library, Everett Sutton of Benkelman, Nebraska, Mrs. Martha Barker and Mrs. Raymond Pyle of the Monroe County Historical Museum, Alva Dorn of Kalamazoo, Richard Wehner of Monroe, and staff members of the following institutions: the Dorsch Memorial Library (Monroe), the Toledo Public Library, the Ohio Historical Society, and the Chicago Westerners Brand Book, were exceedingly helpful.

My secretary Mrs. Jack Jennette deserves special praise. Her great interest and watchful eyes revealed many errors.

My wife Ethel saved me from many hours of toil by assisting me in many ways.

I would be remiss if I did not give particular thanks to William F. Kelleher of Cliffside Park, New Jersey, for his fifteen years of constant encouragement.

And special acknowledgment goes to my companion on a three-day trip over the Smoky Hill stage route to test out various theories—former Seventh Cavalryman Howard B. Berry of Milan, Michigan.

LAWRENCE A. FROST

Monroe, Michigan
June 25, 1967

CONTENTS

ILLUSTRATIONS

THE COURT-MARTIAL
OF GENERAL GEORGE ARMSTRONG CUSTER

"If I were an Indian, I often think that I would greatly prefer to cast my lot among those of my people who adhered to the free open plains, rather than submit to the confined limits of a reservation, there to be the recipient of the blessed benefits of civilization, with its vices thrown in without stint or measure."

—George Armstrong Custer

I. KANSAS
WAS CONCERNED

IT WAS WAR TO THE FINISH for the Kansans. Hostile Indians had murdered, robbed and raped hundreds of their citizens. Construction workers on the Kansas Pacific Railroad had been driven from their work, leaving behind many of their mutilated dead. Travel and communication were at a standstill. The year was 1867.

Governor Samuel J. Crawford did not intend letting the Plains Tribes run Kansans off their lands. He had permission from Lieutenant General William T. Sherman to muster eight companies of volunteer cavalry.[1] This he made known in his July first proclamation.

The Kansas governor was not a man to take the responsibilities of his office lightly. A graduate of law school, having served as an officer in both infantry and cavalry during the Civil War just over, and now thirty-two years of age, he had the vitality, temperament and enthusiasm necessary to meet the peculiar and monumental problems of a new state.

His first term of office, just completed, had been a stormy one, for there were opponents who tried to take over. A dissenting group of politicians known as "The Third House"[2] did everything in its power to obstruct progress and obtain personal profit, but finally it was

---

[1] Samuel J. Crawford, *Kansas in the Sixties*, 258; 40 Cong., 2 sess., *House Exec. Doc. 1*, 35.

[2] Crawford, *Kansas*, 206.

squelched. The term had ended with some improvement, for the chaos Crawford had inherited was now less apparent. His second term had a smoother start.

The Cheyenne Indians had had a taste of the white man's sense of honor at Sand Creek, Colorado Territory, in 1864. Trustingly encamped under an American flag which Cheyenne Chief Black Kettle had raised on his lodgepole, and under guarantees of neutrality, the Cheyennes had been shockingly attacked and massacred by volunteer troops led by Colonel J. M. Chivington. A wave of horror and distrust spread across the plains from tribe to tribe.

They had observed and resented the lawless aggressions and encroachments of the white men, and had witnessed the total disregard for treaties they trustingly had signed. The Sand Creek Massacre was vivid evidence of the white men's forked tongues. This feeling of distrust was evident on the Pawnee Fork in Kansas in April of 1867, when Sioux and Cheyennes abandoned their camp to General Winfield S. Hancock who, mistaking their motives, totally destroyed it.

During 1866 Indians had haunted the old Santa Fe Trail, committing depredations along the valleys of the Smoky Hill, Solomon, Republican, and Platte rivers. The settlers, overland trains, and railroad-grading parties had been the subject of these raids. By July of that year the Kansas Pacific Railroad had been completed to Junction City, from which point the overland stages and wagon trains continued west. The track construction progressed from two to three miles daily whenever the laborers were protected by troops.[3]

In 1867, Indian attacks began to increase with the melting of the spring snows.[4] As the Kansas Pacific reached out to follow the northerly side of the Smoky Hill River across the "Great American Desert," its work crews and surveyors became the subjects of repeated raids. Observers described the Indians as Arapahos and Cheyennes.[5]

The "Great American Desert," so-called because it was a vast plain covered with an overlay of rich grass each summer, extended from

[3] 40 Cong., 2 sess., *House Exec. Doc. 1*, 34; Crawford, *Kansas*, 224, 230–31; Henry B. Carrington, *Ab-Sa-Ra-Ka*, 262.

[4] 40 Cong., 2 sess., *House Exec. Doc. 1*, 28.

[5] *Ibid.*, 34.

4

eastern Kansas to the nearest slopes of the Rocky Mountains. On it grazed millions of antelope, deer and buffalo.[6]

The Indians, though looked down upon as barbarians by their white contemporaries, were intelligent enough to realize that the vast hordes of immigrants following the course of this new railroad along the Smoky Hill would drive the game before them. Game, particularly buffalo, was the Indians' source of food, clothing, shelter and fuel. From the hides they obtained their tipi covers, their clothing, and other leather goods. The flesh served as food, and the bones were used for implements and ornaments. Droppings, or "chips," provided fuel on the woodless prairies. The professional buffalo hunter, who was subsequently to destroy the herds, was not foreseen at this point.

Of immediate concern to the Indians was the encroachment of the immigrants, settlers, and miners and the establishment of military posts and railroads, the latter obviously hastening the advance of an objectionable civilization.

Railroad-grading parties, overland wagon trains, stage lines, and settlers felt the increasing pressure of the raiders. The Indians had developed a distrust because of the white man's disregard for previous treaties. It soon became apparent that the Indians believed they could harass the railroad builders enough to prevent further construction.

Governor Crawford had made repeated requests for federal military aid. Few troops had been shuffled around during the summer of 1866, for there were not many available; and it was not until October that Lieutenant Colonel George Armstrong Custer was sent to Fort Riley to command and prepare the newly formed Seventh United States Cavalry regiment for the field.[7]

Although most of the Indians had entered their winter camps, and

[6] Crawford, *Kansas*, 231.

[7] *Army Register for 1866*, 34. A brevet major general famed as a cavalry leader during the Civil War, Custer reverted to the rank of captain in the Fifth Cavalry at the end of the war. When four additional cavalry regiments were formed in 1866, he was appointed a lieutenant colonel in the Seventh Cavalry. Regardless of these changes in rank, many persons continued to refer to him as "General Custer," both in speaking of and writing about him.

Many of Custer's fellow officers experienced similar changes in rank, sometimes causing a certain amount of confusion of titles. (See also footnote, page 98, below.)

5

raids were infrequent, an overwhelming disaster occurred on December 21, 1866, at Fort Phil Kearny in Dakota Territory. Colonel William J. Fetterman and eighty-one officers and men were completely destroyed by an Indian ambush.[8] This was an emphatic declaration to the whites that they should go back east; as an Indian sign, it meant "White men, go home." The line had drawn thin.

The Cheyenne, Kiowa, and Arapaho Indians began serving notice on the army post commanders, stagecoach drivers, and Indian agents that as soon as the grass grew they would insist on the white man withdrawing from the routes of travel.[9] These three tribes had banded together to oppose the construction of the Union Pacific Railroad on the north side of the Platte River. The five hundred lodges of Cheyennes heartily disliked the government and its inroads, while the Sioux nation, composed of some five hundred lodges, all hostile and warlike, contrived to influence the Arapahos, who had been friendly to the whites until that time. United, they presented a foreboding front.

In response to the increasing number of complaints about Indian raids, General William Tecumseh Sherman became quite concerned about the territory under his supervision. As commander of the Military Division of the Missouri, he decided upon a personal appearance along the Platte. Once in the area, and having observed for himself, he concluded that, "As usual, I find the size of the Indian stampedes and stories diminished as I approach their location." He found the telegraph lines intact, stage coaches traveling without interruption, and overland travelers unmolested. The few Indians he did see were "more to be pitied than feared."[10] However, by the time he had left Fort McPherson and reached Fort Laramie, some killings had occurred along the Smoky Hill route. He recommended to General Grant, who was general-in-chief, that a wide belt of land between the Platte and the Arkansas rivers, including the Union Pacific and Kan-

---

[8] 40 Cong., 2 sess., *House Exec. Doc. 1*, 34; Crawford, *Kansas*, 224, 230–31; *Indian Operations on the Plains*, 50 Cong., 1 sess., *Senate Exec. Doc. 33* (hereafter cited as *Indian Operations on the Plains*), 36–51; H. B. Carrington, *The Indian Question*, 21–28.

[9] 40 Cong., 2 sess., *House Exec. Doc. 1*, 34.

[10] 39 Cong., 2 sess., *House Exec. Doc. 23*, 5–8; Donald J. Berthrong, *The Southern Cheyennes*, 266.

sas Pacific Railroads, be cleared of Indians for the exclusive use of overland transportation. The Indians should be confined to their reservations well away from this area, and be controlled by the army.[11]

Sherman concluded that the farmers and ranchers were exploiting the Indian stories in order to sell their grain, feed, and cattle to the expanding garrisons and cavalry troops. He planned to place the Indians near civilized tribes so they would become self-sustaining through a knowledge of agriculture. This plan had no opportunity to mature before the Sioux took command of the situation.[12]

As previously noted, the Indians, chiefly Sioux, but including some Arapahos and Cheyennes, lured Colonel Fetterman and his detachment five miles out of Fort Phil Kearny, and then killed them. This development caused Sherman to write his brother, United States Senator John Sherman, that it now appeared to him such affairs would be repeated since the Sioux and Cheyennes would not settle down, and the only means by which trouble could be avoided in the future would be extermination of these tribes.[13] At the time, Custer and his newly formed Seventh Cavalry were at Fort Riley, some six hundred miles to the southeast of Fort Kearny.

Singling out Major General Winfield S. Hancock to take charge of a spring campaign against them, Sherman conveyed to him his philosophy of offering "no quarter" to Indians.[14] Hancock followed this philosophy when a party of sixty-five warriors from Black Kettle's Cheyenne camp stole forty cavalry horses from Fort Harker. He ordered the guilty Cheyennes turned in to him, at the same time expressing the hope his command would be refused so he would have cause to exterminate them.[15] He had just been studying reports that indicated the Cheyennes had destroyed the Chalk Bluff stage station on the Smoky Hill River and killed the stocktenders there.[16]

There seems to have been considerable dissatisfaction among the Indians at this time too, apparently because of an unequal distribution

---

[11] 40 Cong., 2 sess., *House Exec. Doc. 1*, 36–37; Berthrong, *Cheyennes*, 267–68.
[12] *Ibid.*
[13] *Indian Operations on the Plains*, 36–51.
[14] Robert G. Athearn, *Sherman and the Settlement of the West*, 130–31.
[15] Berthrong, *Cheyennes*, 268–69.
[16] *Difficulties With Indian Tribes*, 41 Cong., 2 sess., *House Exec. Doc. 240* (hereafter cited as *Difficulties With Indian Tribes*), 138–43.

7

of presents from the whites. Kicking Bird, a chief of the Kiowas, informed Major Henry Douglass, commandant of Fort Dodge, that at a council of the Arapahos, Cheyennes, Comanches, Kiowas, Sioux, and Apaches, it was agreed that they would begin a war as soon as the grass was old enough.[17]

Brigadier General John Pope had written Washington that: ". . . the government every day is stimulating immigration. Where under such circumstances is the Indian to go? It is useless for the government to think of undertaking to subsist large bodies of Indians in remote and inaccessible districts. Whatever may be the right or the wrong of the question our past experiences in America reveal that the Indian must for the most part be dispossessed. The practical question to be considered is how the inevitable can be accomplished with the least inhumanity to the Indian."[18] He knew that as a military commander he was required to protect the immigrants, the mails, and the settlements. The government had to go on or back out in the face of an increasing migratory move to the west. No one seemed to know what was the right thing to do.[19]

Since it had become apparent in military circles, that the Indians were planning action when circumstances permitted, General Hancock issued General Orders No. 16, restricting sale of arms and ammunition to the Indians for their hunting needs. He also ordered a discontinuance of the practice of allowing Indians to visit or loiter about the posts, permitting none but important chiefs in the interior of a military post.[20]

As an on-the-spot observer at Fort Dodge, post commander Major Douglass was keeping General Sherman informed. Early in January he had indicated that the Indians had been supplied continuously with breech-loading carbines, revolvers, powder, lead, and percussion caps. These sales were made by Indian traders over and above the arms and ammunition given out by the Indian agents as authorized by the Commissioner of Indian Affairs. He had observed that several hundred Indians had visited his post and none had less than one revolver and

---

[17] *Ibid.*, 47; 40 Cong., 2 sess., *House Exec. Doc. 1*, 28.
[18] J. R. Perkins, *Trails, Rails and War*, 180.
[19] *Difficulties With Indian Tribes*, 98–99.
[20] *Ibid.*, 41.

some had as many as three. All had more than an ordinary supply of ammunition.[21]

For a revolver, an Indian would give ten to twenty times its value in horses or furs. Similar rates prevailed for the purchase of powder and lead. The anxiety of the Indians to procure them indicated to Douglass that they were laying in a supply preparatory to an outbreak. Between the authorized Indian agents and the traders, the Indians had never been better armed. It was Douglass' observation that the Interior Department did not appreciate the danger of arming Indians, nor did it have any control over the traders who were profiting from such transactions.

At that time there were 1,800 Cheyennes and 750 Arapahos on the Upper Platte River. Kiowas and Comanches numbered about 2,800.

Captain Henry Asbury, Third United States Infantry, had sent a report from Fort Larned, Kansas, noting the combined begging for food and the threats of Satanta, a chief of the Kiowas. He also mentioned that the Indians had cause to complain because they did not get treaty goods from their agent, Colonel J. H. Leavenworth, and added, "I think it only hastens, but will not be the cause of, the impending troubles."[22]

In Washington the Kansas situation was being discussed at President Johnson's cabinet meetings. Secretary of Interior Orville H. Browning, newly appointed to the cabinet, vehemently opposed Secretary of War Edwin M. Stanton's approval of recent military orders.

At a full cabinet meeting on March 19, Stanton justified orders given by western military commanders prohibiting licensed Indian traders from supplying moderate quantities of arms and ammunition to "friendly" Indians, on the grounds that an Indian war was imminent and "that at such a time the Indian agents and traders must be subordinated to the military authorities."

Browning maintained that the arms and ammunition were necessary for the subsistence of the Indians and the withholding order was the cause of the great discontent among them. He opposed Stanton "on the grounds that the supplies were to friendly Indians only, who

[21] *Ibid.*, 46–48; William H. Leckie, *The Military Conquest of the Southern Plains*, 33.

[22] *Ibid.*, 50.

were entitled to have them under existing laws and treaties—that such supplies were necessary to enable the Indians to support themselves and families, and that refusing to furnish them, and thus exposing the Indians to starvation, was well calculated to provoke instead of preventing war." He contended that the Indian agents were best qualified by temper, disposition, and constant contact with their charges to determine what might be safely supplied in the way of arms and ammunition, and to whom it might be issued. He added that all of the Indians were at peace and most anxious to remain so, and that they were under the exclusive control of the Department of the Interior, whose agents were not subject to the supervision of the military: in the event of war he would not interfere with the military—in peace he would manage without military interference. He concluded by asking to have the military orders recalled, since he proposed to issue a circular to his agents embodying his views. Although strongly resisted by Stanton, the President and the cabinet supported Browning.[23]

The cabinet meeting of March 29 was occupied with a discussion of the newly issued Browning circular. Again Browning requested that the military orders subjecting his agents to the supervision of military officers be withdrawn. The entire cabinet agreed with Browning that the orders were wrong and should not have been issued without his approval, but Secretaries Seward and McCulloch doubted the propriety of recalling the orders immediately.[24]

At the cabinet meeting of April 9, Secretary Stanton presented a letter from General Sherman recommending, in view of an Indian war, that three companies of three western regiments be filled to their maximum of one hundred men each. There was also a recommendation from General Grant that the army be increased from fifty thousand up to eighty thousand men. Sherman's request was approved but Grant's request was denied. Grant's suggestion was renewed by Stanton at the next cabinet meeting and again was turned down.[25]

In Kansas, Governor Crawford reacted by declaring that, "There, under the same Government, was the War Department, with an army in the field, endeavoring to suppress Indian hostilities, and at

[23] Orville Browning, *The Diary of Orville Hickman Browning*, 138.
[24] *Ibid.*, 140.
[25] *Ibid.*, 143.

the same time, the Interior Department, furnishing the same hostile Indians with supplies and munitions of war. Back of the Interior Department was a gang of thieving Indian agents in the West, and a maudlin sentimentality in the East, derived from James Fenimore Cooper's novels[26] and impressed upon that department by ignorant but well-meaning humanitarians."[27]

He outlined hundreds of cases in which the Indians killed, scalped, pillaged, captured, and outraged Kansas settlers which, in answer to his protests to the Indian agents, brought forth the statement that their Indians were peaceful and harming no one.

Finally, in April of 1867, Governor Crawford visited General Grant in Washington to offer co-operation in the protection of the Kansas frontier. He also visited Secretary Browning, but found him unadvised and even indifferent to his story of the hostile Indians and their depredations. Browning informed him that *if* there should be any such trouble he would attend to it at the proper time. The energetic Crawford told him *the time had arrived*, for why else was Hancock in the field endeavoring to hold the miscreants back? He continued to say that agents and traders had supplied the hostile Indians with food and clothing during the past winter and were now supplying them with arms and ammunition to be used against the people of Kansas during that spring and summer, and he thought it was about time to let up on that particular "humanitarian" policy. Although Browning agreed to discontinue the issuance of arms and ammunition to the various tribes, Crawford hardly got home before this promise was disregarded.[28]

However, the trip was not unfruitful, for Crawford had first visited New York, where he had sold $130,000 worth of general obligation bonds. This would soothe some of the frontier state's growing pains.[29] And, even though obstructed by Browning, he had made his point with Generals Sherman and Hancock, for he had informed them of the Indian preparations on the plains of Kansas.

He had received numerous letters and petitions asking for relief

---

[26] Cooper was a nineteenth-century American novelist.

[27] Crawford, *Kansas*, 263.

[28] *Ibid.*, 249–50.

[29] *Ibid.*, 249.

from the Indian murders and robberies. By June the situation had worsened to the point of suspending construction of both the Kansas Pacific and the Union Pacific railroads. Over a thousand laborers of the Union Pacific Railroad had been driven in because of the murder and scalping of their men by renegade Indians.[30]

As a result of his appeal to Secretary Stanton for an Indian-fighting army, authority was granted for the issue of necessary supplies and guns to a volunteer force in Kansas. Four companies, designated as the Eighteenth Kansas Cavalry, were mustered in on July 15; some three hundred men in all.[31]

Meanwhile, on March 11 General Hancock advised Colonel Leavenworth, the Indian agent for the Comanches and Kiowas, that he was preparing an expedition to the plains for the purpose of convincing the Indians within the limits of his department (Department of the Missouri) that the government was able to punish any who might molest travelers across the plains or commit any other hostilities against the whites.

He asked Leavenworth to instruct the Indians to keep off the main routes of travel, since their presence tended to bring on difficulties with the whites. The communication ended by inviting him to accompany the expedition in case he was unable to settle the matter satisfactorily, thereby showing the tribes to be visited that the officers of the government acted in harmony. On this same day a similar communication was sent to Colonel E. W. Wynkoop, Indian agent for the Cheyennes, Apaches, and Arapahos.[32]

On March 14 General Sherman sent orders from St. Louis to General Hancock which were, in part:

> The fact that the management of Indian affairs is left by Congress in the control of the Department of the Interior, deprives us of a legal right to control them and prevents our adopting preventive measures. We are compelled to respect the Indian treaties because they are the law of the land, obligatory on all, especially on us who are intrusted with the execution of the law. We are bound also to respect the authority of the commissioners or agents, who are charged

[30] *Ibid.*, 255.
[31] *Ibid.*, 260, 281.
[32] *Difficulties With Indian Tribes*, 16–17.

with the intercourse and control of the various tribes, and to leave them to manage all questions not amounting to actual war. You need not, therefore, make demand on the Cheyennes for the drunken fellow who killed the New Mexican at Zarah last fall, nor for the party who killed the men and carried off the stock at the stage station, at Chalk Bluffs, on the Smoky Hill route, last year. Leave these cases to the agents and so notify them.

Our duty is to protect our own people, while engaged in their lawful and natural pursuits, against all enemies of whatever race or color. This embraces citizens who have made settlements on surveyed lands, or other lands where it is lawful for them to make locations; all mail routes established by law; all roads traveled through Indian country established by competent authority, or to which a right had accrued by former implied consent; and especially we are bound to protect and command the respect due our own authority as represented by forts, stations, and troops on the march.[33]

General Sherman made note of the Cheyennes, Arapahos, and Kiowas assembling in large numbers near the post on Smoky Hill and advised that they be checked immediately, and should they want war to notify them that they could have it at once.

Accordingly, General Hancock gave notice to Colonels Wynkoop and Leavenworth on March 22 that he would make no demands upon the Indians for past depredations, that there would be no war unless the Indians commenced hostilities, and that he was prepared to aid the agents in controlling, arresting, or punishing any who might be guilty of outrages or depredations.[34]

On March 26 General Hancock gave orders that the troops of the expedition, while on march and in camp, would receive orders from Andrew J. Smith, colonel of the newly formed Seventh United States Cavalry. Smith, like Custer, had been brevetted a major general during the Civil War. Instructions, when necessary, would be given Colonel Smith by the major general commanding, (General Hancock) who accompanied the expedition.

Hancock was at Fort Riley, Kansas, at the time. To make his position clear he issued an order stating that:

It is uncertain whether war will be the result of the expedition or

[33] *Ibid.*, 98.   [34] *Ibid.*, 94.

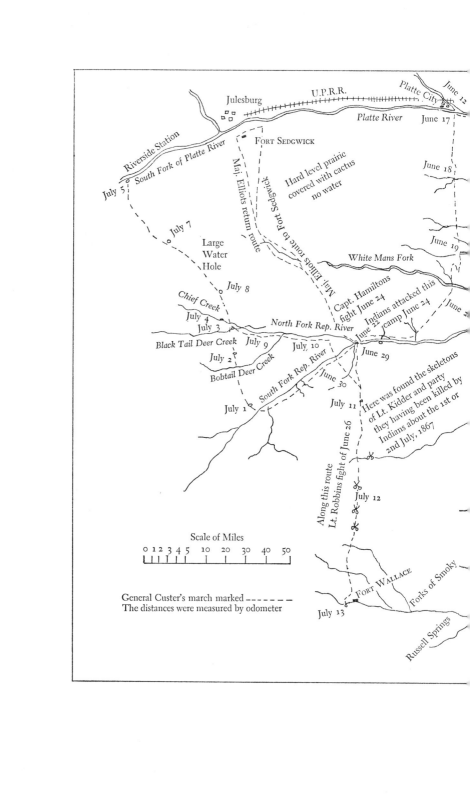

Julesburg   U.P.R.R.   Platte City June 12

Platte River   June 17

Riverside Station

South Fork of Platte River

FORT SEDGWICK

June 18

July 5

Hard level prairie covered with cactus no water

Maj. Elliots route to Fort Sedgwick

Maj. Elliots return route

July 7

June 19

Large Water Hole

White Mans Fork

July 8

Chief Creek

Capt. Hamiltons fight June 24

July 4

Indians attacked this

June 22 camp June 24

June 2

July 3

North Fork Rep. River

June 24

Black Tail Deer Creek   July 9   July 10

July 2

June 29

Bobtail Deer Creek

South Fork Rep. River

June 30

July 11

Here was found the skeletons of Lt. Kidder and party they having been killed by Indians about the 1st or 2nd July, 1867

July 1

Along this route Lt. Robbins fight of June 26

July 12

Scale of Miles

0 1 2 3 4 5   10   20   30   40   50

FORT WALLACE

Forks of Smoky

General Custer's march marked – – – – – –
The distances were measured by odometer

July 13

Russell Springs

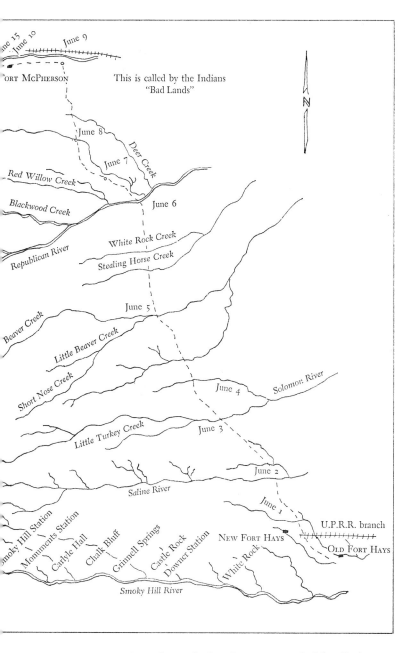

Route of the Custer cavalry column during the summer of 1867. Redrawn from the original linen map in the author's collection.

not . . . We go prepared for war, and will make it, if a proper occasion presents. We shall have war if the Indians are not well disposed toward us . . . .

No insolence will be tolerated from any bands of Indians who we may encounter. We wish to show them that the government is ready and able to punish them if they are hostile, although it may not be disposed to invite war. In order that we may act with unity and in harmony with these views, no one but the commander present, on detachment or otherwise, will have interviews with the Indians.[35]

Custer later wrote, "Of the many important expeditions organized to operate in the Indian country, none, perhaps, of late years has excited more general and unfriendly comment, considering the slight loss of life inflicted upon the Indians, than the expedition organized and led by Major General Hancock in the Spring of 1867."[36]

Hancock took the newly formed Seventh Cavalry, the Thirty-seventh Infantry with Light Battery B, and the Fourth Artillery to the region of Fort Zarah and then to Forts Larned, Dodge, Hays, and Harker. He had three regiments of cavalry in his command, but was short at that time because he was using the Third Cavalry in New Mexico, while the Tenth Cavalry, which was all Negro, was being enlisted. Since the Seventh Cavalry was the only regiment immediately available, it was shifted from the Smoky Hill to the Platte River and back again, as the Indian hostilities shifted from road to road.[37]

United States Indian Agent Leavenworth arrived at Fort Zarah, Kansas, April 3, and General Hancock two days later with his entire command of some fifteen hundred men. Hancock invited Leavenworth to accompany the expedition to the Pawnee Fork about thirty-one miles from Fort Larned, and Hancock arranged a council with the Cheyenne chiefs for April 10.[38] On April 9 eight inches of snow fell and the council was postponed until the return of good weather. From this point Hancock was subjected to a display of Indian diplomacy.

It soon became apparent that the Indians did not intend to approach

---

[35] *Ibid.*, 12–13.

[36] G. A. Custer, *My Life on the Plains*, 22.

[37] 40 Cong., 2 sess., *House Exec. Doc. 1*, 34–35.

[38] G. A. Custer, *My Life*, 22.

the troops, nor did they wish the troops to approach them. They had sent word on the eleventh that they had started toward Hancock's camp but had discovered a large herd of buffalo, which they proceeded to hunt.

On the evening of the twelfth several Cheyenne chiefs and a dozen warriors visited the camp and asked to hold a conference with General Hancock. In General Custer's words:

> A large council fire was built in front of the General's tent and all the officers of his command assembled there. A tent had been erected for the accommodation of the chiefs a short distance from the General's. Before they could feel equal to the occasion, and in order to obtain time to collect their thoughts, they desired that supper might be prepared for them, which was done. When finally ready they advanced from their tent to the council fire in single file, accompanied by their agent and interpreter. Arrived at the fire, another brief delay ensued. No matter how pressing or momentous the occasion, an Indian invariably declines to engage in council until he has filled his pipe and gone through with the important ceremony of a smoke.[39]

Hancock explained the purpose of his expedition, emphasizing that it was to promote peace. He expressed his regret that there were not more chiefs present and announced his intention of visiting the village in the morning to hold a council with all the chiefs. The Indian replies were rather vague.

Edmond Guerrier, one of General Hancock's interpreters, noting the Indians' repeated requests to Hancock not to come any closer to their camp, stated that they thought the visit was not intended to be a peaceful one or Hancock would not have brought so many soldiers with him.[40]

On the morning of April 13 the entire force marched from Fort Larned up Pawnee Fork toward the Indian village, a distance of about twenty-one miles. Shortly before reaching camp they were met by several chiefs and warriors of the Cheyenne and Sioux tribes. They stayed with the troops all night, and on the following morning the Sioux chief Pawnee Killer left camp at an early hour with the avowed

[39] *Ibid.*, 24.
[40] George Bird Grinnell, *Fighting Cheyennes*, 243–44.

purpose of arranging for the return of all the chiefs for a nine o'clock council. No chiefs had arrived by 11 A.M., so Hancock decided to move his forces upstream nearer the village, so the council could be held in his camp that night.

Of this Custer said:

> At 11 A.M. we resumed the march, and had proceeded but a few miles when we witnessed one of the finest and most imposing military displays, prepared according to the Indian art of war, which it has ever been my lot to behold. It was nothing more nor less than an Indian line of battle drawn directly across our line of march; as if to say, thus far and no further. Most of the Indians were mounted; all were bedecked in their brightest colors, their heads crowned with the brilliant war-bonnet, their lances bearing the crimson pennant, bows strung, and quivers full of barbed arrows. In addition to these weapons, which with the hunting-knife and tomahawk are considered as forming the armament of the warrior, each one was supplied with either a breech-loading rifle or revolver, sometimes with both—the latter obtained through the wise foresight and strong love of fair play which prevails in the Indian Department, which seeing that its wards are determined to fight, is equally determined that there shall be no advantage taken, but that the two sides shall be armed alike; proving, too, in this manner the wonderful liberality of our Government, which not only is able to furnish its soldiers with the latest improved style of breech-loaders to defend it and themselves, but is equally able and willing to give the same pattern of arms to their common foe. The only difference is, that the soldier, if he loses his weapon, is charged double price for it; while to avoid making any such charge against the Indian, his weapons are given to him without any conditions attached.[41]

When Hancock saw this strange array on his front the command was given to draw sabers and, at the same time, the infantry brought their muskets to a carry. Hancock rode forward, accompanied by his officers. Through an interpreter he asked the chiefs to meet him half-way, to which they responded. After shaking hands, Hancock inquired about the hostile attitude just presented and declared that if they wanted war he would provide it. They replied that they wanted

[41] G. A. Custer, *My Life*, 25.

no war. Following this Hancock told them he would march to the village and camp near it, but would prohibit any soldiers from molesting it. It was then arranged that the chiefs would meet for council at Hancock's headquarters after camp was made. When they arrived they brought news that the women and children had fled upon the approach of the troops. Hancock asked some of the chiefs to go after their women and children, since he meant them no harm, offering them good horses for that purpose. It was Guerrier who returned the horses that evening with a message from the warriors that their people had scattered so far it was impossible to find them.

When Hancock was informed that the warriors were leaving the village he ordered Custer to surround and search it. The village was found empty except for an old, infirm Indian and a half-blood child that had been horribly mistreated.[42] The Indians had left nearly three hundred lodges, a thousand buffalo robes, and numerous utensils of considerable value to them in their great haste to evacuate.

Concerning this development Indian Agent Wynkoop then wrote to Hancock: ". . . I regard the late movement of the Cheyennes of my agency as caused by fear alone . . . Your movement toward the Indian village terrified the squaws and children, who left with such movable property as they could gather. . . ." He understood that Hancock intended destroying the Indian village and requested that he not do so, since it would result in a serious Indian outbreak. Further, he said that he was certain there was no evidence that this band of Cheyennes deserved any punishment.[43]

It is evident that the Cheyennes and Sioux had just cause for their panic. The approach of so many soldiers was an ample reminder of a similar occasion in which they trustfully observed the approach of soldiers only to be shot down in cold blood. They had no intention of permitting a second Sand Creek massacre. Their solution was flight.

General Hancock's inability to understand the Indians with whom he was counciling and his inability to convince them of his friendly intentions, was a major reason for the Indian mistrust. The Cheyennes and Sioux, too, were having trouble understanding each other.

[42] Henry M. Stanley, *My Early Travels and Adventures in America*, I, 241; *Difficulties With Indian Tribes*, 14, 52, 64–65, 130; G. A. Custer, *My Life*, 82.
[43] *Difficulties With Indian Tribes*, 27.

It seems that dialectal changes in the language of the southern Cheyennes and Arapahos were creating a barrier rather difficult to overcome. Lack of effective communication was the order of that day.

Then Agent Wynkoop reported to his commissioner: "I am sorry to say that the [Hancock] expedition is disastrous. . . . I am fearful that the result of all this will be a general war, which is much deprecated, as there are many unprotected whites on the different roads across the plains and at the mail stations and ranches." Wynkoop was writing from Hancock's camp on the Pawnee Fork.[44]

It was at early dawn on this same day, April 15, that Colonel Custer was ordered in pursuit of the escaping Indians. With him were a number of Delaware Indian scouts and two guides whose special assignment was following the trail. He headed for Walnut Creek and on toward the Smoky Hill River, intending to cover forty or fifty miles each day. Captain William G. Mitchell thought Custer and his eight troops would probably go between Forts Wallace and Hays in pursuit of the Cheyennes. Custer had but two days' forage and rations.[45]

Reporting to Hancock on the sixteenth, Custer told him that they were close on the trail on Walnut Creek; in fact, so close that the Indians' fires were found burning and several of their horses and a mule were found tied to trees, still bearing packs. None of the Indians had been seen by his command, although his Delaware scouts, while in the advance, had seen small numbers watching from the heights at a distance. At times they had been so close that the earth had been damp in the pony tracks and lodgepole drag marks.

Custer had placed the wagons under the direction of a squadron so that he might travel faster. The Indians, seeing him gain upon them, broke up into numerous small bands and separated. The main trail rapidly disappeared and the troops were forced to halt. They had traveled thirty-five miles, stopping only to water the horses. While the troops set up camp, the Delawares scouted six miles beyond, but were unable to continue the trail because the ground was too dry and hard.

Smoke signals were seen ten miles distant to the north, east and

[44] *Ibid.,* 130–31.
[45] *Ibid.,* 64.

west. At 4 A.M. of the sixteenth the soldiers set out to follow the valley of a small stream for some miles, but no sign of Indians was discovered. The search then was directed north toward the Smoky Hill, with the intent of moving toward Fort Dodge.

After some reflection it was Custer's thought that: "The hasty flight of the Indians and the abandonment of, to them, valuable property, convinces me that they are influenced by fear alone, and it is my opinion that no council can be held with them in the presence of a large military force . . . Captain Robert M. West, of the Seventh Cavalry, and possessed of great experience with Indians, is firmly of the opinion that they (the Cheyennes) have gone north or south." Here was sage counsel.[46]

On April 17 Leavenworth reported that General Hancock had decided not to burn the Indian village and had ordered every article taken from the village be returned. He reported further that Custer had *not* seen any of the Indians he had been pursuing, and sarcastically added, "fifteen hundred Indians escape and not one is seen."[47]

Custer's communique of April 17 to Hancock was sent from Downer's Station on the Smoky Hill. In it he stated that his troops had covered twenty-one miles since leaving camp on Walnut Creek, striking the Smoky Hill thirteen miles west of Downer's Station, and there encamped. It was there he ascertained that travel was expected to cease on this route since the Indians had attacked Lookout Station the day before, killing and burning the three men employed there, as well as burning the station and hay and running off with eighteen horses and mules.[48]

General Hancock did not know which way to turn. A strong desire to destroy the Indian village overwhelmed him, because it would look good, according to the military standards of the Civil War, to be able to report in large figures the amount of enemy property destroyed or captured. However, General Smith was adverse to any such action.

Hancock's uncertainty ever since his contact with the village and

[46] *Ibid.*, 68–69.
[47] *Ibid.*, 131.
[48] *Ibid.*, 69–70.

even since the inception of the campaign could be attributed to his in-experience in Indian warfare. "What to do" had been his theme from the beginning. On April 17 he had written General Smith that he "... had better inform General Custer that there is much doubt about the propriety of destroying this camp, that should he pass this way and find that I had not done so, to leave it untouched, unless he has in the meantime met with resistance, in which case he should burn the camp, lodgepoles and all, carrying off all its tools, kettles, iron, etc.

"Whether to attribute the abandonment of this village to a panic entirely or not can scarcely be determined until we hear if the Indians have committed hostilities anywhere; if they have, we will regret not having destroyed this camp."[49]

In another letter to Sherman on that same day he told more of the young Indian girl who had been found raped in the village. The youngster had identified her assailant as an Indian.[50] Agent Wynkoop had said earlier: "I firmly believe that the soldiers ravished the child. It was the conclusion I arrived at when I heard she was ravished...."[51]

An issue over the incident developed between the agents and the military, for Leavenworth immediately reported to his commissioner that it was evident the girl was neither a Cheyenne nor a Sioux. It was mutually agreed, however, that she was eight years of age and horribly mistreated. From this point there was a variation of view: Fall Leaf, a Delaware chief, advised Hancock she was neither Sioux nor Cheyenne, but was a half-blood captive. Hancock was convinced she had been attacked by Indians, since he had taken the early pre-caution of surrounding the village with his guards to prevent any disturbance. In *Tenting on the Plains*, Mrs. Custer quotes her as saying "The Indian men did me bad."[52]

[49] *Ibid.*, 66.
[50] *Ibid.*, 65; Grinnell, *Fighting Cheyennes*, 244; Theodore R. Davis, "A Summer on the Plains," *Harper's Monthly Magazine*, Vol. XXXVI (February, 1868), 296; Stanley, *Early Travels*, I, 39–40; G. A. Custer, *My Life*, 32; *Difficulties With Indian Tribes*, 65, 130; George W. Manypenny, *Our Indian Wards*, 170.
[51] Stanley, *Early Travels*, I, 241.
[52] Elizabeth B. Custer, *Tenting on the Plains*, 577–78.

II. DIFFICULTIES
WITH THE INDIAN TRIBES

Custer's communique of April 17 gave Hancock a way out of his dilemma because it had indicated there was ". . . no doubt but that the depredations committed at Lookout Station were by some of the same Indians who deserted their lodges on Pawnee Fork, and whose trail I followed until they broke up into small bands." All signs pointed to the return of the Indians to the Platte River and signified that the promised time of attacking "when the grass came up," had arrived.[1]

On the nineteenth Hancock received another dispatch from Custer, this time from Fort Hays. A war party of eight hundred Sioux, Pawnees and Cheyennes had been seen there four days earlier, heading north, stripped, painted and armed for war.

Custer had stopped at Lookout Station and found the bodies of the murdered trio. A party of men from the Big Creek Station, the next stop east, had attempted to burn them but, either through fear or lack of proper implements, had only covered them with some poles. The wolves had managed to uncover them and had eaten some flesh off their legs. They had been burned beyond recognition and their intestines had been torn out, the latter not having been done by the wolves.

After properly burying the victims near the station, Custer re-

[1] *Difficulties With Indian Tribes*, 69–70.

ported that "I failed, as did the Delaware Indians, to discover the slightest clue as to what tribe committed the act." He added: "Lookout Station was burned and the men massacred on Monday, the 15th, which clears those Indians and the men massacred at Pawnee Fork the day of our arrival from the charge of being present at the murder. I am confident, however, that the act was committed with their knowledge and approval, which accounts for their hasty flight."[2]

At Fort Hays he was detained by lack of forage; only a day's supply was available. Before Custer left, Hancock had been assured by his chief quartermaster, Captain George W. Bradley, that there would be an eight-to-ten-day supply there. It was impractical to march across country with the limited grazing available, so Custer sent "Wild Bill" Comstock to Fort Harker with an urgent request for four days' forage for the command. To continue pursuing the Indians northward was useless. His only solution was to rejoin Hancock.

Hancock could hold back no longer, so on the morning of the nineteenth he completely destroyed the Sioux-Cheyenne village of 251 lodges. This included 942 buffalo robes, 436 saddles, and numerous housekeeping articles. Reporter Henry M. Stanley wrote that it would take three thousand buffalo to replace the skins used in the wigwams destroyed.[3]

Wynkoop reported to Indian Commissioner Taylor that the Indians had left, in his judgment, with the belief that Hancock had come to perpetrate another Sand Creek affair, stating that "Thus, in my opinion, has another Indian war been brought about which might have been averted by the military authorities pursuing a different line of policy."[4]

Reporting to General Smith on the twenty-first that he was "perfectly satisfied with General Custer's movements," since he had "exercised sound discretion in not returning to join us at Pawnee Fork

[2] *Ibid.*, 72–74.

[3] *Ibid.*, 26, 132–34; Stanley, *Early Travels*, I, 46.

[4] *Difficulties With Indian Tribes*, 132. On November 8, 1864, Colonel J. M. Chivington, with more than eight hundred men and four pieces of artillery, attacked a peaceful camp of one hundred lodges of Cheyennes and eight or ten lodges of Arapahos. Each lodge held about five Indians, over half of whom were women and children. The killing and acts of barbarism continued for over two hours, until more than one hundred bodies could be seen. Three-fourths of the Indian dead were women and children. This dastardly massacre occured in Colorado on Sand Creek.

or at Fort Dodge," he asked Smith to "inform General Custer that we will be at Dodge today or tomorrow, and that we have utterly destroyed the Indian village at Pawnee Fork. . . . It is war against the Cheyennes and Sioux between the Arkansas and the Platte."[5]

Correspondent Henry M. Stanley offered his opinion that General Hancock had been deceived by the Indians, since they had burned three stations on the Smoky Hill route, scalped, disemboweled, and burned three men employed at the Fossil Creek Station, run off with several horses and mules, and alarmed the traders in general—all following his speech to the fifteen chiefs. Hancock then felt compelled to burn the Indian village.[6]

That Hancock was ignorant of the proper method of dealing with Indians was evident in his messages to them and to their agents. That he was unqualified to command such an expedition against them was apparent when he used infantry and a pontoon train to pursue mounted warriors. His demand for a nighttime council made the Indians suspicious because it was their custom to hold friendly talks during the day. Their suspicions grew when he stated his intention of visiting their village on Pawnee Fork, for they had not forgotten the Sand Creek massacre. Unintentionally, he was doing everything possible to stir up a war.

On the same day that Hancock had burned the village, Major Wickliffe Cooper, commanding a squad of Seventh Cavalry near Cimarron Crossing, discovered Indians skulking on his flank. They were endeavoring to steal the command's supply of cattle. Major Cooper ordered Lieutenant Matthew Berry and twenty men to advance and, through an interpreter, demand their surrender. They replied with gunfire. The troopers responded with a charge that carried them across the river in pursuit. Six Indians were killed, one trooper was wounded, and one horse was shot. The guide identified the dead warriors as Sioux and Cheyennes. On one was found the fresh scalp of a white woman.[7]

Colonel Wynkoop was "horrified" to learn of this skirmish a few days later, immediately reporting the incident to his commissioner.

[5] *Difficulties With Indian Tribes*, 76–77.

[6] Stanley, *Early Travels*, I, 47.

[7] *Difficulties With Indian Tribes*, 96–97.

He wrote of it as an attack on six Cheyennes by 130 cavalrymen, and stated that he knew of no overt act these Indians had committed that would require such action. He indicated that he had the feeling the Indians of his agency had been forced into war.[8]

General Hancock had been informed by Wynkoop that "the Arapahos, Apaches, and particularly the Cheyennes, were peacefully inclined, and rarely committed offenses against the laws, but that, most unfortunately, they were charged, in many instances, with crimes which had been perpetrated by other tribes. . . . In this respect they had suffered heavily from the Kiowas of Colonel Leavenworth's agency, who were the most turbulent Indians on the plains and deserved punishment more than any other."[9]

At about that same time, Colonel Leavenworth had reported to him that the tribes of his agency had been greatly wronged by having been charged with various offenses which had undoubtedly been committed by the Indians of Colonel Wynkoop's agency.[10]

It was Hancock's belief that he would be at Fort Hays in about ten days, with the object of showing the Kiowas and Comanches as much strength as possible, even though he felt he had been defeated to a great extent by the failure to have sufficient forage at Fort Hays. He advised General Custer to exercise his discretion as he had done previously, and he would be sustained.[11]

W. H. Cottrell, superintendent of the Smoky Hill Stage Route, sent a telegram to General Hancock dated April 23 stating, "I must have protection for the United States mail from Big Creek to Pond Creek; the Indians have burned Lookout Station, murdered three men, and run off the stock. The United States mail will have to stop unless I can have soldiers at the stations. Will you send a force at once?"[12]

On this same day General Hancock had talked, near Fort Dodge, with the Kiowa Chiefs Kicking Bird, Stumbling Bear, The Man That Moves, and several others. He reviewed what had happened since his

[8] *Ibid.,* 132–33.
[9] *Ibid.,* 118.
[10] *Ibid.,* 117.
[11] *Ibid.,* 77.
[12] *Ibid.,* 57.

approach to the Indian village and repeated that he had not come to make war upon the Indians but to punish only those who had committed the depredations. He said he intended to war with all the Sioux and Cheyennes between the Arkansas and the Platte, and concluded by asking for scouts from the ranks of the friendly Kiowas, Comanches and Arapahos.

Hancock advised them to comply with the Great Father's wishes and they would be fed when the buffalo were gone. He stressed the need for avoiding the Cheyenne camps and for going to their agents when they wished any wrong redressed. Kicking Bird nimbly parried these suggestions with, "There are but a few of my young men with me, but if you could give me some clothing for the tribe, they would all see that what you have said is so."[13] He added that the Cheyennes, Arapahos and Apaches of Colonel Wynkoop's agency, especially the Cheyennes, deserved severe punishment for their numerous misdeeds, many of which had been laid at the doors of innocent tribes.

Hancock held firmly to his belief in the effectiveness of a show of strength. He had thought that a show of his numbers at Pawnee Fork would induce the Indians to accept his terms, not knowing that the panic he created resulted from memories of the Sand Creek massacre. With Custer at Fort Hays, his forces were divided.

On April 24, Colonel Wynkoop advised Commissioner Taylor that the Indians of his agency had not yet retaliated for the "wrongs" heaped upon them, and "if proper action be taken by the Department of the Interior to prevent the military from forcing trouble on, that a general Indian war may be prevented." He enclosed an inventory of the articles destroyed by General Hancock which had numerous discrepancies as compared with General Hancock's official army inventory.[14]

General Hancock then held a "talk" with Little Raven (chief of the Arapahos), Yellow Bear, Beardy, Cut Nose, and some of the warriors at Fort Dodge on April 28. Little Raven maintained that his tribe had been peaceful, had not interfered with the trains or roads, and had not committed any depredations. It was his belief that

[13] *Ibid.*, 101–104.
[14] *Ibid.*, 29.

his people did not belong north at all, with the Sioux or any other tribe, but rather in the south. He said he would remain south of the Arkansas River until the Sioux and Cheyennes went north of the North Platte River.

General Hancock explained his intentions and his past actions, stressing a desire for peace though a willingness for war should the Indians prefer it. Little Raven voiced a very strong feeling for peace and evinced a desire for obtaining it by staying in the south if there is war above the Arkansas, or going north if there is war south of the Arkansas. Hancock concluded by expressing a request for two or three hundred Indians to be used as scouts.[15]

On May 1 General Hancock wrote to General Sherman advising him that there had been no further difficulty in securing grain, although hay was difficult to obtain because of high water and bad roads.

Custer was being actively employed against the Sioux and Cheyennes, according to Hancock, and "As soon as matters are a little more straightened out, General Custer will be an exceedingly valuable officer to pursue the Indians. I desire none better for such service."[16]

Hancock added that he believed he was being hampered by the advice and interests of the Indian agents, although he listened to them when their views were guided by the same public interest that he held. In some cases he had noted that matters had been complicated by the agents giving advice to the Indians as to what they should say and how much they should talk. He states, "I have laid the evidences of outrages and depredations before some of them [the agents] but as yet I have in no instance been called on to make energetic efforts for restitution or redress from the Indians."[17]

It was at Fort Larned, Kansas, on May 1, that General Hancock held a council with Satanta, head chief of the Kiowa Indians. Beginning with the usual overtures of expressing friendship for the whites and the great need for peace between them, Satanta said, "I do not want war at all, but want to make friends, and am doing the best I can for that purpose." He then made a long speech about his greatness as a chief, the poorness of the Kiowas, and the general virtues of

[15] *Ibid.*, 105–107.
[16] *Ibid.*, 108.
[17] *Ibid.*, 110.

his tribe and himself. He ended by asking Colonel Leavenworth (who was present) why he had not received his annuity goods, whereas all the other tribes had.[18]

Hancock replied by outlining what had already transpired since the Pawnee Fork affair and indicated that if the Kiowas were peaceful they should remain south of the Arkansas, since soldiers had difficulty in telling one tribe from another.[19]

Colonel Leavenworth then explained that Satanta's tribe had received no annuities because they had taken part in the killing of the Box family in Texas.[20]

In a report to Commissioner Taylor on May 2, Agent Leavenworth stated that "*Little good*, but a *great deal* of harm, has resulted from this expedition."[21] He followed this with a letter on May 4, stating that Generals Sherman and Hancock were to meet at Fort Harker on the seventh, at which time he would be there to protect the Indians of his agency (Kiowas and Comanches) who, he claimed, were never more friendly, even though in an almost starving condition. He added that up to April 15 he had believed that trouble had been avoided, but was compelled to change his mind because of the course the military took, concluding with, "General Hancock, owing to the mistakes or mismanagement of the military at Fort Larned, has seen but two or three of the leading men of the Kiowas. . . ."[22]

Soon after, General Edward O. C. Ord wrote, "I propose building posts in their [the Indians'] country, as that demoralizes them more than anything else, except money and whiskey."[23]

Colonel A. J. Smith received a notification May 7, that sufficient rations and forage had been shipped to Fort Hays for the army to start an immediate expedition against all Sioux and Cheyennes between the Arkansas and Platte rivers.[24]

On the ninth, Stanley reported an interview with General Han-

[18] *Ibid.,* 119.
[19] *Ibid.,* 123.
[20] *Ibid.,* 124. Also present were Indian agents Colonel Edward W. Wynkoop and Colonel Jesse H. Leavenworth. Leavenworth's father built Fort Leavenworth in the 1820's.
[21] *Ibid.,* 15.
[22] *Ibid.,* 15.
[23] *Ibid.,* 21.
[24] *Ibid.,* 104.

cock relative to the expedition. Stanley had been under the impression that the campaign was intended solely to punish the Indians for their numerous outrages—for such was the common belief in the West. Hancock defined his purpose as that of feeling the temper of the Indians in order that he might obtain evidence against the guilty parties and determine which of the tribes were for war; then punish those tribes. If necessary, he intended to sign treaties with the peaceful tribes and separate them from the warring ones. He particularly wanted to post more troops on the Smoky Hill and Santa Fe roads.[25]

Up to this point, $100,000 worth of Indian equipment had been burned. Congress had voted $150,000 for the expense of the campaign.

Custer and the Seventh Cavalry were to remain at Fort Hays until the grass appeared and his horses were in better condition, after which he was to begin active operations against the Sioux and Cheyennes.

Stanley went on to say:

> Custer is precisely the man for that job. A certain impetuosity and undoubted courage are his principal characteristics. From all we hear from persons qualified to judge, he must be a first-rate cavalry officer, and will no doubt perform any task allotted to him to the entire satisfaction of the western people.[26]

Indian Superintendent Thomas Murphy wrote Commissioner Taylor on May 13 that he had held a conference with Agent Leavenworth relative to the Indian affairs and military operations in the Southwest and had come to the conclusion that:

> It would have been far better for the interest of all concerned had he [General Hancock] never entered the Indian country with the soldiers. Indians who, at the time he got into their country, were peaceable and well-disposed toward the whites, are now fleeing with their women and children, no one knows where to, and what the final results will be is doubtful.[27]

Leavenworth wrote Commissioner Taylor on May 16 that the buffalo were fast disappearing from the plains, forcing the Indians in

[25] Stanley, *Early Travels*, I, 87.
[26] *Ibid.*, 86.
[27] *Difficulties With Indian Tribes*, 29–30.

his district to depend upon small game for subsistence. Traders had reported to him that many of the Indians in the north were in a starving condition. Leavenworth claimed that without ammunition they would starve, and asked if something couldn't be done about it.[28]

A telegram to General Sherman from General Augur was sent from Omaha on May 18, stating:

> I have not reported the many instances of Indian hostilities recently occurring within my lines, hoping they were the result of temporary excitement, and would soon cease; but, instead, they are becoming of almost daily occurrence at some point, either on the railroad, telegraph or mail lines.[29]

Many reports were coming in of Indian attacks near Fort Hays and along the Union Pacific Railroad tracks.

General Hancock, reporting from Fort Leavenworth on May 22, gave detailed information on his campaign thus far, adding recommendations for improvements in the fortifications at Forts Zarah, Larned, and Hays. He expressed his intention of maintaining active operations the remainder of the summer and as late into the winter as practicable against all Sioux and Cheyennes between the Arkansas and the Platte.[30]

Superintendent Murphy wrote to Commissioner Taylor on May 27, "I am creditably informed that General Hancock . . . has virtually declared war upon all the Indians north of the Arkansas and south of the Platte." He then drew attention to the existing treaty that permitted the Cheyennes, Arapahos, and Apaches to roam between these two rivers until a reservation had been provided by the President.[31]

[28] *Ibid.*, 22. The construction of the Union Pacific Railroad was the beginning of a ruthless destruction of the buffalo by the hide hunters, whose only desire was to obtain a dollar per hide, leaving the carcasses to the wolves and buzzards.

In contrast, the Indian rarely killed except as the need prevailed, and he had use for every portion of the buffalo. The hide was used for lodges, moccasins and clothing, the meat for food, and the bones and horns for utensils. It was the ruthless killing and extermination of the buffalo that finally determined the acceptance of the Indians as our wards.

[29] *Ibid.*, 58.
[30] *Ibid.*, 78–92.
[31] *Ibid.*, 25.

On May 28, Commissioner Taylor ordered Superintendent Murphy to issue annuity goods only to those Indians who had not been hostile and had no captives in their possession. In the event part of a band had been hostile, all of the goods would be given to the peaceful members of the band.[32] So ended two months of Indian warfare.

[32] *Ibid.*, 30.

III. TO SQUELCH
A PRAIRIE FIRE

Tнᴇ Iɴᴅɪᴀɴ ᴅᴇᴘʀᴇᴅᴀᴛɪᴏɴꜱ increased in number and intensity. Hancock's expedition had no salutary effect upon the Indian problem. There was no question it had intensified hostilities until they had reached uncontrolled proportions.

Telegrams poured into governmental offices and forts announcing and describing outrages committed on settlers, ranchers, and railroad men. Fear was evident in each message, for everyone questioned the ability of the military to restrain the raiders. Some of the messages read:

> A coach was attacked at Bijou Station; the driver fell pierced by five bullets, and a passenger was shot in the thigh.[1]

> Coach attacked; the passengers were C. C. Caldwell, E. W. Bullock, Alex Benham, division agent of Wells, Fargo & Co., S. W. Phelps, Hiram Facht, Major Talbot. These gentlemen drove the Indians off, and killed one Indian, it is supposed.[2]

> Coach attacked near Moore's Ranche. Stage supernumerary killed, and Captain Davis, of the Post Office department, *en route* to Montana, and a son of General Davis, mortally wounded in the groin.[3]

[1] Stanley, *Early Travels*, I, 119.
[2] *Ibid.*   [3] *Ibid.*

33

Turner and Paxton, of Pole Creek, lost twenty-five mules, which have not been recovered. While chasing them, they picked up a white woman's scalp.[4]

On yesterday, a war party struck the settlements in White Rock Valley, and killed two men and one woman, and wounded one boy, who escaped to tell the sad story. Others are missing; supposed to be killed or captured. Many families are leaving their homes, and cannot return unless they have protection. We appeal to you for help and protection against these merciless savages.[5]

The Indians have killed two more of our men, near Bunker Hill Station, and driven the workmen off the line. Please send us arms and ammunition. Unless you send us protection, our work must be abandoned.[6]

I have just returned from Fort Wallace, over the line of the U.P.R.R. The Indians along the whole line are engaged in their savage warfare. On Saturday, three more of our men were killed and scalped. Our laborers, one thousand or more, have been driven in. General Hancock is away west of Fort Wallace, so I cannot apply to him.[7]

At Fort Sedgwick on the Platte River news was brought in of the killing of three herders near Julesberg. A detachment of cavalry under command of Captain John Mix scoured the countryside for miles until they became tired and hungry and discovered, to their dismay, that they had forgotten their rations and had to return. On their arrival at Fort Sedgwick they were anxiously asked, "What news of the Indians? Did you see any?" To which the dejected captain replied, "Nary a one. I'm durned if I believe there are any Indians in the country."[8]

Another report had arrived telling of the murder of two men just north of Julesburg. This time the troopers took along a two-day supply of rations. That same evening they returned to be greeted by, "What news? What success?" And the reply was, "Nary an Indian."[9]

[4] *Ibid.*, 120.
[5] Crawford, *Kansas*, 253–54.
[6] *Ibid.*, 256.
[7] *Ibid.*, 255.
[8] Stanley, *Early Travels*, I, 110.
[9] *Ibid.*, 111.

Desertion among the cavalry troopers was an everyday occurrence. The men were leaving at the rate of fifty a month and, despite all efforts to prevent it, they would leave with arms, equipment and horses.[10] The Seventh Cavalry alone had lost 512 men by desertion between October 1, 1866, and October 1, 1867.[11]

Mrs. Custer wrote that:

> In one night while I was at Fort Hays, 40 men deserted, and in so bold and deliberate a manner, taking arms, ammunition, horses and quantities of food, that the officers were roused to action, for it looked as if not enough men would be left to protect the fort. A conspiracy was formed among the men, by which a third of the whole command planned to desert at one time. Had not their plotting been discovered, there would not have been a safe hour for those who remained, as the Indians lay in wait constantly. My husband, in writing of that wholesale desertion in the early months of the regiment's history, makes some excuse for them under circumstances that would seem to have put all tribulation and patience out of mind.[12]

Colonel Custer wrote that:

> Unfortunately, desertions from the ranks became so frequent and extensive as to cause no little anxiety. To produce these, several causes combined. Prominent among them was the insufficiency and inferior quality of the rations furnished the men. At the same time the latter were made the victims of fraud, and it was only by zealous care and watchfulness of the officers immediately over them, that their wants were properly attended to.[13]

He related instances where bread baked and dated in 1861 was issued to his regiment in 1867; where huge stones weighing as much as twenty-five pounds were found in unbroken packages of provisions, for which the government had paid a food contractor high prices per

---

[10] Davis, "A Summer on the Plains," *loc. cit.*, 298. Theodore R. Davis and Henry M. Stanley were the first correspondents to accompany a military expedition against American Indians. Davis, as artist-correspondent for *Harper's Weekly*, and Stanley, as correspondent for the *Weekly Missouri Democrat* and the New York *Tribune*, joined the Hancock expedition in March of 1867.

[11] 40 Cong., 2 sess., *House Exec. Doc. 1*, 475. There were 111 apprehensions.

[12] Elizabeth B. Custer, *Tenting*, 695.

[13] G. A. Custer, *My Life*, 46.

pound. He went on to say that, "In-activity led to restlessness and dissatisfaction." Poor food, cholera and scurvy did the rest.[14]

Many of these men had enlisted under assumed names, either to escape some punishment back east or to cover their anticipated desertion. Some of them were heading for the gold fields of Colorado, while others just wanted to see the country and to take advantage of its opportunities. Although many deserters survived some were killed by Indians. For those who wished employment, the Union Pacific railroad needed men to cut ties. There were bands of desperadoes in the area to which some of the men were attracted. In the event of capture by the military, the heaviest sentence imposed on a deserter was six months in the guardhouse.[15]

It was Sherman's wish to clear the area between the Arkansas and the Platte rivers of all unfriendly Indians. By the use of cavalry under the command of Colonel Custer this area would be freed of all impediments to travelers wishing to reach the gold fields of Colorado or California. Pressures on the government had increased since the Hancock expedition had not achieved its objective.[16]

Kiowa Chief Satanta, who previously had held a council with Generals Hancock and Smith and had received a major general's coat and insignia from them because they had been impressed with his "goodness," raided Fort Dodge on June 1 while wearing this same coat.[17] While stampeding most of the post's animals, "he had the politeness, however, to raise his plumed hat to the garrison of the fort, though he discourteously shook his coat-tails at them as he rode away with the captured stock."[18]

[14] *Ibid.*

[15] Davis, "A Summer on the Plains," *loc. cit.*, 288.

[16] Stanley, *Early Travels*, I, 132; G. A. Custer, *My Life*, 48; 40 Cong., 2 sess., *House Exec. Doc. 1*, 35; Mrs. Frank Montgomery, "Fort Wallace and its Relation to the Frontier," *Kansas Historical Collections*, Vol. XVII, (1926–28), 222; 40 Cong., 2 sess., *House Exec. Doc. 1*, 33; Crawford, *Kansas*, 250, 262; J. R. Perkins, *Trails, Rails and War*, 192, 194; Carrington, *Ab-Sa-Ra-Ka*, 286, 290; *Difficulties With Indian Tribes*, 341. The Platte River was generally accepted as the dividing line between northern and southern Indians. The area between it and the Arkansas was to be a neutral zone or "no Red Man's land," if Sherman could accomplish it.

[17] *Ibid.*, 43; Davis, "A Summer on the Plains," *loc. cit.*, 297.

[18] Davis, "A Summer on the Plains," *loc. cit.*, 298.

Custer and six companies of the Seventh Cavalry had been ordered to leave the Smoky Hill River and ride toward the Platte. Leaving Old Fort Hays near the Smoky Hill on June 1, the troops were to scout to Fort McPherson on the Platte, describe a semicircle southward, touching the Republican River, and then toward Fort Sedgwick on the Platte River. Here the supplies would be replenished, and afterward they would move south to Fort Wallace on the Smoky Hill and then to the starting point at Fort Hays—in all, about a thousand miles.[19]

Custer's first day's march, as customary, was short so his men could be toughened gradually for the campaign ahead. The three hundred[20] men and the train of twenty wagons were marched up Big Creek valley fifteen miles, to camp on its north bank in heavy timber.[21] Colonel Smith and his adjutant, Captain Thomas B. Weir, along with two companies of the Seventh Cavalry and some infantry, remained behind to garrison Fort Hays.

Reveille was sounded at 5 A.M. the following day. Men rolled out of their blankets reluctantly, for the air was cold and their muscles stiff. The sergeants called the rolls, then made out their lists of absentees while the men fed and groomed the horses. Ten men from each company were excused from these duties because they were assigned to K.P. While the horses were cared for, the officers made repeated trips to see that all this activity was accomplished in a thorough manner. In Indian country the condition of the horse could determine the continued life of its rider.

About the time the horses had been groomed, breakfast was ready and the men lined up for their coffee and sowbelly. Immediately following breakfast the bugler sounded the "General," upon which all tents were taken down and everything packed for resumption of the march. In a matter of minutes the headquarters bugler sounded "Boots and Saddles," the signal to saddle the horses and prepare the wagons to leave. Five minutes later "To Horse" was blown and the men of each company led their horses to their assigned positions and stood at the head. As "Prepare to mount," was called by Custer, each

[19] G. A. Custer, *My Life*, 48.
[20] *Ibid.*, 298; G. A. Custer, *My Life*, 47, "about three hundred and fifty men."
[21] Lt. Henry Jackson, *Itinerary of the March of the United States Cavalry*, 4.

trooper placed his left foot in the stirrup, and at his command "Mount," the men rose into the saddles in unison. To be out of time with the entire command could mean that a trooper would find himself afoot the first half of that day's march, for such was the punishment meted out.[22]

Once mounted the entire outfit moved forward in columns of fours at the command of "Advance." By this time it was 6 A.M.; the day's march was to be twenty-nine miles. Custer tried to maintain an average daily march of twenty-five miles when not in pursuit of enemy.[23]

The first part of the march was over marshy prairie. After traveling nine miles the troops encountered a broken ridge between two dry creek beds which they used as a trail way for that portion of the march, since it provided an elevated view of the surrounding terrain. They ended the day by crossing the Saline River to camp on its north bank in the Cottonwood timber. Although the grass had been scant along the route traveled, it was abundant in the river bottom. Upon reaching camp the horses were grazed and groomed and pickets were posted to prevent any surprise.[24]

It was soon discovered that the campsite had been used lately by the Indians. Elk bones were strewn everywhere, giving evidence of good hunting and feasting. At a distance of two miles there was visible a prominent knoll on which a scaffold had been erected. Custer took several of his troopers and his guide William Comstock to examine more closely this object of his curiosity. The twenty-foot-high scaffold had been constructed of saplings, on the top of which rested an Indian body. Comstock advised him that some of the tribes in this area disposed of their dead in this fashion. It was the belief of these natives that the spirit of the deceased would pass on to the "happy hunting grounds" where he would engage in the same pleasures he was permitted upon this earth. Because of this belief he was provided with all of the necessary equipment to pursue these ambitions.[25]

[22] G. A. Custer, *My Life*, 51–52.

[23] *Ibid.*, 52; Stanley, *My Early Travels*, I, 85. Stanley indicated that foot soldiers can average fifteen miles a day.

[24] Jackson, *Itinerary of the March*, 40.

[25] G. A. Custer, *My Life*, 52; Davis, "A Summer on the Plains," *loc. cit.*, 289.

It was Comstock's belief that this was the son of some chief, for though he had not reached adulthood, he was provided with all of the arms and apparel of a warrior. Beside him lay a bow and a quiver full of steel-tipped arrows, a tomahawk and scalping knife, and a red-clay pipe with a bag of tobacco. He was well supplied with provisions, a rifle and revolver with ammunition, a saddle and bridle, and a white woman's scalp as an affadavit of his warring prowess. Beneath the scaffold rested the strangled carcass of his favorite war pony.[26]

William Comstock was the "character" of the expedition.[27] Born near Kalamazoo, Michigan, and transplanted to the plains when he was but fifteen, he had become the outstanding scout in that country. Newspaper correspondent Theodore Davis said, "He is quiet and unassuming in manner, small in size, and compact in proportion. He is one of the best riders on the plains, with which he is probably more familiar than any other white man who roams over them."[28]

Custer wrote his wife, Libbie, that he took every opportunity to learn Comstock's tricks-of-the-trade. He had Comstock mess with him and Moylan, thereby using every moment to obtain valuable information regarding the Indians and their habits. He told Libbie that "He [Comstock] brought with him a large dog he has named 'Cuss' ... short for ... ?"[29]

Will, or Medicine Bill, as the Indians called him, was as superstitious as any red man. He had a "medicine" for everything. Like the Indians, Will referred to every object or event in his life as either "good medicine" or "bad medicine." If he had bad luck, he had to do something to change his "medicine." His two fondest wishes were to see George Armstrong Custer and to see a railroad engine. He saw his first locomotive on the Platte River, at which time he shouted, "Good medicine! Good medicine!" He had traveled there with Custer. Of him Custer said:

No Indian knew the country more thoroughly .... He was perfectly familiar with every divide, water course, and strip of lumber

[26] Davis, "A Summer on the Plains," *loc. cit.*, 299; G. A. Custer, *My Life*, 52.
[27] Davis, "A Summer on the Plains," *loc. cit.*, 303; G. A. Custer, *My Life*, 47.
[28] Davis, "A Summer on the Plains," *loc. cit.*, 303.
[29] Marquerite Merington, *The Custer Story*, 200; Elizabeth B. Custer, *Tenting*, 579.

for hundreds of miles in either direction. He knew the dress and peculiarities of every Indian tribe, and spoke the languages of many of them. Perfect in horsemanship, fearless in manner, a splendid hunter, and a gentleman by instinct, as modest and unassuming as he was brave, he was an interesting as well as valuable companion on the march such as was then before us.[30]

The regiment left camp on June 3 at 5 A.M., crossing the south fork of the north fork of the Saline River with a great deal of difficulty. The south banks were high and perpendicular, and while the water in the creek was but six inches deep, its bottom was quicksand. Rolling prairie was reached and the going became easier. After twenty-nine miles of travel, camp was made on the banks of the Solomon River.[31]

The following morning camp was broken at 5 A.M. again, and the march was continued over gradually rising, rolling prairie. Eighteen miles were traveled before camp was made on Bow Creek.[32]

On the morning of the fifth the company broke camp at 5 A.M. and marched in a northwesterly direction over broken prairie, striking Prairie Dog Creek, where the stock was permitted to graze for three hours during the first rainstorm encountered since leaving Fort Hays. The prairie beyond this point was broken by ravines and covered with cactus plants. After covering twenty-two miles the company reached the heavily-timbered north banks of Beaver Creek and made camp for the night.[33]

On June 6 the troops moved out in fours, again at 5 A.M. The course of the day's travel once more was over rolling prairie and the distance was lengthened to thirty-four miles, now that the men had toughened to the saddle.[34] After crossing Stealing Horse Creek and White Rock Creek the troops discovered a four-day-old Indian trail on the south bank of the latter. The band consisted of between ten and fifteen braves and was headed east. The troopers followed the trail far enough to determine that it was futile to continue.[35] Camp was made just two miles from the Republican River.

[30] G. A. Custer, *My Life*, 47.
[31] Jackson, *Itinerary of the March*, 5.
[32] *Ibid.*, 7.
[33] *Ibid.*, 7–9.
[34] *Ibid.*, 9–10.
[35] Merington, *The Custer Story*, 204; G. A. Custer, *My Life*, 53.

On this same day, a dispatch was sent from Fort Sedgwick by General Sherman to Governor Hunt of Colorado, who was concerned about the Indian dangers that threatened his territory. He said, "It is barely possible that the Cheyenne camp, stampeded by Hancock on Pawnee Fork, is now on the Republican south of this. General Custer may strike them in coming across . . . ."[36]

On the following morning the horses and men moved out at the customary 5 A.M., crossing the Republican on a firm, sandy bottom. The water was three feet deep and extended to a width of seventy-five yards. Little difficulty was encountered, though the banks were marshy. After traveling about seven miles the regiment suddenly saw before them on the high ground to their left, about a hundred mounted warriors. Without a second look at the superior numbers of cavalry, the Indians wheeled about and headed westward as fast as horseflesh could carry them. Custer immediately ordered Captain Edward Myers and Company E in pursuit, but this action had to be discontinued because of the superior horses upon which the Indians were mounted.[37] Their tracks revealed that the horses had been stolen from the Overland Stage Company, whose practice had been to pay double the price offered for horses by the government, thereby obtaining the best animals available. Captain Myers circled back to join the advancing column some miles farther on. There were only seventeen miles of travel that day because the discovery and pursuit of the Indians caused some delay.[38]

The column moved out with some difficulty on the morning of June 8, for it was dark and misty. The point led in a northwesterly direction, keeping well to the left of Medicine Lake Creek. Just six miles from camp a small, unnamed creek was encountered. Although the creek was but ten feet wide, the steep, miry banks required bridging. This was the beginning of a trying day.

Eleven miles farther it became possible to cross Medicine Lake Creek with wagons for the first time. The crossing was very bad. Horses sank into the soft mud up to their flanks. Every wagon had

[36] 40 Cong., 2 sess., *House Exec. Doc. 1*, 33.

[37] Jackson, *Itinerary of the March*, 10–11.

[38] G. A. Custer, *My Life*, 53; Davis, "A Summer on the Plains," *loc. cit.*, 300–301.

to be corduroyed separately. Although the tacky, soft, steep banks were only ten yards apart, it took fifty men four hours to accomplish the crossing with the twenty wagons. Despite the fact the grass was poor, and the water in the creek but six inches deep, camp was made on the north bank near an old cavalry camp.[39]

Just as Colonel Custer had risen from his dinner table, Captain Edward Myers rushed into the tent to report that Major Wickcliffe Cooper had shot himself. The Colonel and his brother Tom had been discussing Cooper's excessive drinking, for both thought him an accomplished officer and a most companionable gentleman, destroying himself by the excessive use of rum.

They hastened to his tent and found him lying on his knees and face, his right hand grasping a revolver, the ground near him covered with blood. His body was still warm. In a discussion of the matter among the officers it was determined he had been drunk when he turned the gun on himself.[40]

One by one the officers came to gaze on their companion. Custer, a teetotaler, returned to his tent to prepare a message to Cooper's pregnant widow.[41] To Libbie he wrote afterward, "May the example be not lost on them [the officers]."[42] Major Cooper's body was taken to Fort McPherson by ambulance for burial.

The remainder of the trip to Fort McPherson on the Platte River took another two days. It was uneventful and monotonous although the country became very rough in spots. Davis wrote of the march from Fort Hays to Fort McPherson as being made over one of the most interesting portions of the plains. "The country is broken into bluffs and canyons, never flat and uninteresting.... The banks of the little streams are fringed with trees of all descriptions, ash and walnut being as plentiful as cottonwood. Game was abundant, and furnished a continual and much needed supply of meat for the command."[43] It

[39] Jackson, *Itinerary of the March*, 11-12.

[40] Merington, *The Custer Story*, 204-205; Carrington, *Ab-Sa-Ra-Ka*, 280.

[41] Theodore R. Davis, "With Generals In Their Homes," *Chicago Westerners Brand Book* (1945-46), 119: It was his opinion that: "He [Custer] had given up, as I afterward knew not without an effort, a collection of habits—which to put it mildly are not uncommon among army men—Custer did not swear, drink whiskey or use tobacco in any form—but he drew the line at cards."

[42] Merington, *The Custer Story*, 205.

[43] Davis, "A Summer on the Plains," *loc. cit.*, 299.

42

took all of Comstock's skill and knowledge of the terrain to lead the troopers through the canyons they encountered.

Approaching the Platte River the command reached an area that the Indians called the Bad Lands, "a succession of ridges with deep ravines between them, many of them at best fifty feet deep."[44] A wagon road had to be cut down into some of them. A few of the ridges appeared impossible to cross with loaded wagons. Two wagons rolled off one of these ridges, creating considerable confusion and delay.

Davis was enchanted with one of the campsites on which they had pitched their tents. No sooner had the shelters been pitched than it was discovered they were over an area perforated with rattlesnake holes. The troopers made short work of the rattlers with their sabers and with but one exception every mess enjoyed broiled or fried rattlesnake meat.[45]

A large number of antelope were killed by the command between the Platte and Republican rivers, and several young ones were captured and tamed, becoming favorite pets around the camp.[46]

[44] Jackson, *Itinerary of the March*, 13.
[45] Davis, "A Summer on the Plains," *loc. cit.*, 299–300.
[46] *Ibid.*, 301.

IV. PEACE
ON HORSEBACK

Fort McPherson was located half a mile south of the Platte River, just across the river from McPherson Station on the Union Pacific Railroad. Covering an area of thirty-eight acres, it had been known in 1863 as Cantonment McKean, then as Cottonwood Springs, when it was used by the Overland Stage Company and had a population of a hundred citizens. On February 20, 1866, it became Fort McPherson. It was a five-company post, housed in three log, and two frame barracks. Although there were several wells, most of the water used was hauled from the Platte River. The reservation area was a level plateau about thirty feet above the river level.[1]

The post was commanded by Colonel Henry B. Carrington and was the regimental headquarters of the Eighteenth Infantry which included Company C, Third Artillery, and Company B, Second Cavalry. At this time Colonel Carrington was the subject of much discussion in Washington, having been the commanding officer at Fort Phil Kearny at the time of the Fetterman massacre December 21, 1866.[2]

---

[1] *Barracks and Hospitals Circular No. 4* (hereafter cited as *Barracks and Hospitals*), 334.

[2] Louis A. Holmes, *Fort McPherson, Nebraska*, 25–26; Stanley, *Early Travels*, I, 109.

44

The total distance from Fort Hays to Fort McPherson was just 215 miles. At McPherson the wagons were refilled with supplies, rations, and forage, and then moved out with the troops to a new camp some ten miles to the west, on the south bank of the Platte River where the grass was more abundant and the ground a little higher and drier.[3] This camp was near Jack Morrow's ranch.

The river was half a mile wide at this point, and ranchman Jack Morrow had the only ferry available. His fee of $5.00 a head for man or beast was the result of his known monopoly. The current was so swift that the flat-bottomed ferryboat would land from one to two miles below its starting point. It then was taken out of the water and hauled back to a new starting point.

All along the Platte were evidences of the raiding Indians. Abandoned ranches and numerous graves were to be seen. Many of the graves were simple mounds of unmarked earth standing as graphic evidence of a venturesome pioneer. Some graves were more pretentious, marked by a crude board on which had been inscribed, "Unknown Man Killed By Indians," and a date.[4]

No sooner was camp made than the Sioux chief Pawnee Killer, with a few other Oglala Sioux chiefs, appeared for a "talk," with the obvious purpose of obtaining rations, ammunition, and information. Custer's object was to induce Pawnee Killer and his band to bring their lodges into the vicinity of the fort and remain at peace with the whites. To encourage this move he gave them liberal quantities of coffee, sugar and other desirable articles. They left Custer's council with strong expressions of their desire to live at peace with the whites, promising to bring their families in under the protection of the fort so they would not become embroiled in the war which, obviously, was about to spread over the entire plains.[5]

Pawnee Killer made several attempts to discover where Custer was heading, but was unsuccessful. While the council was in process, "Little Bill," one of the pet antelopes, satisfied his curiosity by inspecting the beadwork on the Indian's clothing. His tameness, and

---

[3] Jackson, *Itinerary of the March*, 15; G. A. Custer, *My Life*, 54.
[4] Davis, "A Summer on the Plains," *loc. cit.*, 301.
[5] *Ibid.*, 301; G. A. Custer, *My Life*, 54; Jackson, *Itinerary of the March*, 15.

45

then the ferocity with which he attacked one of the dogs when it
sniffed his heels, astonished them so that they expressed their admira-
tion for him with a series of, "How, how, how!"[6]

The chiefs left the camp with strong promises to bring their bands
under the protective custody of Fort McPherson, to remain there
until the Cheyennes were subdued. But as Custer stated many months
later, "Pawnee Killer and his chiefs never attempted to keep their
promises."[7]

General Sherman, who was at Fort Sedgwick, seventy-five miles
due west, was informed immediately of the conference with the Sioux.
Without hesitation he ordered Custer to hold Pawnee Killer and
three of his men as hostages until the Sioux under him could be
brought to Brady's Island opposite Fort McPherson, where they
would be fed and guarded until Chief Spotted Tail would make a
consolidation at Fort Laramie.

Custer had faith in Pawnee Killer's promises; Sherman had none.[8]
He had seen Hancock duped on Pawnee Fork and thought he was
about to see history repeat itself. He intended sending a company of
men south to the Republican River to test the truth of Pawnee
Killer's story.

Previous to this exchange with Sherman, Custer had advised
Libbie:

> I can write you but a few lines to send to Platte City by Captain
> West, who goes to send a dispatch for General Sherman by telegraph
> to Sedgwick. We are all well. Left McPherson this morning where I
> was treated with the utmost kindness and consideration. I feel much
> more hopeful than I did a few hours ago, for the reason that six of
> the principle Sioux Indians have just come in to see me to sue for
> peace for their whole tribe who are now collected and waiting our
> reply. One of the Sioux Chiefs was "Pawnee Killer" who was at the
> pow-pow on the Pawnee Fork where the lodges were burned. He
> recognized me and I him of course. I encouraged peace propositions
> and have sturdy hopes of a successful and satisfactory settlement with
> the Sioux which will leave us only the Cheyennes to deal with. I am
> telegraphing the result of my peace talk with the Sioux to General

[6] Davis, "A Summer on the Plains," *loc. cit.*, 301.
[7] G. A. Custer, *My Life*, 60.
[8] G. A. Custer, *My Life*, 54; Carrington, *Ab-Sa-Ra-Ka*, 285.

46

Sherman and hope as another result to follow that I will see my little girl much sooner thereby. If I can carry out my present plans I will be at Wallace probably within fifteen days, certainly within twenty. I will write you positively from Sedgwick. I wrote you from Mc-Pherson giving account of the suicide of Colonel Cooper. Oh, I am so grateful that I never gave my little sweetheart anxiety on my account from reason of intemperance . . . I am going to remain in this camp until day after tomorrow to await a reply from General Sherman . . . I will write to you tomorrow . . . Write to me at Wallace unless you are there yourself. . . . Notify me of any change in your residence.[9]

On that same day Colonel Henry B. Carrington wrote Custer from his command post at Fort McPherson, advising him that the Oglala Sioux were on the Republican and that many of them wished to cross the Platte River where there were no hostilities. He claimed that all had been advised to keep off the road and that no friendly Indian would be on it between Julesburg and a day's march west of Fort McPherson. He also advised Custer to place no confidence in traders with Indian wives.

Fort Sedgwick was located a quarter of a mile south of the South Platte River, eighty-six miles west of Fort McPherson. The nearest town was Julesburg, a railroad station, three miles north on the Union Pacific Railroad. The men were housed in two adobe barracks with walls two feet thick. Four smaller buildings, two of which were adobe, served as quarters for the officers. There were no water closets or bathrooms; water was obtained from the river or from a well in the rear of the quarters. The immediate vicinity of the post was level, the ground gradually rising to some bluffs and hills a mile distant, and then on to tablelands as far as the eye could see.[10]

The river could be forded most of the year, although it was very high from June to the middle of August. The ford was five hundred yards below the post and was about half a mile wide. Wagons could cross almost every day, even though the water would come above

[9] Letter of G. A. Custer to Libbie Custer, dated June 12, 1867. Original in author's collection.

[10] *Barracks and Hospitals*, 338–40.

their bottoms.[11] The major problem was the changing channel, with the resulting possibility of quicksand.

This post was commanded by Major Lewis C. Hunt, with a garrison composed of Companies K, F, G, and B of the Fourth Infantry, two companies of the Thirtieth Infantry, one company of cavalry, and a small squad of artillery.[12]

On June 13 during the Carrington–Custer–Pawnee Killer conference at Custer's camp near Morrow's ranch, Sherman, from Fort Sedgwick, wired Custer to advise Pawnee Killer that there were men out to exterminate him and that he should come in to Fort McPherson at once to answer charges for recent murders at O'Fallon's Bluff and Plum Creek.

Custer's courier carried a reply to Sherman advising him that Pawnee Killer had left camp at 4 P.M. but was being pursued. With less than three hundred active men left of his six companies—since one-sixth were dismounted and unserviceable—Custer questioned the advisability of dividing his force into three units and sending them on their separate ways. Two companies to pursue Pawnee Killer, two to go up to the Republican, and two to meet Sherman, seemed unwise.

Sherman's response was to order Custer to retain his *status quo*, since Pawnee Killer had gone too far to pursue. As a neophyte in Indian warfare Custer was learning a valuable lesson—never trust an Indian if it is to his advantage to deceive.

General Sherman now knew where the Sioux were. His next step was to determine the location of the Cheyennes. On June 15, again he wired Custer from Fort Sedgwick:

> A good many people believe that the Cheyennes are still on the upper Republican, Captain Mix started out last night with 50 men, all he could raise, and will send back word which General Potter will [send on] to me and you. If the Cheyennes are still there you must be ready to start at the drop of a hat for the Upper Republican.

[11] 40 Cong. 2 sess. *House Exec. Doc. 1*, 28. The following number of trains passed the fort between February 1 and September 28, 1867: 124 trains, 3,074 wagons, 4,587 men, 556 women, 587 children, 5,738 mules, 1,062 horses, 948 led animals, and 11,096 oxen.

[12] *Ibid.*, 41.

Major General George Armstrong Custer. From an oil miniature painted by R. T. Lux in New Orleans, on a vase owned by the J. C. Custer family. July, 1865.

Major General Winfield S. Hancock, commander of the Kansas Indian campaign of 1867.

I will be down to North Platte today and see you at your camp tomorrow.[13]

That same day Custer marched his troopers east along the south bank of the Platte River and camped two miles from Fort McPherson.[14] No sooner had General Sherman arrived in camp to confer with Custer the next day than a heavy rain began to fall. The men used this opportunity to take horses into the Fort to have them shod.[15] The grass being poor, the following day the troops moved the camp nine miles to the west, near the forks of the Platte. Sherman rode with them.[16] Here Custer was to await further orders, pending information available to Sherman when he reached Sedgwick.

Before Custer left Fort McPherson, General Sherman had received a message dated June 16 from General Hancock, who sent it from Fort Wallace. This missive gave Captain Myles W. Keogh's verbatim report, which indicated that every station garrisoned by men from Fort Wallace—ninety-five miles east to some seventy-five miles to the west—had been attacked an average of four times.[17]

Having received numerous reports that the Arapahos were on the warpath Sherman wired Custer to begin a forced march south twenty miles to the Republican. After scouting it thoroughly for some fifty miles west of Fort Sedgwick, he was to strike for the South Platte and into Sedgwick for further orders.[18] No fault would be found in killing horses if a good many Indians were killed. He was to kill as many Indians as he could, capturing and bringing in the women and children.

The command moved out at 5 A.M. on June 18, passing through Morrow's Canyon on their way southward over a succession of hills, the valleys between these hills varying from one to four miles in width. About fourteen miles from camp the men observed a small lake covering some four acres, three feet in depth, resulting from the rain of two days before. After traveling about twenty-six miles, the

---

[13] Sherman's telegram to Custer dated June 15, 1867; original in author's collection.

[14] Jackson, *Itinerary of the March*, 15.

[15] *Ibid.*, 17.

[16] *Ibid.*, 17.

[17] *Difficulties With Indian Tribes*, 60.

[18] G. A. Custer, *My Life*, 54.

command made camp on the south side of Medicine Lake Creek where the grass was good. The distance that day was estimated on the basis of the hours of marching, the odometer being out of order.[19]

The regiment moved out early the next day proceeding over level prairie most of the forenoon. After traveling ten miles the troops encountered the miry banks of Red Willow Creek and found it necessary that they be corduroyed. After this delay the command moved onto rolling prairie again, finally calling it a day when they struck Blackwood Creek. There were heavy patches of timber providing ample firewood, but the water was bad.[20]

The morning of the twentieth was very misty and foggy. Visibility did not extend beyond a hundred yards in any direction, which accounted for the command's passage into a dead-end ravine six miles out of camp. The route had been southerly, but upon emerging from the ravine the command moved westerly for a mile and then southward, reaching and crossing White Man's Fork of the Republican River. After traveling a few miles south, they made camp on the left bank of Palader Creek, where the water was good, the brush plentiful, and the grass abundant. Distance traveled that day was nineteen miles.[21] No Indians had been sighted up to this point, and it was on this same day that Indian Superintendent Murphy wrote Commissioner Taylor that a portion of the Cheyennes south of Fort Zarah were peaceful. He added, "Recollect that war was declared on all Indians found south of the Platte and north of the Arkansas Rivers."[22]

Assistant Adjutant General Chauncey McKeever received word from Major Henry Douglass at Fort Dodge that the country in his vicinity was alive with depredating Indians operating in bands of fifty to two hundred. He described a raid led by Satanta that had cleaned out his cavalry herd, leaving him completely immobile. He concluded by requesting that a "competent force of cavalry be sent to operate in this section of the country with as little delay as practicable."[23]

[19] Jackson, *Itinerary of the March*, 17.
[20] *Ibid.*, 19.
[21] *Ibid.*, 20.
[22] 41 Cong., 2 sess., *House Exec. Doc. 240*, 34.
[23] *Ibid.*, 62–63.

General Sherman had received word from General Hancock that Fort Wallace and every one of the stage stations east and west of it had been attacked repeatedly, one soldier killed, and four citizens killed, scalped and mutilated within four miles of the fort.[24]

General Smith, from Fort Harker on June 19, had advised General Sherman:

> I believe the Cheyennes are now all on the Smoky going south, Old Satanta is on the warpath with all his tribe of Kiowas, and I urgently request that Custer be sent back to the line of the Smoky Hill at once if his services can possibly be spared. We want cavalry and will require several regiments on north and south of the Arkansas. Now that the Kiowas have gone over, it is my impression that there will be a grand combination on and south of the Arkansas.[25]

Smith then wired Custer that:

> The Cheyennes are already on the Smoky from Harker to Wallace and beyond in small parties and have committed depredations. I have already asked General Sherman to send you back and will telegraph him again. We need you here very much. Old Satanta is on the warpath with all his tribe the Kiowas, and has already hit us a hell of a lick. The people are here with me and all well.[26]

Smith's reference to "the people" obviously meant Custer's wife Libbie, from whom he had received no letters because of the interrupted communications along the mail routes. He had received word of the increasing incidence of cholera at the various posts, and this was of considerable concern to him. The first evidence of cholera had been at Fort Leavenworth and then it had spread westward to Fort Riley and Fort Harker.[27] No letters from Libbie could mean that cholera had struck home. Smith's reference to "the people" being well, since he could not use a military message for private use by being as obvious as to call Libbie by name, was welcome news.

[24] *Ibid.*, 60.
[25] *Ibid.*, 61.
[26] Copy of telegram, A. J. Smith to G. A. Custer, from Fort Harker, June 18, 1867, Mrs. E. B. Custer collection, Custer Battlefield National Monument.
[27] 40 Cong., 2 sess., *House Exec. Doc. 1*, 12, 34; William A. Bell, *New Tracks in North America*, I, 77; Elizabeth B. Custer, *Tenting*, 667–68.

V. CHOLERA
ON THE SMOKY HILL

O N THE TWENTY-FIRST, camp broke at the usual 5 A.M., the troops traveling southwesterly over rolling prairie to reach the Republican River and then due west.[1] And on the twenty-second camp broke at the usual time, the troops moved westerly along the bottom land of the Republican River and finally encamped on the west side of a small stream called Forwood's Spring Creek. This camp was selected to be used as a base for a thorough search of the surrounding country for Indians. This matter would require at least several days, and wood, water, good grazing, and facilities for defense were available.[2]

Custer had understood when he left General Sherman that he was to thoroughly search this area, then march his command to Fort Sedgwick and there either meet Sherman or receive further instructions from him.

At this time he was seventy-five miles southeast of Fort Sedgwick, and about the same distance northeast of Fort Wallace. His guides agreed that the country between the camp and Fort Sedgwick was almost impassable for heavily-laden wagons, whereas that toward Fort Wallace was generally level and unbroken. And since they were equidistant from both forts, Custer decided to send his wagon train south to Fort Wallace for supplies, and a trusted officer with an

[1] Jackson, *Itinerary of the March*, 23.
[2] *Ibid.*, 25.

escort to Fort Sedgwick with his dispatch to Sherman, explaining his suggested plan for a continuous march of twenty or more days.

Major Joel A. Elliott was selected to carry the dispatches to Fort Sedgwick. Since it was to be an extremely dangerous mission embodying a round trip of almost two hundred miles over unknown terrain infested by hostile Indians, he was instructed to choose his own detail and plan his movements according to his best judgment. Realizing that small detachments were more mobile and could move more rapidly than larger ones, he limited his detail to ten men and included Lieutenant James T. Leavy and one scout. On the twenty-third, leaving by stealth at 3 A.M. so that their movements could not be detected in the dark, they moved rapidly to an area outside the center of danger.[3]

It will be recalled that the appearance of Custer's forces on the Republican had quieted action to the north on the Platte River, the Indians becoming more active on the Smoky Hill. On returning to St. Louis, General Sherman learned that Custer had sent to Fort Wallace for supplies. He sent orders to Custer through Lieutenant Henry G. Litchfield (General Augur's chief of staff at Omaha) stating:

> I don't understand about General Custer being on the Republican awaiting provisions from Fort Wallace. If this is so, and all the Indians be gone south, convey to him my orders that he proceed with all his command in search of the Indians towards Fort Wallace, and report to General Hancock, who will leave Denver for same place today.[4]

Lieutenant Litchfield transmitted these orders to Lieutenant Colonel Joseph H. Potter, who commanded Fort Sedgwick. He, in turn, gave the orders to Lieutenant Lyman Kidder along with a detail of ten men and an Indian guide, to carry to General Custer at his camp on the Republican.[5] There will be further discussion of this detail below.

On the afternoon before, Captain Robert M. West with Company

---

[3] *Ibid.*, 25; G. A. Custer, *My Life*, 55–56; Davis, "A Summer on the Plains," *loc. cit.*, 302.

[4] 40 Cong., 2 sess., *House Exec. Doc. 1*, 35.

[5] *Ibid.*, 35.

K left with the train of twelve wagons under command of Lieutenant William W. Cook and accompanied by Lieutenant Samuel M. Robbins and Company D, heading for Fort Wallace. West and Company K were to escort the wagon train as far as midway Beaver Creek, where he and his men were to use the waiting interval to scout up and down Beaver Creek.[6]

Cook had a letter for Mrs. Custer, who was expected to be at Fort Wallace, instructing her to return to the command and her husband in company with the loaded wagons. As matters went, she had not received her husband's earlier letters instructing her to be at Fort Wallace. A letter dated June 22 was published in "Tenting on the Plains" in which his anxiety for her is clearly stated and obviously stemming from his information of the rapidly spreading cholera.[7]

According to Bell in his *New Tracks in North America*, the Thirty-eighth Regiment of Infantry, a Negro regiment, had been ordered from Fort Leavenworth to Fort Union while showing the first signs of the dread disease.[8] From the records it appears that as they moved the disease accompanied them. An examination of burial records and of the markers in the post cemeteries clearly indicates that cholera had moved rapidly westward from Fort Leavenworth, the apparent point of origin. Post records of Fort Wallace for the year 1867 indicate that twenty-four individuals were killed by Indians and thirty died from cholera.[9]

Although the advance of the Negro troops westward was the reason offered for the spread of the dreaded cholera, numerous civilians, also became the victims of the disease. Their movements were not as easily traced even though it was evident the traffic of prospectors and pioneers westward had diminished slightly. Unquestionably they, too, aided the spread of the disease, for many of them succumbed to it along the way.

Custer and his men had received verbal reports from the outside world in their contacts with Forts McPherson and Sedgwick. Rumor of the spread of cholera was on every tongue. Concern for the safety

[6] G. A. Custer, *My Life*, 56.

[7] Elizabeth B. Custer, *Tenting*, 582–83.

[8] Pages 77–78.

[9] Records of Deceased Citizens, Fort Wallace, Kansas; Records of Deceased Soldiers, Fort Wallace, Kansas.

of their families was evident. There was a desire to complete the job they had set out to do as rapidly as possible, for only then would they be free to return to the post to meet their families and friends or receive regular mail from them. The receipt of mail in the field was a matter of extreme irregularity.

At dawn of the twenty-fourth Indians attempted to stampede Custer's horses. The pickets and the stable guards of the different troops had been posted as usual—the horses and mules having been tethered near the tents after their grazing. Suddenly the sharp crack of a carbine rang out, immediately followed by the cry "They are here!" The alert had been shouted by the officer of the day, Lieutenant Thomas W. Custer, the colonel's brother.[10]

The first shot brought every man from his tent armed and ready for battle. Custer burst through the tied tent flaps robed only in red flannels and holding his Spencer carbine. Rushing hatless and shoeless to the spot where the action seemed to have started he was told that one of the pickets had discovered the Indians just before they attempted to stampede the animals, and had opened fire. They, in turn, had shot him through the body and had ridden over him as they retreated before the brisk fire of the troopers. Although they had carried off his carbine and ammunition, they had not had time to scalp him or to discover that his wound was not fatal.

A mile away they reassembled, obviously awaiting another opportunity. Custer wanted to learn the identity of his attackers and the tribe to which they belonged. One of the interpreters was directed to advance to a point midway between the two adversaries and give the parlay signal at that point by riding in a circle. A small party of Indians responded to this signal, and through them it was arranged that seven of their chiefs would meet with Custer and six officers at the bank of the river, equidistant from the two factions.

Custer, his six officers and interpreter, and a bugler, proceeded to the appointed spot and dismounted. The horses were left in charge of the bugler, who was ordered to watch every move and in the event of treachery to sound the "Advance," a signal to the remaining troops.

Loosening their revolvers from their leather cases and thrusting

[10] Jackson, *Itinerary of the March,* 25; Davis, "A Summer on the Plains," *loc. cit.,* 302; G. A. Custer, *My Life,* 56–58.

them in their belts, Custer and his men descended the river bank to await the Indians. The seven chiefs soon arrived on the opposite bank, removed their leggings, and waded across. The river at this season of the year was but a shallow trickle.

Custer, in relating the episode to Libbie, stated:

> Imagine our surprise at recognizing as the head chief Pawnee Killer, our friend of the conference of the Platte, who on that occasion had overwhelmed us with the earnestness of his professions of peace, and who, after partaking of our hospitality under guise of friendship, and leaving our camp laden with provisions and presents, returned to attack and murder us within a fortnight. This too, without the slightest provocation, for surely we had not trespassed against any rights of theirs since the exchange of friendly greeting near Fort McPherson.[11]

Pawnee Killer and his Oglala Sioux companions immediately extended their hands with the familiar "How," while the suspicious Custer kept one hand on his revolver. The chiefs gave every evidence of forgiving him for his interference with the success of their raid on his camp. No reference was made to the matter, for Custer wanted to determine the location of their village and of their future movements.

Near the end of the conference a young brave emerged from the foliage on the opposite bank, crossed over, and greeted them in a friendly fashion. This maneuver was repeated until four had joined the original party. Custer drew attention to this violation of the terms under which they were to meet. Pawnee Killer made light of it, saying; "They like to meet friends. Their hearts are good." At this point another party of warriors was seen approaching the ford, whereupon Custer, who by this time was well aware of impending treachery, told Pawnee Killer, "No more warriors can cross. See my bugler out of gun range. At my signal he will call all of my men to my side in a few moments. What chance would you have?"

Pawnee Killer immediately signaled the Indians on the other side to remain there. After a bit of verbal sparring, in which each tried to obtain information from the other and which satisfied Custer that the Indians were intent upon mischief, Pawnee Killer made it evident

---

[11] G. A. Custer, *My Life*, 58.

that he was going to rejoin his warriors. Custer was extremely anxious to detain him or to locate his village. This concern was prompted by the absence of his own two detachments. Major Elliott and his party of eleven would be no match for these warriors. The detachment to Fort Wallace was larger and better able to protect itself. When Pawnee Killer seemed ready to leave, Custer told him that he would march with him to the village. The chief countered by asking for sugar, coffee and ammunition. Custer refused. He had witnessed a strange repayment for the last such gifts.

Since there was nothing more to be said, the Indians recrossed the river and galloped off to join their main body some two miles away, while the troopers returned to camp. His command was in readiness, so Custer ordered them to follow the Indians at top speed—determined, if possible, to locate their village. After several hours of pursuit it became evident the heavier horses of the cavalry could not maintain the speed of the small Indian ponies, so they returned to camp.

A short time later a small party of Indians was observed approaching from a different direction than the one taken by those they had been following. Captain Louis Hamilton was immediately ordered to take his troops and pursue the Indians in order to learn of their intentions. The six Indians sighted had disappeared over a ridge. When this ridge was reached by the troops the Indians were seen on the next ridge beyond. After this course of events was repeated a number of times the cavalry found themselves several miles from camp, at which point the Indians divided into two parties, each going in a different direction. Captain Hamilton divided his forces, placing Colonel Custer's brother, Lieutenant Tom Custer, in command of a detachment to follow one party, while he followed the other with his twenty-five men. When they had become so widely separated in their pursuits that they could be of no assistance to each other, Captain Hamilton suddenly saw forty-three Indians spring out of a hiding place in a ravine and fill the air with arrows and war whoops. Then the Indians began circling the soldiers and throwing themselves upon the sides of their horses, firing their carbines or their bows as they rode by at breakneck speeds. With great coolness Captain Hamilton formed his men into a position of defense while the Indians, with growing boldness, rode closer to send in their showers of bullets and arrows.

The medical officer, Dr. Coates, had accompanied Captain Hamilton, but in the division of the command had joined Lieutenant Tom Custer. Somehow he had become separated from both parties. When but half a mile from Captain Hamilton he heard the firing, saw what was transpiring, and wisely chose to head four miles back to camp as fast as his spurred horse would take him. The Indians, seeing him escaping, decided to alter his plans. Though the Indians had faster mounts, the doctor had the advantages of a head start and a desire to live. A broken cinch or a fall could quickly lose the race. As the Indian ponies narrowed the gap, the yells grew louder, terrifying the doctor's horse. When his pursuers were almost within arrow range, the camp came into view a mile away. The grief of the Indians was apparent as they sent a volley of bullets after him and then turned away to avoid pursuit from the fresh animals they knew were in the cavalry camp.

When Coates reached camp, he threw himself from his horse and had to lie on the ground, speechless from exhaustion and excitement. As soon as he had recovered sufficiently to tell the astonished cavalrymen of the plight of their comrades, the bugle blared out "To Horse," and the men were on their way.[12] Since they had at least five miles to cover to reach the point where Captain Hamilton last had been seen, the reinforcements pushed forward at a trot to conserve their horses for the conflict that seemed inevitable. After traveling about two miles they observed in the distance Captain Hamilton and his troopers returning leisurely, having beaten off their assailants, killing two warriors and wounding several others. The Indians had wounded one cavalry horse.

This action occurred within the course taken by Major Elliott and his men, leaving no doubt that the area between the Arkansas and Platte rivers was infested by warring Indians. This loss of two warriors would increase their activities and inflame their desire for revenge. Major Elliott and his men were a matter of concern. No reinforcements could be sent to meet them, since their exact route

[12] *Ibid.*, 60–62; Davis, "A Summer on the Plains," *loc. cit.*, 303.

was unknown. There was nothing to do but wait, and wait they did, for the next few days.

On June 28 Major Elliott and his escort arrived, their mission accomplished. They had ridden two hundred miles through enemy territory at night, concealing themselves in ravines during the day. A guide and a compass had made it possible.[13]

Anxieties were transferable, and, with Elliott safely back, all thoughts turned to the larger party that had headed to Fort Wallace for supplies. Since Major Elliott had not come into contact with hostile Indians on his journey to the north, the probability was that they had moved to the south, between the command and Fort Wallace.

Custer reasoned that a wagon train could not get to Fort Wallace without being seen. The Indians would permit them to go through, knowing they would return loaded with supplies. They would observe that the larger portion of the escort remained at Beaver Creek while the wagon train proceeded to the fort, guarded by only forty-eight men. The time and place to attack the loaded wagon train would be on its return trip, somewhere between Fort Wallace and Beaver Creek. Custer's apprehension grew when he realized that his wife, in response to his letter, probably would be at the fort when the wagon train arrived, in which case she would return with it.

Because of his great Indian experience, Custer had placed Captain Edward Myers in charge of a squadron of men, with orders to follow the trail of the wagon train until he had joined Captain Robert M. West's command at Beaver Creek nearly fifty miles away. Leaving on the night that Captain Hamilton had his engagement with the Sioux, Myers carried written orders for West to join the two commands and march toward Fort Wallace until they should meet the train and its escort.

Myers marched his men to Beaver Creek without halting.[14] They joined Captain West, and under his command as the senior officer they proceeded toward Fort Wallace. There was little difficulty in following the trail of the wagon train, because the tracks were easily discernable in the dry soil. Once the combined squadrons united with

---

[13] G. A. Custer, *My Life*, 62; Davis, "A Summer on the Plains," *loc. cit.*, 303.
[14] Jackson, *Itinerary of the March*, 28; G. A. Custer, *My Life*, 63.

the wagon train escort there would be little likelihood of surprise or defeat, since Captain West was an experienced Indian fighter with a thorough knowledge of their tactics.

The wagon train and its escort of forty-eight men was under the command of Lieutenant Samuel M. Robbins, with the wagon train itself under the command of Lieutenant William W. Cook. They proceeded to Beaver Creek without incident, where they were met by Captain West and his command.

Leaving at dawn the next day, the entire command moved toward Fort Wallace.[15] Captain West sent out portions of his command as scouting parties searching for Indians. There had been no indication of hostility from the Indians, and none was contemplated. They were totally unaware of Hamilton's engagement with hostile Indians to the north.

While moving over a large, level plateau which gave the appearance of unruffled terrain for many miles around, Will Comstock, their guide, remarked, "If the injuns strikes us at all, it will be just about the time we are comin' along back over this very spot. Now mind what I tell ye all."[16]

Although level in appearance, the tabletop-like surface of the plateau was covered with ravines, imperceptable at first glance, but running almost up to the very trail over which they traveled. These natural hiding places became deeper as they progressed away from the plateau, terminating in a distant valley of some running stream. They were excellent hiding places for Indian ambush, as the veteran scout Comstock was quick to perceive.

The remainder of the trip to Fort Wallace was uneventful.[17] The wagons were quickly loaded with fresh supplies, the mail was obtained, and preparations were made to return the following day. Neither Libbie Custer nor her mail was found at the fort. The General's letter to her from Fort McPherson, requesting her to be at Fort Wallace, had miscarried.

[15] G. A. Custer, *My Life*, 63.
[16] *Ibid.*, 64.
[17] *Ibid.*, 64.

VI. ATTACK
ON THE WAGON TRAIN

THE RETURN OF THE DETACHMENT was slower, because the wagons were loaded with the sorely needed supplies. Lieutenant Robbins was mindful of Will Comstock's warning as they had approached Fort Wallace. Patrols were constantly on the alert for Indians, particularly when they reached the level plateau where Will had made his prophetic statement. The monotony of the march had been uninterrupted until suddenly Comstock, who had been searching the horizon with eyes as keen and as trained as any Indian, observed strange figures on the crest of a hill to the far right.[1] Using his field glasses he pronounced the figures to be nothing less than Indians, an observation soon corroborated by the officers. The command had traveled half the distance back to Beaver Creek.

Soon the Indians realized they had been discovered. Since further concealment was valueless, they boldly rode to the crest of the hill for all to see. At first a few dozen made their appearance, but gradually the number increased to a hundred. If the fifty troopers had wondered whether these were hostiles or friendlies, any doubts soon were dissipated.

Observing the leisurely advancing warriors through his field glasses, Comstock noted that they were arrayed in full war costume—

[1] G. A. Custer, *My Life*, 64.

war bonnets, war paint and all.[2] Some of them carried long lances with colorful pennants, and hanging from their left arms were the round, almost bullet-proof buffalo hide shields adorned with bright paint and feathers of varied design. Most of them were armed with carbines and revolvers, and many carried bow and arrows besides.

As they approached down the slope, seemingly confident in their superior numbers, the soldiers formed a rough estimate of their full strength. Reinforcements beyond the hill on which they were first seen had gradually increased their numbers until they now had between six and seven hundred warriors in their party. Adding to their advantage was a terrain extremely favorable to the Indian method of warfare.

Lieutenant Cook ordered the wagon train into two parallel columns, wide enough apart to permit the cavalry horses between them as they moved along or stopped.[3] The plight of the fifty men was precarious. Defense being the only recourse, the men were dismounted to fight on foot in the form of a circle around the wagon train. Every fourth man was assigned the job of horse-holding between the two columns of wagons. The wagonmaster had orders from Lieutenant Cook to keep the wagons moving and close together, though these orders were hardly necessary, since the savage screams of the advancing warriors had the frightened teamsters involuntarily doing just that.

When the first attack came it was made on one flank. The men coolly held their fire until the Indians were within short range of their Spencer repeating carbines. Dropping to one knee, they took deliberate aim and poured such a volley into the oncoming Indians that they were forced to swerve to one side and pass by. Several of them reeled in their saddles, while others went down with their wounded ponies but had hardly touched the ground before their comrades dashed to their rescue, snatching them up to their running ponies to prevent them from losing their scalps to an enemy—for it was their belief that by losing a scalp in such a fashion all chance of reaching the happy hunting ground was lost forever.[4]

[2] *Ibid.*, 64.
[3] *Ibid.*, 65; Davis, "A Summer on the Plains," *loc. cit.*, 303.
[4] G. A. Custer, *My Life*, 65–66; Davis, "A Summer on the Plains," *loc. cit.*, 303.

Unnerved by the fierceness of the fire, the Indians withdrew out of carbine range to parley. The troopers, jubilant in their obvious success, gave vent to their feelings in a rousing cheer. Comstock lost no time in shouting his taunts to the retreating Sioux in their native tongue. He concluded that:

> There's no sich good luck for us to think them Injuns mean to give it up so. Six hundred red devils ain't agoin to let fifty men stop them from gettin' at the sugar and coffee that is in these wagons. And they ain't agoin' to be satisfied until they get some of our scalps to pay for the bucks we popped out of their saddles a bit ago.[5]

It took little time to decide, for the attack was quickly renewed. The first charge had been in a body; this time the warriors had elected to fight individually in the habitual Indian method of "circling," but exercising great caution. The chiefs led off, followed at regular intervals by the warriors in single file until all six or seven hundred had formed a huge circle around the fifty troopers and their wagons, appearing to engulf them completely. The ponies were ridden at full speed as their riders hurled savage war whoops and epithets toward their prey. There was no response. Gaining more courage because of the silence of the soldiers, the Indians contracted their single file circle. Suddenly the soldiers opened fire. Although the results were satisfactory, it appeared that it would be only a matter of time before the small force would run out of ammunition and succumb to superior numbers. At no time did the wagon train come to a halt.[6]

The unparalleled horsemanship of the warriors was a sight to behold. Riding at high speed in single file, they held themselves on the far sides of their ponies, only exposing their heads and a single foot, and from this position were able to aim their weapons from over or under the necks of their ponies, using their ponies as shields against the carbine fire of the troopers and thus offering a most difficult target. This running battle lasted for three hours without a letup. Cavalry ammunition was running low. The only sources of relief would be nightfall or reinforcements, and both seemed far away.

The Indians had posted scouts on the high bluffs that paralleled

[5] G. A. Custer, *My Life*, 66.
[6] *Ibid.*, 67.

the trail, to watch for any possible interference from the outside. Although apparently turning all of their attention to the fight below, they were not long in observing something on the horizon some ten miles away that only the practiced frontiersman or Indian would have seen. By careful watching, what at first appeared to be a stationary dark line on the horizon was seen to be moving. It slowly assumed more definite shape until the searching eyes of the scouts determined that it was a column of cavalry moving toward the very point they were occupying. Once it was determined, it took only moments to impart the knowledge to the besieging warriors. It was theirs to decide whether they could overcome the besieged in the two hours it would take for the fresh cavalry detachment to arrive. Prudence overruled desire, for their mounts were exhausted after three hours of hard riding. Sending a final volley of bullets and arrows into the train, they withdrew to the bluffs and disappeared.

The surprised and uninformed troopers took the intermission in their fight for survival to give their few wounded every possible attention. Their exultation at the withdrawal of the Indians lasted but an hour when fresh fears arose. Far ahead of them there was another cause for alarm—a body of unidentified horsemen had appeared. These fears soon were dispelled, however, for field-glasses indicated that these were not Indians—they wore the blue blouses of the cavalry. Lieutenant Cook, Bill Comstock, and a few troopers dashed out to meet them. These men were known. Captain West and his detachment, sent to relieve the wagon train's escort, had arrived. This explained the Indian's abandonment of what had seemed to be a sure thing. The score: at least five Indians known to have been killed and many wounded; of the cavalrymen only a few were wounded.[7] On the morning of the twenty-eighth all were back in the main camp on the Republican River.[8]

[7] *Ibid.*, 68; *Difficulties With Indian Tribes*, 110–11.

[8] G. A. Custer, *My Life*, 69; Jackson, *Itinerary of the March*, 28. Jackson records Companies E, D, and K as returning to camp June 27, with Major Elliott and party returning June 28. G. A. Custer's *My Life*, 62, indicates that on June 27, "our fears for the safety of the Major and his escort were dispelled by their safe return to camp. . . . our anxiety [now] became centered in the fate of the larger party which had proceeded with the train to Fort Wallace for supplies." Then on

Hancock's encampment at Fort Harker, April 2, 1867. Custer's headquarters and the cavalry camp on the left, the artillery camp in front, and the general head-quarters, right background. *Harper's Weekly*, April 27, 1867.

Burning the Cheyenne village near Fort Larned, Kansas, April 19, 1867. Lodges, saddles, furs, and clothing were destroyed. *Harper's Weekly*, June 8, 1867.

Meanwhile, Custer had his men break camp, cross the north fork of the Republican River, and then cross the south fork of the Republican and camp on its bank. Leaving there at 5 A.M. of the following day, June 30, they moved in a southwesterly direction along its bank between the rolling hills on either side of the river and made camp on the border of a creek twenty miles from their camp of the morning.[9]

The march was continued in the same direction the following morning. After crossing several dry creek beds emptying into the Republican River, the command made a crossing to the north side of the Republican and went into camp surrounded by scattered timber. The horses had traveled twenty miles that day. Sleep came easy to all, for the day had been hot and the trail arduous.

The beginning of the next day's march came at 5 A.M.[10] Moving in a northwesterly direction they crossed Bob Tail Creek after traveling fourteen miles. The crossing was good, because the banks were low and the bottom of firm sand. A series of bluffs commenced on the south side of the creek a mile east of this crossing, and continued from there to its mouth. They were utterly impossible for wagons, since they were perpendicular, of solid stone, and from thirty to fifty feet high.

Camp broke at the usual time the next day and the troopers, heading in a northerly direction, traversed some very rough country until they struck bad prairieland, which continued for some miles before they reached Black Tail Deer Creek.[11] The ravines leading to the creek were found to be impassable, forcing the men to travel eastward until a suitable avenue was discovered. Even so, the crossing bottom was soft and the creek banks soggy and miry. Continuing along the northerly border eastward they found a campsite in an area having sandy soil. At this point sand hills came almost to the creek's edge on the north side, while on the south side the banks consisted of bluffs of

page 69 he writes: ". . . on the morning of the 28th the train, with its escort, returned to the main camp on the Republican."

Dispatches brought by Major Elliott from General Sherman directed Custer to strike out for Riverside Station west of Fort Sedgwick.

[9] Jackson, *Itinerary of the March*, 28.
[10] *Ibid.*, 28.
[11] *Ibid.*, 28.

solid stone thirty to fifty feet high. The day had been warm and windless. As the tents were being pitched, a slight breeze arose which gradually increased in velocity. In a short time the sand-ridden air had moisture added to it, for the rain came. Wind, rain, and sand pounded the troopers with increasing intensity, tearing down one tent after another until nearly everyone was exposed to the raging elements. Seeming to wait just for this moment, hailstones added to the general discomfort. Horses became difficult to manage—having traveled twenty-one miles that day over exceedingly troublesome terrain, they were tired and uncomfortable. Some broke away from the picket line but were found within the camp lines. The night was too dark for them to travel far.

Daybreak was a welcome relief; the wind had abated and the damage was adjusted. The column moved out at the usual time and continued north, crossing Chief Creek and camping at the site of a magnificent spring surrounded by luxurious grass and sandy soil.[12] The remainder of the day was used for resting the command—the fact that it was the Fourth of July playing no part in the decision to stop early. Although there was no celebrating in the cavalry camp, such was not the case elsewhere.

At midnight the command moved forward through a break in the sand hills and out onto a hard, level prairie.[13] The march continued across several arroyos and dry creek beds. Water could be obtained by digging, but was in quantities sufficient only for the men. The burning sun and arid land were causing untold suffering among the horses and mules and some of the dogs died from thirst and exhaustion. Custer decided to press on to the Platte River that day. Leaving Major Elliott in command he took Lieutenant Moylan, Dr. Coates, and an orderly with him, intending to push on to the river in order to select as good a campsite as darkness would permit.[14] At that point the river appeared to be four or five miles distant, but they traveled mile after weary mile and found no sign of the all-important stream. At eleven o'clock, after having covered fifteen miles, they reached the riverbank. First watering their horses and then quenching their own thirsts they discussed the possibility that the command might reach that point soon. Since the hour was late and the distance between them

[12] *Ibid.*, 30.   [13] *Ibid.*, 32.   [14] G. A. Custer, *My Life*, 68.

great, it was not expected that the men would arrive before morning.

Selecting a grassy area for their bivouac they picketed the horses by fastening the halterstrap to the hilt of a saber and then forcing the blade into the ground. The horses grazed a bit, but soon yielded to fatigue.

Using the saddles for pillows and the saddle blankets for covers, the men soon fell asleep. Wisely, they covered their blankets with their rubber ponchos to keep off the dew; by doing so, they protected themselves from a heavy shower that night. So weary were they that none awakened during the shower, although it did arouse them to the point of pulling their ponchos over their faces so they could sleep undisturbed.

At the first sign of daylight, all awakened as if by a bugle call, and attended to hasty toilet in the river nearby. By the time they were through there was sufficient light to examine the surrounding countryside. Their field glasses revealed the bivouac of the troops three miles down-river. In a matter of minutes their rested horses carried them to the troops, where they learned that the column had turned off the trail in the darkness and headed for the river at this point, some of the men not reaching the riverbank until that morning.[15]

After breakfast a detachment went on to Riverside Station, one mile to the east, where Custer learned that the preceding evening Indians had attacked the next stage station west, killing three men.[16]

It was Custer's belief that General Sherman had sent on to Fort Sedgwick later orders than those he was acting under, so he sent a telegram of inquiry to the commanding officer there. Great was his surprise when the reply indicated that the day after Major Elliott and his detachment had left Fort Sedgwick with dispatches a second detachment, consisting of ten troopers of the Second United States Cavalry under the command of Lieutenant Lyman Kidder, had left Fort Sedgwick with dispatches from General Sherman. These dispatches were to be delivered to Custer at his camp near the forks of the Republican River, but, failing to find him there, were to be delivered to him wherever he could be overtaken on the trail.

[15] Jackson, *Itinerary of the March*, 33.
[16] G. A. Custer, *My Life*, 69.

VII. THE KIDDER
MASSACRE

In February of 1867, Lyman S. Kidder had been appointed a second lieutenant by President Johnson.[1] His previous military experience had been in the east during the Civil War, following which he had been mustered out as a first lieutenant. Arriving at Fort Sedgwick in late June as a member of the Second United States Cavalry, he soon was assigned to extremely hazardous duty, despite the fact that he had had no experience in fighting Indians.

On June 29 Kidder was ordered to the commandant's quarters and detailed to carry to Colonel Custer important dispatches received from General Sherman. His post commander, Lieutenant Colonel Joseph H. Potter, gave him written instructions as follows:

> You will proceed at once to the forks of the Republican, with an escort of ten (10) men of Co. M. Second U.S. Cavalry, where you will deliver to General Custer the dispatches with which you will be intrusted. Should General Custer have left that point, you will take his trail and overtake him. After delivering your dispatches you will return to this post. Until you reach General Custer you will travel as rapidly as possible.[2]

A Sioux Chief, Red Bead, was assigned as his guide. Kidder, al-

[1] E. A. Brininstool, "The Kidder Massacre," *Hunter-Trader-Trapper*, Vol. LXV, No. 6 (December, 1932), 12.
[2] *Ibid.*, 12.

though only twenty-five years of age, was older than nine of his men, four of whom were only nineteen. About half of them were foreign-born.³ Why this detail of boys under the command of an officer with absolutely no experience in Indian warfare was sent on a suicidal mission—for such it was in Indian country—always has remained a mystery.

Custer had become greatly concerned—both for the safety of Kidder and his small command and for intelligence of the orders Kidder was carrying to him. He telegraphed Fort Sedgwick advising the commandant that no contact had been made with Kidder and requesting that a copy of the orders carried be procured for him. The reply transmitted orders from General Sherman directing Custer to march his command "across the country from the Platte [River] to the Smoky Hill River, striking the latter at Fort Wallace."⁴

Custer started his command for Fort Wallace at daybreak.⁵ The early start was occasioned by a feeling of anxiety for the Kidder party and the scarcity of supplies. Though promised, no supplies had been delivered, either to Fort Sedgwick or to Riverside Station. It was time to move.

Davis mentions that there was considerable uneasiness in the minds of the officers—a feeling that since Kidder had not succeeded in overtaking the command it was certain some misfortune had befallen him.⁶ Comparisons had been made between Elliott and Kidder. It was evident that Elliott was an officer of experience, who had the good fortune to accomplish his mission before it was known that the Indians were on the warpath. Kidder was without experience, and perhaps without luck.

Tragedy was about to strike the cavalry column. Inferior and insufficient rations, nearness to the overland route of travel to some newly-discovered mining claims in Colorado Territory, and the supposed opportunity to amass great wealth as prospectors or miners

³ *Ibid.*, 12.
⁴ *Ibid.*, 13; G. A. Custer, *My Life*, 70–71; Davis, "A Summer on the Plains," *loc. cit.*, 306; Montgomery, "Fort Wallace and its Relation to the Frontier," *loc. cit.*, 217.
⁵ G. A. Custer, *My Life*, 73.
⁶ Davis, "A Summer on the Plains," *loc. cit.*, 306.

proved too great a temptation to many of the enlisted men. Forgetting that they had sworn allegiance to the flag, that they were in enemy country and in a state of war, and that the penalty for desertion under those circumstances was death, a number of them made plans to desert.

Davis indicated that, "The stay of a single day on the banks of the Platte River cost the command a loss of thirty-five men by desertion. This out of a force of less than three hundred was a serious misfortune."[7] The deserters left early on the morning of July 7, causing much concern. However, there was no time for pursuit. The column started southward at 5 A.M., retracing their previous path across a prairie covered with cacti.[8]

Having marched fifteen miles by noon, the command halted to rest and graze the horses for a short time. Not knowing that they were going to march an additional fifteen miles, and believing that they would be encamped for the rest of the day, about a third of the remaining troopers conspired to seize their horses and arms that night and escape to the mountains. When orders were given to repack for continuation of the march, thirteen soldiers, seven of them on horseback, were seen to leave camp traveling in a northerly direction as rapidly as they could move. Neither the shouts of the officers nor the "Recall" sounded by the bugler diminished their speed. Desertion in broad daylight under such circumstances was a sight the officers never before had encountered. The only horses saddled were those of the guard and a few of the officers. Orders were given the officer of the guard to pursue and overtake the deserters.[9] Major Elliott, Lieutenant Custer, Lieutenant Cook, and seven of the men began the pursuit at a gallop. They soon discovered that the deserters had taken seven of the fleetest horses in the command, making it impossible, with the lead they had, to overtake them. Not so with those on foot. After a chase of several miles they came within hailing distance and were ordered to halt. Major Elliott repeated the order several times and obtained no response. As they neared the men the ringleader raised his carbine to fire on his pursuers, which was the signal for the latter

[7] *Ibid.*, 306.
[8] Jackson, *Itinerary of the March*, 33.
[9] G. A. Custer, *My Life*, 72–73.

to open fire. Three of the deserters were brought down in the first volley, and the remaining three surrendered immediately.[10]

While resuming the march, a trusted sergeant informed Custer that a large portion of his command intended to desert that night. Realizing the seriousness of being left stranded with a diminutive force of men, Custer proceeded to place every officer on guard duty that night, advising his men accordingly. Since the expected break did not occur, it became evident that the summary measures of that afternoon had produced a satisfactory effect. There were no more desertions for the remainder of the campaign.[11]

The column moved south the next day and then began heading eastward into the "prickly pear country." As far as the eye could see, the countryside was covered with cacti. As strangely beautiful as this country was, it caused considerable discomfort to both the men and the animals. The dogs were glad to be kept in the wagons, although occasionally they escaped and went howling along the column, painfully paying for their moments of freedom.[12]

The troopers finally reached a place of rest on the west side of Ironwood Spring Creek at its confluence with Chief Creek (north fork of the Republican River). Here the bottom land on the south side of Chief Creek was, at most, half a mile wide and backed by perpendicular stone bluffs impossible for the passage of wagons; on the north side were sand hills, running down to the banks.

The command left camp at 5 A.M. on the tenth and traveled the south bank of Chief Creek, crossing a number of dry creeks with no great difficulty. They made several short rest stops. When they reached Bob Tail Deer Creek, the stone bluffs were replaced with rolling hills to the south.

After crossing the three-foot banks of Bob Tail Deer Creek and proceeding easterly, they crossed several gulches with dry bottoms, all of which emptied into what was now called the North Fork of the Republican River. The ground traversed was hard-back prairie, intersected by ravines or gulches formed by winter rains in the hills lying from one to four miles back from the river. It was impossible for the

---

[10] *Ibid.*, 73.

[11] *Ibid.*, 73; Davis, "A Summer on the Plains," *loc. cit.*, 306.

[12] Davis, "A Summer on the Plains," *loc. cit.*, 306.

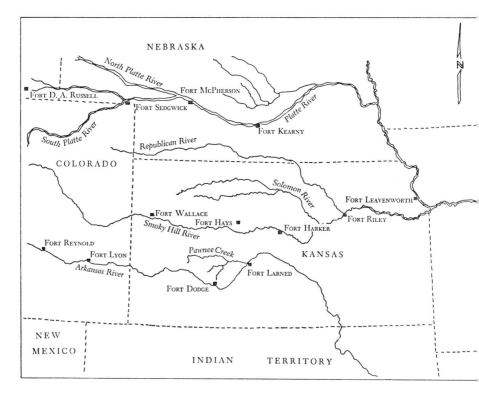

NEBRASKA
North Platte River
Fort D. A. Russell
Fort McPherson
Fort Sedgwick
South Platte River
Fort Kearny
Platte River
Republican River
COLORADO
Solomon River
Fort Leavenworth
Fort Wallace
Fort Hays
Fort Harker
Fort Riley
Smoky Hill River
Fort Reynold
Fort Lyon
Pawnee Creek
KANSAS
Arkansas River
Fort Larned
Fort Dodge
NEW
MEXICO
INDIAN   TERRITORY
N

Principal western cavalry forts in 1867.

wagons to travel along the low ground at the river's edge because of its extremely miry condition.[13]

That evening, after camp had been made secure and the men had congregated around their campfires discussing the events of the day, one of the officers sat on the ground beside Will Comstock as he reached for a burning ember to light his pipe and said, "Will, you've heard us discuss the chances Lieutenant Kidder and his men have in getting through to us, and you've heard us make bets on the chance the youngster has. Now you usually have something to say but you've been mighty silent through it all. Don't you have an idea on the subject?"

Will didn't lift his head, but just kept looking into the fire as he

[13] Jackson, *Itinerary of the March*, 36–38.

72

puffed on his pipe. After several moments of silence—for no one spoke as they waited to hear from the one man whose opinion on Indians they respected most—Will turned toward the group and said,

Well gentle*men*, [emphasizing the last syllable as was his manner] before a man kin form any ijee as to how this thing is likely to end, thar are several things he ort to be acquainted with. For instance, now, no man need tell me any p'ints about Injuns. Ef I know this young lootenint—I mean Lootenint Kidder—ef I know what for sort of man he is, I could tell you might near to sartainty all you want to know, for you see Injun huntin' and Injun fightin' is a trade all by itself, and like any other bizness a man has to know what he's about, or ef he don't he can't make a livin' at it. I have lots of confi-*dence* in the fightin' sense of Red Bead, the Sioux chief, who is guidin' the young lootenint and his men, and ef that Injun kin have his own way thar is a fair show for his guidin' 'em through alright; but as I sed before, thar lays the difficulty. Is this lootenint the kind of a man who is willin' to take advice, even ef it does cum from a Injun? My experience with you army folks has allus bin that the youngsters among ye think they know the most, and this is perticu-larly true ef they hev jest cum from West P'int. Ef some of them young fellars knowed half as much as they b'lieve they do, ye couldn't tell thim nothin! As to rale book larnin, why I suppose they got it all, but the fact of the matter is, they couldn't tell the difference twixt the trail of a war party and one made by a huntin' party to save thar necks. Half uv 'em when they first cum here can't tell a squaw from a buck, just because both ride straddle; but they soon larn. But that's neither here nor thar. I'm told that the lootenint we're talkin' about is a newcomer, and that this is his first scout. Ef that be the case, it puts a mighty onsartain look on the whole thing, and twixt you and me gentle*men*, he'll be mighty lucky ef he gits through alright. Tomorrow we'll strike the Wallace trail, and I kin soon tell ef he has gone that way.[14]

Nearing the North Fork's confluence with the South Fork of the Republican the following day, the column turned to the southeast about ten miles above the junction. The march was over very rough, broken hills, and then over rolling prairie. After a good crossing on the South Fork of the Republican River, where the banks were low,

[14] G. A. Custer, *My Life*, 74.

the bed of firm sand, and the water a foot deep, the country to be traversed presented a series of arroyos, deep ravines, gullies, and ridges, and then another hard, rolling prairie. Following a four-hour rest on Thickwood Creek the column pressed forward, finally striking Captain West's old trail toward Fort Wallace. They followed this trail southward over level prairie covered with cacti, and made camp without benefit of water and with but little grass.

Continuing along Captain West's trail the following morning, the men found a resting spot halfway to Beaver Creek that provided an abundant supply of water. Following a four-hour halt during which Comstock and his Delaware Indian scouts had moved in advance to examine the various tracks seen on the trail toward Fort Wallace, the column moved on in the same direction. After following Comstock's party a few miles the command overtook them as they were concluding their appraisals.

"Well, what do you find, Comstock?" was Colonel Custer's first question. Comstock replied:

> They've gone to Fort Wallace for sure. The trail shows that twelve American horses, shod all round, have passed at a walk, goin' in the direction of the fort; and when they went by this p'int they were alright, 'cause their horses were moving along easy like, and there are no pony tracks behind 'em, as wouldn't be the case ef the Indians had got an eye on 'em. It would be astonishin' ef that lootenint and his layouts gits into the fort without a scrimmage. He may, but ef he does, it will be a scratch ef ever there was one, and I'll lose my confidence in Injuns.[15]

The column pressed on in blistering heat, for the sun was high in the heavens and not a cloud was visible. The interest of the men and the anxiety of the officers had increased since all had heard the opinion and observations of Comstock. With Fort Wallace only two days away, the fate of Kidder and his party soon would be known.

Pursuing the trail of Captain West and ordering Comstock and his scouts to keep a close watch on Kidder's trail, Custer forgot time and distance as the tension increased. Then a strange object was seen on the trail a mile or more in the distance. Comstock and some of his Delawares galloped toward it and discovered that it was the carcass

[15] *Ibid.*, 75.

of a white horse. Closer examination revealed that it carried a U.S. brand, and that it had been shot by a bullet within the past few days. Major Elliott remembered seeing a company of cavalry mounted on white horses at Fort Sedgwick. All evidence led to the conclusion that this was one of the horses belonging to Kidder's command.[16]

A careful examination was made of surrounding ground in an attempt to determine whether or not the dead horse had been a victim of an Indian skirmish. The horse had been stripped of all his equipment—whether by friend or foe it could not be resolved—but it was generally concluded that it had been destroyed by Indians. Some of the men thought the horse might have been taken ill on the trail, a common occurrence, and one in which orders were given to kill the animal rather than leave it behind and have it fall into the hands of the Indians.

Two miles down the trail another dead horse was found, apparently killed in a similar manner. Near this one Comstock discovered some pony tracks that clearly indicated the presence of Indians. The terrain was that of a level plateau, such as Indians would choose so they could easily encircle their victims. Not a break or a depression could be found behind which a defense could be made.

Here were indications that both horses and ponies were running at full speed. Prior to that the horses had been walking. The trail began to descend into a valley through which meandered a small stream known as Beaver Creek, some two miles distant.

Custer noted several buzzards floating lazily over an area within a mile of this creek and slightly to the left of the trail. Noticeable, too, was a rank stench that he had encountered many times upon the battlefield, that of decaying corpses.

Comstock, the Delawares, and several of the officers separated from the main column and conducted a search. Finally, one of the Delawares uttered a whoop and, at the same time, jumped to the ground to examine something. Custer, in his *Life On The Plains*, wrote:

> Hastening, in common with many others of the party, to his side, a sight met our gaze which even at this remote day makes my very blood curdle. Lying in irregular order, and within a very limited

[16] *Ibid.*, 75.

circle, were the mangled bodies of poor Kidder and his party, yet so brutally hacked and disfigured as to be beyond recognition save as human beings.

Every individual of the party had been scalped and his skull broken —the latter done by some weapon, probably a tomahawk—except the Sioux chief Red Bead, whose scalp had simply been removed from his head and then thrown down by his side. This, Comstock informed us, was in accordance with a custom which prohibits an Indian from bearing off the scalp of one of his own tribe. This circumstance, then, told us who the perpetrators of this deed were. They could be none other than the Sioux, led in all probability by Pawnee Killer.[17]

Red Bead was less disfigured than the rest—he could be recognized. The tendons of the arms and legs had been severed, the nose of every man was hacked off, and their faces were so disfigured that none was recognizable. All of their clothing had been removed, and some of them were lying in beds of ashes, indicating that they had been put to death by torture. All of the bodies were bristling with arrows, varying in number from twenty to fifty. Try as they might, after the most painstaking scrutiny, the men could find not one shred of evidence that could lead to the identity of any of the victims. A trench was dug near the spot where they lost their lives, and all were buried in a common grave.[18]

As the troopers moved south toward the headwaters of Short Nose Creek, where they were to camp that evening, they debated varying theories as to what actually transpired at the scene of the massacre. No Indian account was given for many years, for fear of retribution. In reconstructing Kidder's movements, Custer recalled the encampment of the Seventh Cavalry at the fork of the Republican on its north bank, waiting for the return of the wagon train from Fort Wallace, which arrived on the day Kidder left Fort Sedgwick.[19] The

[17] *Ibid.*, 77.

[18] *Ibid.*, 78; Davis, "A Summer on the Plains," *loc. cit.*, 307; *Harper's Weekly* (August 17, 1867), 513; *Custer's Report to the Adjutant General*, August 7, 1867, AGO files No. 94.

[19] Grinnell, *The Fighting Cheyennes*, 252–53; George Bent, "Forty Years With the Cheyennes" (edited by George Hyde), *The Frontier* (February, 1906), 4–5.

following morning Custer moved south on the Fort Wallace trail for five miles and then he bore west at right angles to it.[20]

After breaking camp the next morning the column marched along Captain West's trail across rolling prairie, striking the Solomon Holes which during the winter were the headwaters of the Solomon River.[21] After resting here, the command moved southerly again, crossing Black Butte Creek and later Lake Creek, reaching the north bank of the Smoky Hill River half a mile west of Fort Wallace to make camp late in the afternoon of July 13. Since June 1 the main column had marched 705 miles.[22]

[20] Jackson, *Itinerary of the March*, 42–43; 40 Cong., 2 sess., *House Exec. Doc. 1*, 35.

[21] Jackson, *Itinerary of the March*, 42.

[22] *Ibid.*, 43.

VIII. FORT WALLACE
BESIEGED

Fort Wallace was situated on the south fork of the Smoky Hill River, the nearest settlement being Pond City, two miles to the west. First called Camp Pond Creek in 1865, its name was changed to Fort Wallace on September 18, 1866. It was the last and westernmost military post in Kansas and was on the Butterfield Overland Despatch route to Denver.[1]

Initially, the post was built for four companies and could accommodate about five hundred men. At no time, though, did it house a full complement, since the troops stationed there were constantly moved about to act as guards at the various stations of the Smoky Hill stage route, to escort the stagecoaches and wagon trains, or to protect the railroad surveyors and construction crews. It provided more military service than any other post in Kansas.

During June and early July the fort had been the center of repeated Indian raids. Captain Myles W. Keogh, who was to die with Custer at the Little Big Horn in 1876, had been in command of the post and Company "I" of the Seventh U.S. Cavalry since November, 1866. His was the arduous task of spreading the already too few troops over the long line of communication and supply on the Smoky Hill, for the telegraph lines had not yet reached Fort Wallace.[2]

[1] *Barracks and Hospitals,* 309–12.

Although fourteen square miles had been reserved for the fort, not more than one square mile was occupied by buildings and parade ground, in an area on a bluff some three hundred yards north of the Smoky Hill River. There was no timber within sixty miles, the surrounding country being rolling prairie covered with buffalo grass.

There were four barracks—two constructed of lumber and two of marl—seven sets of officers' quarters built of frame, a hospital consisting of two wards holding twelve patients each, a guardhouse, a magazine, stables, a storehouse, granaries, and a few other buildings. Since there was no flowing water, there were no bathrooms. Enlisted men were compelled to bathe in the Smoky Hill River once a week during the summer. In winter, tubs were placed at the end of each dormitory for compulsory regular use.[3]

Scurvy had become commonplace because of the poor quality of food provided the men, the constant presence of salt pork and bacon in the diet contributing greatly to its cause. Dishonest contractors had provided hardtack obviously old, as the dates of the Civil War years still were visible on the containers. Bacon was rotten, moldy, and rancid. It had been stored where rats, warm weather, and alkali dust easily could take their toll.[4]

Nearby Pond Creek Station was a good example of the fortified stations along the Smoky Hill route. The stage station, in which the hostler and drivers lived was built of stone and wood, and next to it was the stable, of similar construction. The two were joined by a covered trench three feet wide and five feet deep. Behind these dwellings was a corral protected by a stone wall. Another covered trench led some ten yards from the stable to a ten-foot-square pit, roofed with stone supported by wood on a level with the ground, with portholes opening on all four sides. A similar trench led from the station house to a pit on the other side, and a third such arrangement led from the corral to a larger pit in the rear. The station was well armed with

[2] Bell, *New Tracks*, 52; Montgomery, "Fort Wallace and its Relation to the Frontier," *loc. cit.*, 205–206.

[3] *Barracks and Hospitals*, 310–12.

[4] Merington, *The Custer Story*, 207–208; Elizabeth B. Custer, *Tenting*, 687–88; Montgomery, "Fort Wallace and its Relation to the Frontier," *loc. cit.*, 219; G. A. Custer, *My Life*, 79–80.

seven-shot Spencer and eighteen-shot Henry rifles, both highly respected by warring Indians.[5]

On June 26 a band of three hundred Cheyennes led by Chief Roman Nose attacked the Pond Creek Station, running off with the stock of the Overland Stage Company. Then, turning toward Fort Wallace, they were met by Company G of the Seventh Cavalry, commanded by Captain Albert Barnitz. In the hand-to-hand fighting that followed, the overwhelming numbers of the Indians and their unusual daring forced the troopers to retreat to the fort with a loss of seven men killed, seven men wounded, and half their horses killed or captured.

Roman Nose was particularly evident in the action. At one point he had unhorsed a trooper with his spear and was about to impale him as he lay upon the ground when Corporal Harris struck him with the saber he held in his left hand. As Roman Nose turned to deal with him, Harris placed his Spencer carbine muzzle against the breast of the chief and fired. Roman Nose fell forward on his horse, blood spurting from his chest wound.[6]

One powerful Indian was seen to pick up Bugler Charlie Clark, who had been knocked off his horse by three arrows, strip him as he rode along, mash his head to a jelly with his tomahawk, and then throw his body under the feet of his horse.

Sergeant Frederick Wyllyams was shot through the head, scalped, cut over the right eyebrow with a hatchet, his nose cut off and his throat cut, his heart laid bare, his legs cut to the bone, and his arms gashed.

General Hancock arrived at Fort Wallace on June 15, staying long enough to appraise the situation and send the message noted previously: "Every one of the stations garrisoned by men from this post, east ninety-five miles and west seventy-five miles, has been attacked on an average of four times."[7] Several days later he left fewer than fifty men at the post when he headed west for Denver.[8] There, they

---

[5] Bell, *New Tracks*, 65–67; Davis, "A Summer on the Plains," *loc. cit.*, 307.

[6] Bell, *New Tracks*, 60–63; G. A. Custer, *My Life*, 79.

[7] *Difficulties With Indian Tribes*, 60; Bell, *New Tracks*, 51.

[8] Bell, *New Tracks*, 52.

were crying for help—provisions were becoming scarce and trade was almost at a standstill because the Smoky Hill blockade had stopped communications with the east.

While the Seventh Cavalry set up camp, Custer rode over to Fort Wallace to determine if additional orders from General Hancock had arrived. From Captain Albert Barnitz he learned that the fort had been attacked by Indians twice within the past few days. The fort was in a virtual state of siege, for the Indians had been so active along the Smoky Hill that travel had ceased and neither mail nor dispatches had been received for a considerable period of time.[9]

Cholera had made its appearance among the men, and deaths were occurring almost daily. Medical supplies were low, the food available was unfit to eat, and reserve supplies of food were near depletion. It was apparent that more abundant and better food was imperative if the cholera epidemic was to be checked. The end of the railroad was two hundred miles away, and the supply depot much farther.[10]

Custer decided to select about one hundred of his men to break through the two hundred miles to Fort Harker. With them he believed he could protect the sorely needed supplies he intended to bring back to the post. Selecting the best of the horses—all of which were generally unfit for service without rest—he left Fort Wallace at sunset on July 15.[11]

He followed the Smoky Hill stage route east, with the intention of covering the 150 miles to Fort Hays as rapidly as feasible. Once across this most dangerous area, he expected to continue to Fort Harker with half a dozen men, while Captain Hamilton followed leisurely with the rest of the command. By the time the latter would arrive at Fort Harker, Custer expected to have the train load of supplies ready for the return trip.

There were twelve stage stations between Fort Hays and Fort

[9] G. A. Custer, *My Life*, 79–80.

[10] *Ibid.*, 80; *Fort Wallace Post Returns*, 1867, indicate that twelve enlisted men died and thirty were ill, whereas desertions totaled sixty. On July 24 Fort Larned reported that fifteen soldiers had died from cholera, and Fort Harker reported some twenty-five deaths from cholera in twelve days of the same month. Asiatic cholera had become epidemic at Fort Riley and at many other frontier posts during the summer of 1867. At Fort Riley alone, seventy-nine had died.

[11] G. A. Custer, *My Life*, 80.

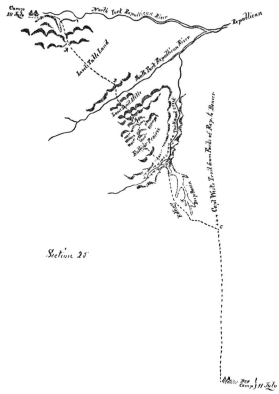

One of the maps made each day and entered into Lieutenant Henry
Jackson's log of the march of the Seventh Cavalry, June–July, 1867.

Wallace, the distances between them varying from five to thirteen
miles. Downer's Station and Monument Station were designated as
"Home" stations, supplying meals for passengers and drivers. The
others were "Way" or "Swing" stations, providing a change of horses
and a place to rest. Home stations were located from forty-five to
seventy-five miles apart. About every hundred miles there would be
a "General Home Supply Station."[12]

Some of the stations, such as Carlyle and Monument, were dug-

[12] *Court of Claims, Indian Depredations; Wells, Fargo Co. vs United States–
1867*, 67 (hereafter cited as Court of Claims); Montgomery, "Fort Wallace and
its Relation to the Frontier," *loc. cit.*, 194–96.

82

outs eight to ten feet in circumference, with a long tunnel leading to
a rifle pit ten feet in diameter. Although dugouts and rifle pits were
round and covered with planking and dirt, the other Way stations
were constructed either of sod or wood, in a rectangular form. The
stations had a small fort at each corner, similar in shape to a well or
cistern and covered with boards and dirt. There was a subterranean
tunnel, or board and dirt-covered trench, containing a well and providing a passageway to the stable. The roof of the stable consisted of
planking covered with dirt as an insurance against the firebrands and
burning arrows of the Indians.[13]

Most of the horses were purchased in St. Louis, and some others
came from Denver. Weighing 1,100 to 1,300 pounds, they traveled
seven to eight miles an hour. Quality was essential, so price was no
objection. Selling for approximately $350 at the delivery point, they
were, as former stage-line employee George Tritch put it, "as fine a
lot of horses as I saw anywhere—large, fine, well-shaped, high-lifed
animals; good travelers. They used to run from one station to another, and the horses would fairly laugh at the idea of going. I never
saw such beautiful animals in my life."[14]

The Concord coaches used were made by Abbott-Downing Company of Concord, New Hampshire. They carried nine passengers
inside and one on the seat with the driver. At a cost of $925 each at
Concord, they were unequaled for sturdiness and durability.[15]

Hay frequently had to be hauled up to 150 miles to a station, and
it ranged in price from $25 to $70 a ton. Hay at Fort Wallace happened to be $28 a ton. Lumber for the stations was hauled some four
hundred miles from the Missouri River, at $50 to $60 a thousand
feet. One-hundred-pound sacks of corn or oats sold for $5 each; flour
sold at $35 a hundred-pound sack. Meals were one dollar. The fare
from Atchison to Denver was $175—meals extra. The express rate
was one dollar a pound on everything but gold dust, coin, or
currency.[16]

During the peak period of the overland stage days, the entire 650
miles from the Missouri River to the Rocky Mountains along the

[13] *Court of Claims*, 5, 9–10.
[14] *Ibid.*, 54.
[15] *Ibid.*, 32; Margaret Long, *The Smoky Hill Trail*, 57.
[16] *Court of Claims*, 19–21, 49.

stage route presented an almost continuous panorama of fully loaded, white-covered "prairie schooners." Most were drawn by six yoke of oxen, the others by four to six horses or mules. One stage driver, while seated on the box of his stage coach making a trip from Denver down the Platte, counted in one day, nearly six hundred freight wagons bound for Denver and various western mining camps.[17]

The encroachment of the railroad, as its construction crews moved it westward, caused the Smoky Hill stage line to roll up before it. When the railroad reached Denver, the stage route was no more.[18] It had followed ridges wherever possible, in order to avoid most of the wet, soggy lowlands. Today one can see sections of the old stage route a hundred feet wide, rutted with wagon tracks.

The marching was done at night as Custer's command traveled from station to station along the stagecoach line. These stations were about ten miles apart and each, in times of peace, was occupied by about six employees. Approaching them at night was no small feat, for the occupants were chary of everyone, firing toward the sound of a voice even though it spoke English. The Indians had resorted to so many tricks that the stage employees took no chances.[19]

While resting for a few minutes near Downer's Station, Custer noted that:

> A small party of our men, who had without authority halted some distance behind, came dashing into our midst and reported that twenty-five or thirty Indians had attacked them some five or six miles in the rear, and had killed two of their number. As there was a detachment of infantry guarding the station, and time being important, we pushed on toward our destination. The two men reported killed were left to be buried by the troops on duty at the station. . . . Had they offered any defense this would not have occurred. Instead, they put spurs to their horses and attempted to escape by flight.[20]

"At every station along the route we received intelligence of Indians," says Davis; "sometimes they had been in large bands,

[17] Root, F. A. and Connelley, W. E., *The Overland Stage to California*, 609.
[18] Long, *The Smoky Hill Trail*, 42.
[19] G. A. Custer, *My Life*, 82; Merington, *The Custer Story*, 209.
[20] G. A. Custer, *My Life*, 82; Davis, "A Summer on the Plains," *loc. cit.*, 307.

sometimes in small."²¹ Custer was certain that the Indians were watching his movements, though none were seen until the skirmish near Downer's Station.

Frequent halts and rests were made along the way. Even so, the column reached Fort Hays at 3:00 A.M. on July 18—one hundred and fifty miles in fifty-five hours, including all halts.²²

Custer continued his ride toward Fort Harker accompanied by Lieutenants Cook and Tom Custer and two troopers, reaching there at 2:00 A.M. on July 19. He had made the ride of sixty miles in less than twelve hours, without a change of animals. Telegrams were sent to headquarters and to Fort Sedgwick, announcing the fate of the Kidder party. Since Colonel A. J. Smith (a brevet major general during the Civil War) was in command of this military district and was stationed here, Custer immediately reported to him the details of his expedition and arranged for Captain Hamilton's arrival as well as for the preparation of a train of supplies for the return trip. He writes:

> Having made my report to General Smith as my next superior officer, and there being no occasion for my presence until the train and escort should be in readiness to return, I applied for and received authority to visit Fort Riley, about ninety miles east of Harker by rail, where my family was then located.²³

There is some difficulty in obtaining the complete story of the termination of Hancock's expedition. Custer proceeded to Fort Riley on the morning of July 19, and had barely arrived when he received a telegram from Colonel Smith ordering him to return to his command.

He attempted to return on the next train but was delayed until the twenty-first through no fault of his own. An erratic train schedule on an incomplete railroad—the Kansas Pacific Railway was complete as far west as Fort Harker—made earlier service impossible. As soon as he reported to Smith, he was placed under arrest.²⁴ Smith was friend-

²¹ Davis, "A Summer on the Plains," *loc. cit.*, 307.
²² G. A. Custer, *My Life*, 82.
²³ *Ibid.*, 82.
²⁴ 40 Cong., 2 sess., *House Exec. Doc. 1*, 35; Merington, *The Custer Story*, 212, quotes Libbie Custer to Rebecca Richmond, September, 1867: "He [General Custer]

ly to the Custers and, seeing that he had Libbie with him, ordered him to Fort Riley, to remain there under arrest to await his court-martial on charges of leaving his command at Fort Wallace without authority.

Captain Hamilton had left Fort Hays with his detachment, arriving at Fort Harker on the twentieth. Smith immediately ordered him in readiness as an escort for the first train returning to Fort Wallace. On the twenty-second, Hamilton, with Lieutenants Cook and Custer, returned with a supply train to Fort Wallace. Major Elliott was directed to assume command of the Seventh Cavalry while Custer was under arrest.

On August 27 General Grant ordered a general court-martial to try Colonel Custer at Fort Leavenworth, Kansas, on September 17, 1867. The charges were preferred by Colonel A. J. Smith, commander of the Seventh Cavalry. It should be noted at this point that the charges preferred by Smith were instigated and pressed by General Hancock. Telegrams of the period indicate that Smith had a tendency to overlook Custer's indiscretion, whereas Hancock was "on the muscle." Additional charges were signed by Brevet Colonel Robert M. West, at that time a captain in the Seventh Cavalry.[25]

Captain West was motivated by several previous actions of his commanding officer. Lieutenant W. W. Cook had been placed in charge of the wagon train to Fort Wallace, whereas the higher ranking Captain West commanded only the troopers that guarded it. And at Fort Wallace, West had been placed under arrest by Custer for intoxication while on duty. Although he was a capable Indian fighter, West was equally known for his battles with the bottle.[26]

The Leavenworth (Kansas) *Daily Conservative* of August 31, 1867, mentioned the charges placed against Custer and concluded that: "We presume he will not be dealt with very severely if this is all the Government has against him."

---

took a leave himself, knowing none would be granted him, and General Hancock ordered his arrest. It sounded quite solemn to unaccustomed ears, but officers look on it as an ordinary occurence. . . ."

[25] *Proceedings of a General Court Martial at Fort Leavenworth, Kansas for the Trial of Brevet Major-General G. A. Custer, September 15, 1867.*

[26] *General Court Martial of Captain Robert M. West at Fort Leavenworth, Kansas, December 23, 1867.*

Congress had become quite perturbed over the ineffective results of the Hancock expedition. On July 16, Mr. Henderson of Missouri had stated in the Senate that: "The war was now costing daily at least $150,000 and, if it lasted through the summer, (and at the present rate it will certainly do that) it will cost us $100,000,000 without having accomplished anything."[27]

Soon after this (July 20, 1867), Congress authorized a mixed commission of army officers and civilians to communicate with all the hostile Indian tribes and negotiate terms of permanent peace. This peace commission was authorized to meet with certain hostile tribes with a view:

1. To remove, if possible, the cause of war.
2. To secure as far as is practicable, our frontier settlements and the safe building of our railroads looking to the Pacific; and
3. To suggest or inaugurate some plan for the civilization of the Indians.[28]

General Hancock had endeavored to explain his summer campaign in an issue of the *Army and Navy Journal,* a circumstance that Colonel E. W. Wynkoop took exception to. Several days before Custer's court-martial (September 14) Wynkoop advised Indian Superintendent Murphy that the Hancock course of action had been a mistake, and then elaborated upon his views.[29]

Whatever Wynkoop wished, he did not realize, for the cards had been shuffled prior to his attempt at controversy. On September 12, General Hancock was replaced by Major General Philip H. Sheridan.[30]

So ended a summer of campaigning against depredating Indians. The Seventh Cavalry had been faced with a shortage of supplies, Indian conferences and attacks, a suicide, mass desertions, the massacre of a message party, cholera, and a besieged Fort Wallace low on medical supplies, food, and forage. And they had given their best.

[27] *Harper's Weekly* (August 3, 1867), 481.
[28] *Report, Commissioner of Indian Affairs* (1868), 486.
[29] *Difficulties With Indian Tribes*, 37–41.
[30] P. H. Sheridan, *Personal Memoirs of P. H. Sheridan* (2 vols., New York, Chester L. Webster and Co., 1888), II, 282–83.

IX. PREPARATION
FOR TRIAL

CUSTER HAD BEEN OVERWHELMED by the conditions he had encountered at Fort Wallace. Wretched, inedible food; inadequate
medical supplies; insufficient forage for the horses; troops rapidly
succumbing to cholera or being killed by Indians; and no word from
General Hancock who, seemingly, had retired from the scene of tra-
vail and conflict to the comforts of Fort Leavenworth, the country's
third most desirable post.[1]

True, Custer had left Fort Wallace without direct orders, so he
acted under the last orders he had received; those sent to him by
General Sherman desiring him to *move toward Fort Wallace to meet
General Hancock, who would give him further orders.*[2] He probably
would have been court-martialed if he had not made an attempt to
alleviate the devastating and demoralizing conditions at Fort Wallace. It was for him to decide whether or not he was to obtain these
orders from Hancock in person.

Custer had pressed Hancock considerably for the Quartermaster's
Department's failure to have forage and supplies available at the

---

[1] G. A. Custer, *My Life*, 79–80; Elizabeth B. Custer, *Tenting*, 701; Montgomery, "Fort Wallace and its Relation to the Frontier," *loc. cit.*, 219.

[2] 40 Cong., 2 sess., *House Exec. Doc. 1*, 35; G. A. Custer, *My Life*, 71.

various forts he visited, because they were within Hancock's command.[3] The lack of supplies had prevented Custer from waging an all-out campaign. The campaign had ended as a costly failure, heaping ridicule and censure on the War Department and the army.

Hancock, acting as the prosecutor, had directed Colonel A. J. Smith to prefer charges against Custer, and had requested that General Sherman convene a court-martial at Fort Riley.[4] Thus some of the heat was taken off Hancock. He was slightly embarrassed, however, when the Court was transferred to his home post, Fort Leavenworth, for the convenience of the officers detailed to court duty.[5] The embarassment was short-lived, since he was replaced by General Sheridan before the court convened.

To the surprise of Hancock and Smith, Captain Robert M. West attached serious additional charges to those ordered by Hancock. West had been smarting under the reprimand given him by Custer on the day they had arrived at Fort Wallace, for "becoming so drunk as to be unfit for the proper performance of his duty." He had reason to believe that Custer's tolerance had reached its limit. The useless suicide of Colonel Cooper, the desertions, the massacre of Lieutenant Kidder's party, and then the conditions evident at Fort Wallace during its state of siege by the Indians were problems enough. For a senior officer to fail in his duty at such a time could only result in court-martial—of this West could be sure. And when he learned a week later that Custer himself faced court-martial, his alcohol-numbed mind could think only of revenge. Additional charges of misconduct were the answer.[6]

As word spread eastward and to the various garrisons, both Libbie and the Colonel received numerous letters from old friends offering assistance, advice, or good cheer. Captain Thomas Weir, in a note to Custer wrote: "Will any little favor I may be able to give be kindly

[3] G. A. Custer, *My Life*, 46; *Difficulties With Indian Tribes*, 107.

[4] Hancock's communication of August 13, 1867, to General W. A. Nichols, Assistant Adjutant General, Military Division of the Missouri.

[5] August 17, 1867, endorsement of General W. A. Nichols.

[6] *West Courtmartial*. General Hancock's initial charge against Custer was "absent himself from his command without proper authority," and "executing an unauthorized journey on private business." West attached the additional charges.

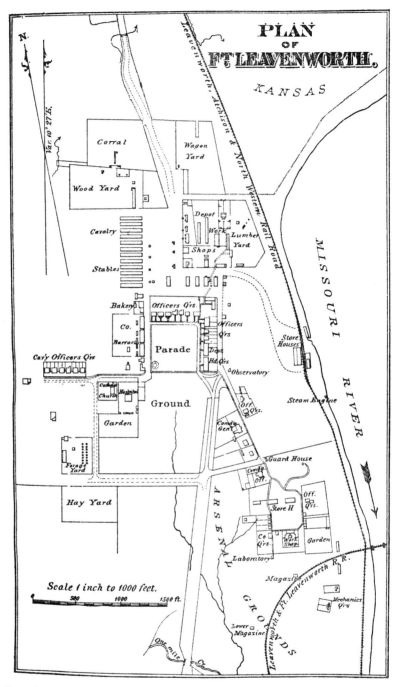

Fort Leavenworth, supply depot and headquarters for the Department of
the Missouri. Because of its size and comforts, "11-Worth" was preferred by "armchair generals" over all other western assignments. From
Military Posts Division of the Missouri, Washington, 1876.

received? I am anxious in the affair to go on your side."[7] And a little
later Lieutenant Charles Brewster advised Custer:

> Lieutenant Wallingford has expressed to me that if subpoenaed,
> he should give everything the best coloring for you, that he could.
> That is also my resolution.
>
> There is not another officer here (at Fort Wallace) whom you
> could count on. Neither Elliott, Meyers, Robins, Barnitz, Com-
> magere, Hale, Jackson nor Levey. Nor Coates either. Hamilton I
> think is friendly to you. Keogh is not. West is very bitter it seems; and
> you may expect the worst from him.
>
> . . . Lieutenant Moylan tells me that your orders were to report
> to District Headquarters after your arrival at Fort Wallace—take
> advantage of this point. I mention this because I thought that pos-
> sibly you may not have seen or heard from Lieutenant Moylan.[8]

A friend in Washington who had served on Autie's staff during
the Civil War wrote him that:

> As far as I have heard, nothing but the utmost astonishment and
> unbelief has been expressed. With the exception of a few old fogies
> it seems to be the general belief that the whole proceeding against
> you is but an outbreak of the smoldering enmity and envy which has
> existed and still exists on the part of some fossils whose names appear
> upon the Army Registers, toward you.[9]

Custer and a group of young army officers had distinguished themselves during the Civil War and had been rewarded with high rank.
Previously, "seniority rule" had prevailed, merit having no place in
the promotions. President Lincoln had recognized the deficiency in
the seniority system, blaming it for the Union's losses in the early
part of the conflict. The debilitating effect and lack of *esprit de corps*
resulting from older officers bogged down with incapacity, lack of
imagination, courage, or drive, was well-known to him. He had
remedied the problem by placing talented young officers where they

---

[7] Letter from T. B. Weir to G. A. Custer, Fort Harker, August 14, 1867. Author's
collection.

[8] Letter from Charles Brewster to G. A. Custer, Fort Wallace, September 7, 1867.
Author's collection.

[9] Letter from S. W. Barnhart to G. A. Custer, Washington, D.C., September 9,
1867. Author's collection.

could do the most good. This won battles and a war, but lost friends for the young officers. The jealousy of the older officers they had by-passed never subsided.

Whittaker in his biography of Custer makes a reference to Sherman, Sheridan and Custer as they relate to this problem: "As a matter of course, all three of these officers were then, and are today (1876), hated most cordially by most other officers, especially by those who graduated from West Point before them and found themselves at the close of the war junior to them."[10] He goes on to say, "Not an Indian fight comes off, not an attack of yellow fever visits the post, but every officer in the army falls to calculating how many "steps" he will gain by so many deaths."[11]

Captain Charles C. Parsons, Fourth U.S. Artillery, was obtained as counsel. A West Point classmate of Custer, he had a fine record as a military lawyer. Libbie referred to him as "a Christian gentleman ... and a Churchman."[12] Then, too, he was a fellow Ohioan, who had received his commission at the same time as Autie.[13]

There was much to do and not much time to do it in. Consideration had to be given to the composition of the Court. Both Custer and Parsons were quite familiar with the seventy-fifth Articles of War which clearly stated that, "No officer shall be tried but by a general court-martial, nor by officers of an inferior rank, if it can be avoided."[14] Of the nine members selected for the Court, only four outranked Custer. This posed a problem. There were other high-ranking officers available, since Fort Leavenworth[15] was a large post and had been

[10] Frederick Whittaker, *A Complete Life of Gen. George A. Custer*, 407.
[11] *Ibid.*
[12] Merington, *The Custer Story*, 211.
[13] *Army Register* for 1867, 44.
[14] S. V. Benét, *A Treatise on Military Law and the Practice of Courts-Martial*, 407.
[15] *Barracks and Hospitals*, 284–86: Fort Leavenworth, Kansas, was established by Colonel Henry Leavenworth in 1827 on the right bank of the Missouri River about two miles above Leavenworth City. Situated on the highest point of an undulating prairie some 150 feet above the river, it commanded an extensive view of surrounding country.

A six-company post acting as a supply depot for the Department of the Missouri, it was considered, in 1867, to be the third largest military establishment in the country.

selected in place of Fort Riley[16] because of the greater number of officers and facilities available. However, a challenge on this point might develop animosity. Ignoring it might be best, unless some member was discovered to be prejudiced.

Various witnesses were developed; their testimony carefully weighed. A page of Parsons' notes evidenced the care he used:

Memoranda—Points to be Shown on Trial—

Moylan (Lt. M.)—Will show that deserters retained only arms and ammunition—dispensing with clothing, camp and garrison equipage, etc., etc.—showing that they had hostile intentions.

Armes (Capt. G.)—Will show that white men were in company with Indians at a recent engagement, encouraging, inciting, etc.

Hamilton (Capt. L.)—Will show that the rate of march from Wallace to Harker was slower than usual on the expedition. The leading Sergeant was on a slow-stepping horse as shown in conversation between witnesses, etc., etc.—probable average —3½ miles per hour.[17]

A court-martial is by law the highest judicial body in the military service, having the power to arrest any guilty party in the enforcement of the article under consideration, no matter what his rank. The president of the court is the senior officer by virtue of his rank, and the judge advocate, by law, is directed to prosecute in the name of the United States. He is not a judge as are members of the court. The court alone administers justice according to the Articles of War, and in case of doubt, according to their consciences, the best of their understandings, and the custom of war in like cases.[18]

While Custer and Parsons were preparing their case the Indians

---

[16] *Barracks and Hospitals*, 287–90: Fort Riley, Kansas was established in 1852 on the left bank of the Kansas River, immediately below the confluence of the Smoky Hill and Republican rivers. Situated on a high plateau overlooking both the Kansas River and the surrounding prairie, it provided quarters for six companies. Three miles to the west of the fort was Junction City.

[17] Original in author's collection.

[18] Benét, *A Treatise*, 8.

were working on theirs. Their activity had increased on the Republican River and along the Smoky Hill. One incident occurred that had everyone talking.

An Englishman, William Thompson, and five others, had taken a handcar and started up the track from the Plum Creek Station on the Union Pacific in search of a break in the telegraph lines.[19] At the point that the break was discovered, a pile of railroad ties was found on the track. As they approached, Indians jumped up from the tall grass all around and opened fire. One Indian on a pony singled out Thompson and galloped toward him, firing when within ten feet. Thompson, though wounded in the right arm, managed to run, but was clubbed down by the Indian's rifle. The Indian then stabbed him in the neck. Thinking his victim dead, he grasped his hair by twining it around his hand and then began to hack and saw away at his scalp with a dull knife. Thompson feigned death, although he was sick and dizzy and the pain was agonizing. When the last bit of scalp over his temple failed to yield to the scalping knife, the Indian gave a final jerk that made the victim think his head was coming off. The Indian then mounted his pony and rode away, but unknowingly dropped the fresh scalp a few feet from Thompson, who managed to conceal it. Since there were numerous Indians in the area, escape was impossible. In fear and in pain, he found a hiding place in the brush nearby.

After several hours a train came along and was derailed when it struck the barricade. The fireman and engineer were shot and scalped, and the boxcars were plundered and then set afire. By this time it was nine o'clock at night. The Indians confiscated everything that appealed to them: boxes of tobacco, sacks of flour, bonnets, hats, boots and shoes, saddles, ribbons, and bales of calico. Their horses were covered with colorful strips of muslin, the tails decorated with ribbons of various colors. The fire was made brighter by the addition of the emptied boxes.

A barrel of bourbon was discovered, and this find quickly added to the ferocity of the raiders. Following a scalp dance, the bodies of the fireman and engineer were thrown into the flames. Soon afterward, Thompson crawled away and managed to find his way to Willow Island Station, where a rescue party brought him to Omaha. He

[19] Stanley, *Early Travels*, I, 155–58.

arrived with a pail of water by his side containing his scalp. The nine-by-four-inch scalp was sutured back on by a hopeful physician, and although it did not "take," the sturdy Thompson survived to tell of his experience for many years thereafter.

X. COURT-MARTIAL

THE COURT-MARTIAL CONVENED at Fort Leavenworth, Kansas, on September 15, 1867, at 11:00 A.M., under Special Orders No. 426 under date of August 27, 1867, at Washington, out of the Adjutant General's Office by order of the commanding general, Ulysses S. Grant. The Court was detailed as follows:

Brevet Major General William Hoffman; colonel, Third U.S. Infantry.

Brevet Major General John W. Davidson; lieutenant colonel, Tenth U.S. Cavalry.

Brevet Major General Benjamin H. Grierson; colonel, Tenth U.S. Cavalry.

Brevet Brigadier General Pitcairn Morrison; colonel, U.S. Army (retired).

Brevet Brigadier General Michael R. Morgan; major, commissary of subsistence.

Brevet Brigadier General Franklin D. Callender; lieutenant colonel, Ordnance Department.

Brevet Lieutenant Colonel Thomas C. English; major, Fifth U.S. Infantry.

Brevet Major Henry Asbury; captain, Third U.S. Infantry.

Brevet Major Stephen C. Lyford; captain, Ordnance Department.

Brevet Lieutenant Colonel Robert Chandler; captain, Thirteenth U.S. Infantry, judge advocate of the Court.

Although ordered to sit without regard to hours, after half an hour they adjourned until Monday, September 16, at 10:00 A.M. Colonel Grierson had not appeared; the cause of his absence was unknown.

Meeting at the prescribed time the next day, all members of the Court were present. Seniority of rank became an opening issue. Lieutenant Colonel Callender questioned whether he or Major Morgan had the right of position in regard to each other on the Court. Since voting was in the sequence printed in the special order composing the Court, it was his feeling that an officer of lower rank would preceed him in any vote called for. To substantiate his question he quoted *Army Regulations*, paragraph five, clause three: "In case of equality of rank by virtue of a brevet commission, reference is had to commissions not brevet." Both held the same brevet rank of Brigadier General of April 9, 1865. Major Morgan had been placed on the Court listing just above him.

The Court reversed the order of the two names, placing Lieutenant Colonel Callender just ahead of Major Morgan, basing the decision on regular army rank. The judge advocate, Captain Chandler, presented a written opinion that this decision was erroneous, and if not "corrected before a finding, the proceedings *may* be declared invalid." He continued, "Paragraph 884, of the *Revised Army Regulations* expressly declares that a 'decision of the proper authority in regard to the rank of members cannot be reversed by the Court.' The proper authority (being the order itself by which the Court is convened) had decided the rank, as set forth in said order, and this cannot be changed except upon application to the authority which convened the Court. In voting, the law directs (72nd *Article of War*) that the youngest member in commission will vote first, and so on to the highest rank. If higher authority than this Court, should decide that Gen. Morgan ranks Gen. Callender, then there *might* be apprehensions or doubts as to the validity of the proceedings . . . ."

The Adjutant General was asked by telegraph for the correct answer. Following an exchange of messages dealing with associated technicalities, Assistant Adjutant General Edward D. Townsend, on September 21, 1867, advised that "The 'Secy' of War affirms the decision of September ninth that General Morgan ranks Genl. Callender and that Bvt. Maj. Asbury ranks Bvt. Maj. Lyford." It had been ascertained that Morgan ranked Callender by virtue of his commission as a brevet colonel, thereby ignoring regular army rank.[1]

In the interim of the telegraphic exchange, the Court proceeded to the trial of Custer, who was called before the Court, and having heard the order of the Court read, was asked if he had any objections to any member named on the order. The accused, Custer, having first asked permission to introduce his military friend and legal counsel, Brevet Lieutenant Colonel Charles C. Parsons, captain of Fourth Artillery, which was granted, presented an objection to Brevet Major General Davidson.

Davidson was represented as a most important and material witness in the case, and it was believed that his testimony would compel him to decide between the degree of credit to be attached to the evidence of other witnesses as compared with his own. Various authorities were quoted to substantiate this claim. Then the Judge Advocate stated that the member objected to was a witness for the defense.

Davidson stated: "I know of nothing at the present time that would incapacitate me from sitting as a fair and impartial member of this Court, but on the general principle of desiring the accused to be satisfied in his own mind of the impartiality of the proceedings I desire to be excused from sitting on the case."

The Court, after taking into consideration the objections and statements, decided not to sustain the objection of Custer's counsel. Custer then offered a further objection to Davidson on the grounds that he had expressed an opinion prejudicial to the accused. According to Custer, Davidson had used "language to the effect that he did not see 'how General Custer expected to get out of these charges. He is a young man—a newcomer in the service—he only graduated in '61,

---

[1] *Brevet*—a commission giving an officer higher nominal rank than that for which he receives pay. Conferred by the advice and consent of the Senate for meritorius service or heroism, it permitted the officer to bear the title of highest rank conferred upon him but did not carry with it the command, pay and emolument. Though brevets were intended to be temporary, they never were recalled, the officer retaining the rank and requiring its application whenever he was addressed. For example, as noted earlier, Brevet Major General George Armstrong Custer, although a major general of Volunteer Cavalry during the latter part of the Civil War, was dropped to his regular army rank of captain, and then made a lieutenant colonel of the Seventh U.S. Cavalry in 1866. And although he was addressed as "General," he only received the command, pay and emolument of a lieutenant colonel.

and never commanded a company, and he must be taught that he cannot come out here and do as he pleases.' "

Observations then were made that General Davidson and Judge Advocate Chandler occupied the same office, giving the former an opportunity to hear Chandler examine his witnesses. This fact was admitted by Chandler, although he attached no importance to it.

Davidson again requested that he be permitted to be excused. After due deliberation the Court announced that it acceded to the request of Davidson, and that he was thereby excused from sitting as a member of the Court.

The accused having no further objection to any member of the Court, the Court was duly sworn by the Judge Advocate and the Judge Advocate was duly sworn by the President of the Court, both in the presence of the accused.

After the Official Reporter was sworn in, the accused, Brevet Major General G. A. Custer, Lieutenant Colonel Seventh U.S. Cavalry was arraigned upon the following charges and specifications, which were read aloud in his presence:

Charges and Specifications preferred against Bvt. Maj. Gen. G. A. Custer, Lieut. Colonel 7th U.S. Cavalry.

Charge first. Absence without leave from his command.

Specification first. In this, that he, Brevet Major General G. A. Custer, Lieut. Col. 7th U.S. Cavalry, did at or near Fort Wallace, Kansas, on or about the 15th day of July 1867, absent himself from his command without proper authority, and proceed to Fort Harker, Kansas, a distance of about 275 miles, this at a time when his command was expected to be actively engaged against hostile Indians.

Charge second. Conduct to the prejudice of good order and military discipline.

Specification first. In this, that he, Bvt. Major General G. A. Custer, Lieut. Col. 7th U.S. Cavalry, immediately after the troops of his command had completed a long and exhausting march, and when the horses belonging thereto had not been rested, and were in an unfit condition for said service, did select a portion of such command consisting of three Commissioned officers, and about seventy-five men with their horses, and did set out upon and execute a rapid march from Fort Wallace, Kansas, to Fort Hays in the same state; the said march being upon private business, and without proper authority or any urgency or demand of public business; and in so doing did seriously prejudice the public interest by overmarching and damaging the horses belonging to the said detachment of his command.

Specification second. In this, that he, Brevet Major General G. A. Custer, Lieut. Col. 7th Cav., while executing an unauthorized journey on private business from Fort Wallace, Kansas to Fort Harker in the same state, did procure at Fort Hays in the same state, on or about the 17th July, 1867, (two ambulances and) four mules belonging to the United States, and did use such (ambulances and) mules, for the conveyance of himself and part of his escort from said Fort Hays to Fort Harker in the aforesaid state.

Specification third. In this that he Bvt. Maj. General G. A. Custer, Lieut. Col. 7th U.S. Cav. when near Downer's Station in the state of Kansas, on or about the 16th day of July 1867, after having received information that a party of Indians had attacked a small party detached from his escort near said Station, did fail to take proper measures for the repulse of said Indians, or the defense or relief of said detachment; and further, after the return of such detached party of his command with report that two of their number had been killed, did neglect to take any measures to pursue such party of Indians, or recover or bury the bodies of those of his command that had been killed as aforesaid—

[Signed] A. J. Smith
Col. 7th U.S. Cavy.
Bvt. Maj. Gen. U.S.A.

Witnesses:

Capt. L. M. Hamilton, *7th U.S. Cavalry*
Lieut. Thos. W. Custer, *7th U.S. Cavalry*
2nd Lt. W. Cook, *7th U.S. Cavalry*

Additional Charges and Specifications preferred against Lieutenant Colonel George A. Custer, Brevet Major-General, U.S.A.

Charge—Conduct prejudicial to good order and Military discipline.

Specification first. In this that Brevet Major General George A. Custer, Lieutenant Colonel 7th U.S. Cavalry, while en route commanding and marching a column of his regiment, six companies or thereabouts, strong, from the valley of the Platte River, to the valley of the Smoky Hill River, did, when ordering a party of three Commissioned Officers and others of his Command in pursuit of supposed deserters who were then in view leaving camp, *also order* the said party to shoot the supposed deserters down dead, and to bring none in alive.

This on "Custer's Cavalry Column Trail," while traveling southward, about fifty miles southwest from Fort Sedgewick, Colorado, on or about the seventh day of July, 1867.

Specification second. In this that Brevet Major General George A. Custer, Lieutenant Colonel, 7th U.S. Cavalry, did order (the following named and designated Soldiers of his regiment, viz. Bugler Barney Tolliver, Company K., Private Charles Johnson, Company K., Private Alburger, Company D., and other) enlisted men of his command, *to be shot down* as supposed deserters, but without trial; and did thus cause three men to be severely wounded.

This on "Custer's Cavalry Column Trail" while traveling southward, between fifteen and forty miles South of Platte River, and between fifty and seventy miles Southwest from Fort Sedgewick, Colorado, on or about the seventh day of July 1867.

Specification third. In this that Brevet Major General George A. Custer, Lieutenant Colonel 7th U.S. Cavalry, after the following named and designated soldiers of his regiment, viz. Bugler Barney Tolliver, Company K., Private Charles Johnson, Company K., and Private Alburger, Company D., had been summarily shot down and severely wounded by order of him the said Custer, did, order and cause the said soldiers to be placed in a government wagon, and to be hauled eighteen miles, (and did then and there neglect and positively and persistently refuse to allow the said soldiers, to receive treatment and attention from the Acting Assistant Surgeon with his command or any other Medical or Surgical attendance whatever).

This on "Custer's Cavalry Column Trail," traveling southward between fifteen and forty miles south of the Platte River, and between fifty and seventy miles Southwest from Fort Sedgewick, Colorado, on or about the seventh day of July 1867.

Specification fourth. In this that Brevet Major General George A. Custer, Lieutenant Colonel 7th U.S. Cavalry, while commanding and marching a column of his regiment, six companies or thereabouts, strong, did, on or about the seventh day of July 1867, at a point about fifteen miles South of Platte River, and about fifty miles southwest from Fort Sedgewick, Colorado, order and cause the summary shooting, as a supposed deserter, but without trial, of one Private Charles Johnson, Company K., 7th U.S. Infantry, a soldier of his command; whereby he, the said Johnson was so severely wounded that he soon after—to wit, on or about the 17th day of July 1867, at or near Fort Wallace, Kansas—did decease; he the said Custer thus causing the death of him the said Johnson.

[Signed] Rob. M. West
Capt. 7th U.S. Cav.
Bvt. Col. U.S.A.

Witnesses:

Major Joel Elliott, *7th U.S. Cavalry*
1st Lt. Thomas Custer, *7th U.S. Cavalry*
2nd Lt. W. W. Cook, *7th U.S. Cavalry*
2nd Lt. Henry Jackson, *7th U.S. Cavalry*
Acting Assistant Surgeon I. T. Coates
Citizen Thomas Atkins, *Qr. Mr. Emplye.*
1st Sergt. John T. Athey, *Company K, 7th U.S. Cav.*
Private Clement Willis,   *do.*   *do.*

To which charges and specifications the accused pleaded as follows:

To the Specification, first Charge	Not Guilty
To the first Charge	Not Guilty
To the first Specification, second Charge	Not Guilty
To the second Specification, second Charge	Not Guilty
To the third Specification, second Charge	Not Guilty
To the second Charge	Not Guilty
To the first Specification, additional Charge	Not Guilty
To the second Specification, additional Charge	Not Guilty
To the third Specification, additional Charge	Not Guilty

To the fourth Specification, additional Charge   Not Guilty

To the additional Charge   Not Guilty

The accused then presented the following communication:

"The accused asks that the counsel be allowed to question witnesses either upon direct or cross examination, without rendering the question in writing.

"That he be allowed to request the Judge Advocate to interrupt any statement being made by a witness or other person present when the accused objects to such statement proceeding any further on legal grounds.

"And that the counsel for the accused be allowed to state directly to the Court, and without rendering it to writing, any objections made and the grounds thereof, and in such cases to address the Court, subject to such rules as the Court may provide.

"The accused makes these requests because a Phonographic Reporter[2] is employed to facilitate the transaction of business before this Court, and the accused believes that when Phonographic Reporters have been so employed, the accused himself, or by his counsel, has been allowed to address the Court as above requested, and that in such way the accused is allowed the same privileges upon the part of the Defense as are allowed to the Judge Advocate for the Prosecution.

"And the accused represents that if these requests be denied, the Prosecution will be allowed a greater benefit than the Defense in that it will be permitted to cross examine witnesses directly, and to make its own statements directly, and that moreover, the objections of the accused will not at times be regarded unless he can directly state such objections to the Court.

"And the accused believes that thereby the business of the Court will be expedited and that the dignity of the Court will not be impaired."

The Court was cleared for deliberation, and upon re-opening of the doors it was announced that as to the first proposition, the accused would be excused from putting his questions in writing, but they

[2] Stanley, in *My Early Travels and Adventures*, Vol. I, page 217, refers to a "George Willis, phonographer" who accompanied the Peace Commission from Fort Larned on October 13, 1867. *Funk and Wagnall's Dictionary* states that a phonographer is a phonetic stenographer. Phonography was a system of phonetic spelling or a form of shorthand then in common use.

would be written by the phonograph, and answered by the witness when directed to do so by the Judge Advocate.

The Court declined to accede to the second request as a rule.

The Court declined to accede to the third request as a rule.

At 3:40 P.M. the Court adjourned till 10:00 A.M., Sept. 17, 1867.

FORT LEAVENWORTH, KANSAS
10:00 A.M. Sept. 17, 1867

The Court convened with all present, including General Custer and his counsel.

The Proceedings of yesterday were read and approved.

Capt. Louis M. Hamilton,[3] 7th U.S. Cav., a witness on the part of the prosecution being duly sworn, testified as follows:

Q. State your name, rank and regiment.

A. L. M. Hamilton, Captain 7th U.S. Cav.

Q. Do you recognize the accused, if so as whom?

A. I do, as Gen. Custer.

Q. In what command were you in the month of July 1867?

A. A portion of the time I was with the Regiment and a portion of the month with a detachment away from the Regiment.

Q. Who commanded the Regiment at that time?

A. While I was with the Regiment, Gen. Custer commanded it.

Q. Were you with the Regiment on the march?

A. Yes sir.

Q. In June and July?

A. Yes sir.

Q. State what that march was.

A. From Fort Hayes,[4] which we left on the first of June, till we reached Fort Wallace about the middle of July.

---

[3] A lineal descendant of Alexander Hamilton; he was killed at the battle of the Washita in 1868.

[4] *Barracks and Hospitals,* 304–309: *Hays* and *Hayes, Sedgwick* and *Sedgewick,* were used synonymously throughout the testimony. *Hays* and *Sedgwick* were in general, and approved official, use at that time.

Old Fort Hays, on Big Creek, was first established in the autumn of 1866 as Fort Fletcher. Troops were stationed there to protect the employees of the Kansas Pacific Railroad against the attacks of Indians. That winter the name was changed to Fort Hays. During the summer of 1867 the post was abandoned because of the serious

Q. State as near as you can remember, the points in the march from Fort Hayes till you reached Fort Wallace.

A. A portion of the Regiment—six companies—left Fort Hayes on the first of June, and reached the Platte on the ninth. We remained about a week in the neighborhood of Fort Mc-Pherson, then turned and went back to the Republican River and laid there about a week. We then returned to the Platte and remained one day and then recrossed to Fort Wallace.

Q. Who was in command of the detachment at that time?

A. Gen. Custer.

Q. What time did the Regiment reach Fort Wallace?

A. I forget the exact date; it was about the middle of July—I think the 13th or 14th.

Q. What time did the Regiment leave Fort Sedgewick?

A. The Regiment did not go to Fort Sedgewick. It went to near Valley Station, which was the nearest point we got to Fort Sedgewick. We reached there at midnight on the fifth and left there on the seventh.

Q. How far is it from that point to Fort Wallace?

A. About 200 miles I think.

Q. How long was the regiment coming from near Valley Station to Fort Wallace?

A. It left there on the seventh and reached Fort Wallace on the 13th or 14th.

Q. In what condition were the horses of the Regiment when they arrived at Fort Wallace?

flooding of the area when Big Creek overflowed its banks. Consequently, on June 22, 1867, General Hancock authorized moving the post to the present site of Fort Hays.

The 7,500-acre military reservation was slightly rolling. The barracks in 1867 were of timber and built to house four companies. Officers quarters, hospital, storehouses and guardhouse were of frame construction. There were no bathrooms. The creek was used as a source of water brought by wagon to the officers' quarters and emptied into barrels placed nearby. Enlisted men bathed in the creek. Four wells provided an additional supply of drinking water. A medical inspection of the post determined that the cemetery was poorly located. Its removal was recommended, since it was between two ravines, both of which drained into the creek above the place where water was obtained for the post.

Hays City, the amusement center for troopers with time and money on their hands, was less than a mile from the post.

A. They were in very bad condition.

Q. How long did the command remain at Fort Wallace before leaving?

A. It remained there until the 14th of August, at the time I rejoined it.

Q. Did any portion of the Regiment leave Fort Wallace to come east?

A. A detachment left there about the 15th of July.

Q. For what point?

A. It came as far as Fort Harker.

Q. How many of the Regiment left?

A. There were between 70 and 75 men. There was a detail of 72 men and officers.

Q. What was the detail made for?

A. For an escort to Gen. Custer.

Q. What was the condition of the horses of the escort, when they left; were they fit for service or otherwise?

A. They were fit for service, but were not in high condition.

Q. How was the escort selected?

A. There was a detail of six men and a non-commissioned officer from each company.

Q. Who had charge of the escort?

A. I commanded it.

Q. Did the escort accompany Gen. Custer; if so how far?

A. It escorted Gen. Custer as far as Big Creek, about nine miles south of Fort Hayes and then Gen. Custer left and came as far as Fort Harker.

Q. Did you come as far as Fort Harker?[5]

A. Yes sir.

[5] *Barracks and Hospitals,* 290–99: Fort Harker, some sixty-nine miles west of Fort Hays, was situated upon an open prairie one mile north of the Smoky Hill River, and on the route of the Kansas Pacific Railroad. There were four quarters for companies, two of frame and two of log. Three of the seven officers' quarters, the hospital, and the guardhouse were of stone. The soil was rich, though dry; highly suitable for grazing. Two springs supplied water for the post.

On June 28, 1867, cholera made its first appearance. A herder and beef contractor's butcher was the first case, several other cases appearing in the garrison immediately thereafter.

Q. When did the escort leave Fort Wallace for Big Creek?

A. About the 15th of July.

Q. What time did the escort reach Big Creek?

A. Early on the morning of the 18th.

Q. State the nature of the march from Fort Wallace to Fort Hayes, as to rapidity.

A. The marching was continuous but not rapid.

Q. How much rest had the escort during the trip?

A. About five hours.

Q. In what condition were the horses when they reached Big Creek, near Fort Hayes?

A. They were in bad condition.

Q. State more explicitly, as to the condition of the horses, whether fit for service or not.

A. They were not fit for immediate service. They were exhausted.

Q. Were there any ambulances on the trip from Fort Hayes to Fort Harker?

A. No sir.

Q. Were there any ambulances in any part of Gen. Custer's command from Fort Hayes to Fort Harker?

A. I came from Fort Wallace to Fort Hays, and Gen. Custer left the command there and I remained over one day.

Q. Did the command cross through Downer's Station on the Journey from Fort Wallace to Fort Hays?

A. Yes sir.

Q. State what you know, if anything, about an attack of Indians near that point.

A. About two o'clock in the afternoon of the day succeeding our march, a Sergeant Connelly who reported that he had been sent back by Gen. Custer, came into Downer's Station and reported to me the Indians had succeeded in killing two of his men about four or five miles back. The horse he was riding was wounded and his party was very much demoralized.

Q. How many men were of his party?

A. Six.

Q. Was any report of that attack made to Gen. Custer?

A. Yes sir.

Q. Who made it?

A. I did.

Q. Were any measures taken for the repulse of the Indians or any action whatever taken by Gen. Custer for the relief of the detachment?

A. The detachment was all in. I afterward learned one man had succeeded in secreting himself.

Q. Was any action taken for the pursuit of the Indians?

A. No sir.

Q. Were any measures taken by Gen. Custer to recover the bodies of the men reported wounded and dead?

A. None that I know of.

Q. How soon after that report spoken of, reached you, did Gen. Custer leave?

A. In about three-fourths of an hour or an hour.

Q. On his way to the east?

A. Yes sir.

Q. Do you know of any horses having been abandoned or shot on that trip?

A. Yes sir, there were two shot, but the exact number of those abandoned I could not ascertain.

Q. For what reason were they abandoned or shot?

A. I considered it advisable to shoot them rather than let them fall into the hands of the Indians on the road. They could not keep up with the command, but might have been of service to them if they had found them.

Q. By whose order were they shot or abandoned?

A. By my order.

Q. Directly from you?

A. Yes sir.

Q. Was Gen. Custer aware of the order you had given?

A. I have forgotten whether I had mentioned it or not; I don't think I did.

Q. Was Gen. Custer aware they had been shot or abandoned?

A. My impression is he was not.

Q. At what point did this attack of the Indians occur?

A. At a point about half way between Castle Rock and Downer's Station.

Q. Did you state what day it was?

A. It was on the 16th or 17th.

Q. Do you know how many men were killed or wounded in the attack of the Indians?

A. One was killed and one was wounded.

Q. Was the body of the killed man recovered or buried?

A. I only know that Capt. Carpenter reported to me that he had recovered the wounded man and buried the dead man.

Q. In regard to the detail of the escort at Fort Wallace, can you state whether the men were selected on account of their having good horses or not?

A. I know my own detail was selected for that reason; I am not able to say for the others.

Cross Examination
Questions by the Accused

Q. How strong were the six companies when they left Fort Hays?

A. They averaged about 50 men each.

Q. How strong were they when they got to Fort Wallace?

A. There was but little difference, about 35 men missing out of the whole command.

Q. How did the condition of the horses, when you reached Fort Wallace, compare with their condition when they left Fort Hays?

A. They were in worse condition.

Q. How did the condition of those 75 horses compare when you left Fort Wallace, with their condition when you first set out from Fort Hays?

A. They were in worse condition.

Q. Who were the four officers who left with the detachment?

A. General Custer, Lieut. Custer, Mr. Cook and myself.

Q. Were you ordered to report as an escort?

A. I received no written orders to report as an escort. My orders were verbal.

Q. Did you regard the horses selected for the detachment as fit for the march?

A. Yes sir.

Q. How far is it from Fort Wallace to Big Creek, where the accused left you?

A. About between 140 and 150 miles.

Q. How far is it from that point to Fort Harker?

A. About 60 miles.

Q. Did the five hours you mentioned include all the rest the horses had from Fort Wallace to your camp on Big Creek?

A. Yes sir.

Q. How were the rests arranged?

A. They were arranged into three long rests and several short ones.

Q. When were the three long rests made?

A. The first was at Smoky Hill Station.

Q. How far is that from Fort Wallace?

A. About 40 miles.

Q. How many hours had you marched?

A. From about seven o'clock the preceding evening till about daylight.

Q. Where was the next rest?

A. The next long rest was at Monument's.

Q. How long had you marched and how far?

A. About 20 miles and from about six till 11 o'clock.

Q. Then you rested how many hours?

A. About an hour and a half.

Q. Where was the next rest?

A. At Downer's Station.

Q. How far was that from the last resting-place?

A. About 45 miles.

Q. How many hours were you marching it?

A. We reached there about half past one or two o'clock the following day.

Q. How far is it from there to Big Creek?

A. About 50 miles.

Q. When did you reach Big Creek?

A. About daylight the following day.

Q. How many intermediate rests did you make?

A. About every hour we had a short rest.

Q. What was the character of those rests?

A. The men were wheeled front into line and dismounted without unsaddling. I recollect we had 4 rests. The third was at Chalk Bluffs. We stopped and made coffee, and rested about three-fourths of an hour.

Q. Did you unsaddle there?

A. Yes sir, and grazed.

Q. Did you have a guide leading the march in the column?

A. There was a guide with the column.

Q. Was there a sergeant directing the march of the column as to gait?

A. They were in their proper places.

Q. Who was the leading enlisted man who marched at the head of the column?

A. A sergeant of Co "E".

Q. Did he have anything to do with directing the gait of the march?

A. That was one of his duties as guide.

Q. About what was the rate of the march—was it fast or slow?

A. It was in an ordinary walk.

Q. How did it compare with the rate of marching on the trip from the Platte and back again?

A. When we started it was faster, but the time was about the same.

Q. Do you mean it is 200 miles in a direct line from near Valley Station to Fort Wallace, or by the route you marched?

A. By the route we marched.

Q. Did you at any time apply to the accused to halt the command?

A. Yes sir.

Q. Did he refuse?

A. Yes sir.

Q. Where was it?

A. At Downer's Station. The column was not in motion at the time.

Q. State the circumstances of that request.

A. I stated to him that I thought it would be better if we would remain there till evening. That was after we were halted.

Q. Had the accused at any time previously, when in motion, refused to halt the command at your request?

A. No sir.

Q. How long had you been halted at Downer's Station when that sergeant reported he had been attacked by Indians?

A. About half an hour.

Q. Were you saddled and ready to march at the time he came in?

A. No sir.

Q. How strong a force of Indians did the sergeant report had attacked him?

A. He reported 18.

Q. Did he report that he took any measures to repulse the Indians?

A. He reported that he intended to do so but did not succeed. He reported that he ordered the men into a gallop towards Downer's Station. I understood him he tried to get back where he could fight them, but two of his men acted very badly.

Q. Were they the two who were killed?

A. No sir; they deserted after that.

Q. What do you mean by saying the men were demoralized?

A. They seemed very much excited about it.

Q. Do you refer to the party who came in with the sergeant?

A. I mean the whole command—there was a great deal of talking about it.

Q. Who did you hear talking about it?

A. I don't know the men. I heard a great deal of talking.

Q. How many men came in with the sergeant?

A. Four; two were left behind.

Q. When you reported to the accused the circumstances related to you by the sergeant, what answer did he make to you?

A. I don't remember.

Cut banks of the Smoky Hill River, in a sketch made with General Hancock's command, April 17, 1867. Original in author's collection.

Sioux and Cheyenne attack on a wagon train. Custer's train, thus attacked, proceeded in a double column surrounded by skirmishers, who successfully held off the Indian charges. *Harper's Weekly*, August 17, 1867.

Indian attempt to drive the stage hands out of the Smoky Hill Station. The adobe fortification was excellent protection against everything except grass fires and starvation. *Harper's Weekly*, April 21, 1866.

Q. Did he make any answer at all?

A. Not that I remember.

Q. How did you learn one of the men was wounded?

A. I learned it from Capt. Carpenter.

Q. Did you learn it at the time?

A. I only heard one of the men say he thought one of the men got off.

Q. Did you report that to Gen. Custer?

A. I think he was standing by at the time and heard the remark.

Q. How near was he to you?

A. Within 10 or 15 feet, either sitting in the door of the house or near it.

Q. If he was sitting in the house do you think he could have heard the remark of the man that it was possible one of the men had escaped?

A. Yes sir.

Q. When did you learn for certain that only one man was killed and one wounded?

A. Between two and three weeks after.

Q. Were you satisfied at the time that only one of the men was dead?

A. I was satisfied both were killed.

Questions By The Judge Advocate

Q. You stated that it was one of the duties of the guide to regulate the gait of the march; did the guide have any particular orders from you or otherwise to regulate it?

A. No sir.

Questions By The Court

Q. Were you so well satisfied that both those men were dead that you thought it unnecessary to make any further inquiries?

A. I was satisfied both were killed.

Q. Why did you make the request of Gen. Custer to make a longer halt at Downer's Station?

A. I thought it would be of importance to the command to stay there if there were any Indians in the neighborhood of the post at that time, and I thought it would have a bad effect on the morale of the command to leave the post when there had been a fight so recently.

Q. When you asked Gen. Custer to make a longer halt at Downer's Station, what reply did he make?

A. He said he would have to go along.

Q. Between what two halting places is Chalk Bluffs?

A. Between Monument's and Downer's Stations, about half way.

Q. How long after the arrival of the command at Fort Wallace did the detachment referred to, leave for Fort Hays or Big Creek?

A. Two days.

Q. Did your verbal order direct you to report to the accused with your detachment as an escort, or simply to report to the accused for duty?

A. Gen. Custer said I am going to take you through to Fort Hays, and told me the number of men though he did not mention the word escort; it was my belief it was for an escort.

The witness having heard his testimony read over then retired.
At 1:00 P.M. the Court adjourned till 10:00 A.M. Sept. 18, 1867.

FORT LEAVENWORTH, KANSAS
10:00 A.M. Sept. 18, 1867

The Court met with the same members present as on yesterday. The Judge Advocate, the accused and his counsel were also present.

Before the proceedings of yesterday were read, the Court was cleared at the request of the Judge Advocate, who stated that he wished to present his views upon the decision of the Court on the subject of the seniority of rank of certain members, regarding Generals Morgan and Callender and referred to earlier.

The Court, upon duly considering the matter presented by the Judge Advocate in reference to the action of the Court on the question of rank as between Bvt. Brig. Gen. Callender and Bvt. Brig. Gen. Morgan, decided to adhere to the decision already made; but to guard against the possibility of error, the Court directed the Judge Advocate to telegraph to the Adjutant General of the Army, to have the question of rank decided by the proper authority, and to inquire also whether an error in the order of precedence of members may be corrected by the Court, which telegrams were at once forwarded as required.

The Court was then opened, and the proceedings of yesterday were read and approved, then adjourned at 11:30 A.M. to meet the following day at 10 o'clock A.M. to await answers to the telegrams sent to the Adjutant General of the Army.

FORT LEAVENWORTH, KANSAS
10:00 A.M. Sept. 19, 1867

The Court convened with the same members present as yesterday, the Judge Advocate, the accused and his counsel also being present.

After the proceedings of yesterday were read and approved and it was announced that no replies had been received to the telegrams sent yesterday, the Court recessed until 2 P.M. There being no further information at that time the Court adjourned until the following morning.

FORT LEAVENWORTH, KANSAS
Sept. 20, 1867

The Court met at 10 A.M. with all members present as before. The Judge Advocate announced that he had received an answer to the telegrams sent to the Adjutant General of the Army, which he read to the Court.

The Court was then cleared for deliberation, and upon reopening the doors it was announced by the Judge Advocate, that the Court, after due deliberation on the reply of Bvt. Maj. Gen. E. D. Townsend, Assistant Adjutant General, decided that it is not a decision by the proper authority, as prescribed by Paragraph 884, Revised Army Regulations; that it does not therefore meet the question, and that he be again telegraphed to by the Judge Advocate and requested to obtain the decision of the proper authority as to the precedence of rank between Bvt. Brig. Gen. Callender and Bvt. Brig. Gen. Morgan, and of Bvt. Major Lyford and Bvt. Major Asbury.

And further, it was announced that the Court had decided not to proceed with the trial until an answer should be received from the telegram above mentioned. The Court adjourned at 11:30 A.M. to meet at 10 A.M. Sept. 21, 1867.

FORT LEAVENWORTH, KANSAS

10:00 A.M. Sept. 21, 1867

Again the Court met with everyone present excepting Brevet Major Asbury, whose absence was unexplained. The Judge Advocate announced that he had received no answer to the telegram sent yesterday to Bvt. Maj. Gen. Townsend.

Whereupon the Court took a recess until 2 P.M. to await an answer to the telegram.

The Court reassembled at 2 P.M., including Brevet Major Asbury. Bvt. Major Asbury explained that his absence in the morning was occasioned by indisposition, so that he did not arise in time for the meeting of the Court.

Following the reading and approval of yesterday's proceedings the Judge Advocate announced the arrival of the reply to his telegram of yesterday which was read to the Court.

Upon the receipt of this telegram, it being considered definite upon the question under discussion, the members took their seats in accordance with that decision.

The Court then, on motion, adjourned until 10 A.M. Sunday, Sept. 22, 1867.

FORT LEAVENWORTH, KANSAS

Sept. 22, 1867

Meeting with everyone present in the Court the proceedings of yesterday were read and approved.

Lieut. William W. Cook, a witness on the part of the prosecution, being duly sworn, testified. With the usual preliminary to identify him, the Judge Advocate proceeded with his questions:

Q. Were you with the Regiment on the march in July?
A. I was.
Q. What march?
A. I was with them on the march during July; We marched from the Platte to the forks of the Republican and back to

the Platte again—that was in June. In July we left the Platte, near Riverside Station, about the fifth or sixth, coming toward Fort Wallace.

Q. What time did you arrive at Fort Wallace?

A. About the 14th or 15th of July—I could not say exactly.

Q. What time did you leave Fort Wallace, after arriving there?

A. I left there two days after.

Q. For what place?

A. Fort Harker.

Q. By whose authority did you leave?

A. The commanding officer's.

Q. Who was the commanding officer?

A. Gen. Custer.

Q. How many troops moved from Fort Wallace to Fort Hays?

A. I understand there were 70 odd men.

Q. Was that a detail from the Regiment?

A. It was, I believe.

Q. Give an account of the march from Fort Wallace to Fort Harker or when the detail stopped.

A. We left Fort Wallace about five or six o'clock in the evening —I could not say exactly what day, but it was about the 17th —and marched through Henshaw. The next place was Russell's Springs and we halted there about three-fourths of an hour. There was an army wagon and six mules going down with provisions to ration up the stations on the Smoky Hill route. The route had been closed up some time and they took that opportunity to send down rations to the troops on the route and we halted about three-fourths of an hour distributing rations—that was about 12 or one o'clock at night. Then at daylight the next morning we were halted for about two hours and the command unsaddled, and the horses were grazing and the command were sleeping. That was in the vicinity of Smoky Hill Station where the wagon stopped and left the remainder of rations; it went no farther. After a rest of about two hours we continued the march till we arrived at Monument's Station, about the middle of the day. We remained there two or three hours. We had gone but about two miles from the Post when we met a train of forage for Fort Wallace and as our horses had had no forage for some weeks we took that opportunity of feeding them, and getting two or three feeds for every horse besides. We then went on till that evening before sundown when we halted about an hour, an hour and a half, or two hours, and the men cooked coffee and some slept for a short time. I dont think we fed the horses there, as the grazing was good. We continued the march, halting several times for a few minutes during the night, till the next morning, when we halted again about eight miles west of Downer's Station. We halted there an hour or an hour and a half. While there some coaches passed going west, with a strong escort. We then proceeded to Downer's Station where we arrived about noon I should say. I suppose we were there two hours; the men unsaddled, we had dinner and I was smoking after dinner. We then went on and stopped that evening about sundown on the banks of the Smoky Hill, I cant exactly say where; we had tea and the horses were grazing and the men got a little rest. We then continued the march that night and arrived early the next morning at Big Creek.

Q. How far is New Fort Hays from Big Creek?

A. About nine or 10 miles.

Q. How far is it from Fort Wallace to Big Creek?

A. Between 140 and 150 miles.

Q. Do you know about how long the command halted during that march from Fort Wallace to Big Creek?

A. I think they halted at least 10 hours, not including the short halts every hour or hour and a half, where we rested five or ten minutes.

Q. How long were you traveling from Fort Wallace to Big Creek?

A. I believe it was 57 hours.

Q. What was the condition of the horses when the command arrived at Big Creek?

A. We arrived there early in the morning, and I had nothing to do with the command and I went to the Station and got breakfast and took a nap and was busily engaged in getting mules for the command and did not see any horses but my own and I dont know. The command was about one-fourth mile from the Station.

Q. For what purpose were you getting the mules?

A. To go to Fort Harker that evening.

Q. For the command to ride, or what?

A. For Gen. Custer to go down.

Q. For riding or driving?

A. Driving.

Q. In what?

A. An ambulance.

Q. How many mules did you obtain?

A. I got one new team there.

Q. Two or four mules?

A. Four.

Q. Who did you obtain them of?

A. The Quartermaster at that Post—I got no ambulance.

Q. Was there more than one ambulance?

A. There were two.

Q. To what use was the ambulance put?

A. It went to Fort Harker that evening.

Q. Who rode in it?

A. Myself and Gen. Custer and Lieut. Custer.

Q. What time did you leave Ft. Hays in the ambulance?

A. About one o'clock in the afternoon; I can't tell the date.

Q. What time did you arrive at Fort Harker?

A. About two o'clock the next morning.

Q. What is the distance from Big Creek to Fort Harker?

A. It is about 67 miles.

Q. You made it in about 12 hours?

A. Yes sir, in 12 or 13 hours.

Q. From Fort Harker where did Gen. Custer go?

A. To Fort Riley I think.

Q. Did he go in the ambulance to Fort Riley?

A. No sir, he went in the cars.

Q. At Downer's Station what occurred in relation to an attack of Indians, if anything?

A. After dinner I was in front of a house, and I heard a noise made by the arrival of a party of horsemen outside the door. I went outside and found Sergt. Connelly and some men who had been attacked by Indians as I understood. I did not hear the report of the Sergeant. There was a private Young with the party who spoke to me about it. I did not hear any report made to Gen. Custer.

Q. Do you know whether any measures were taken by Gen. Custer or otherwise for the repulse of the Indians, or pursuit of them?

A. Not by his own troops. I was under the impression that some men from Capt. Carpenter's command were going out in that direction.

Q. How was that impression produced?

A. By hearsay.

Q. Do you know whether any of the command of Gen. Custer or any detachment from the command were sent out for the relief of the detachment sent out?

A. I do not know of any being sent.

Q. Do you know whether any measures were taken to pursue the Indians, by Gen. Custer?

A. No sir; it was considered inexpedient to pursue the Indians that distance, as that had happened to those men some two or three hours before.

Q. Do you know when the report came in, or did you see any of the detachment come in and hear them say anything?

A. I saw two of the men after they were in and I understood they were out and had been fired on.

Q. How soon after that report came in did the command leave Downer's Station?

A. I could not say exactly; it was half and hour at least, if not more.

Q. How many of the detachment left Ft. Hays and started to Fort Harker with Gen. Custer?

A. One soldier and three officers.

Q. Did you proceed in an ambulance?
A. Yes sir.
Q. The one you obtained at Fort Hays or otherwise?
A. I could not say—we went in an ambulance.

Questions By The Accused

Q. You stated you went to Riverside Station?
A. Yes sir.
Q. Is that the same as Valley Station?
A. I believe not.
Q. Did you go to Valley Station?
A. No sir.
Q. How many halts, exceeding a half-hours time, do you positively remember to have been made from Fort Wallace to Big Creek?
A. The first place we halted was at Russell's Springs, that was about half and hour; the first place where we unsaddled was at Smoky Hill; the next was Monument's Station; the next was that evening at White Rock or Castle Rock; the next was about eight miles west of Downer's Station; and at Downer's Station; and once between that and Big Creek. There were five or six halts where we halted more than half an hour.
Q. Was it five or six?
A. Six.
Q. Besides those did you have intermediate halts?
A. Yes sir, while marching every hour were halts of five or ten minutes.
Q. Do you state positively you obtained an ambulance at Fort Hays?
A. No sir; not an ambulance, but four mules.
Q. On what terms did you obtain them?
A. Till I returned again; then I was to return them.
Q. Did you give any mules in exchange?
A. I left some there that were brought from Fort Wallace.
Q. The soldier you spoke of as accompanying you; was he a soldier or a servant?
A. A servant.

121

Q. A soldier used as a servant?

A. Yes sir.

Q. You spoke of a wagon filled with commissary stores; did it have any difficulty in keeping up with the column?

A. No sir; not the slightest.

Q. What authority did Gen. Custer give you to leave Fort Wallace; verbal or written?

A. Verbal. I went with him.

Q. Did he say why you were going?

A. There was no commissary stores at Fort Wallace and I was going down to bring up a train of supplies for the Post. This is what I understood was the cause of my going down.

Questions By The Court

Q. Were the ambulance or wagon or mules obtained at Fort Hays, the property of the Government?

A. I believe they were.

Q. Why did you exchange mules at Fort Hays?

A. Because it would be better to take fresh animals than to keep those that came down from Fort Wallace.

Q. Were the mules you brought from Ft. Wallace in condition to go to Ft. Harker?

A. They certainly could have gone without trouble.

Q. Did you obtain any wheeled vehicle of any kind at Fort Hays?

A. I did not.

Q. Did you obtain any wheeled vehicle of any kind at Big Creek or old Fort Hays?

A. I did not.

Q. You stated that you left Ft. Wallace with 70 men; how many were in the command when you arrived at Big Creek?

A. I don't know.

Q. Where did you get the vehicle in which you say you rode from Big Creek to Ft. Harker?

A. I brought it from Fort Wallace with me.

Q. How many ambulances did Gen. Custer's party have in traveling between Big Creek and Fort Harker?

A. Two.

Q. How many ambulances did you take from Fort Wallace?

A. Two.

The accused then offered the following: "In the testimony of Lt. Cook this day taken, evidence has been admitted which is irrelevant to the question at issue before this Court, and the record of the Court is thereby encumbered, and occurrences which are not connected with the case are introduced. The accused therefore asked that all questions relating to ambulances not taken at Fort Hays be expunged from the record."

The Judge Advocate said the Court can consider the relevancy of the questions or not when they finally consider the case and come to a finding. As to the encumbrance of the record, that makes no difference.

The Court was closed for deliberation and upon reopening it was announced that the Court had decided not to accede to the request of the accused.

The accused then offered the following: "The accused asks that before a question be put by the Court, and when it is proposed by a member, the question be read and the accused thus be allowed an opportunity to object to it if it be illegal. Benét, page 129, holds that a question put by the Court cannot be objected to by either party, etc., but following: 'a question put by an individual member, if accepted is recorded as by the Court, if rejected, as by a member.' Now this plainly contemplates that the question should be put, placing it on record and then accepted or rejected. And the accused makes this application because he thinks it is essential to the security of his rights."

The Court was closed, and upon reopening the doors, it was announced that the Court had decided that when a question is proposed by a member, it will be read and submitted to the Court by the Judge Advocate. If the accused has any objections to the question he may now offer them before the question is accepted by the Court.

The witness having heard his testimony read over then retired.

Captain Thomas B. Weir, a witness on the part of the prosecution was sworn in, identified and then questioned:

Q. What are your present duties in the Regiment?

A. As long as Gen. Smith commanded the District of the Upper Arkansas I was his Adjutant. I dont know what position I occupy now, not having been assigned to any company.

Q. What was your position in May, June and July last?

A. Acting Assistant Adjutant General District of Upper Arkansas.

Q. Examine this paper and state if you recognize it. (Handing the witness a paper)

A. Yes sir; it is an official copy of an order I issued by Gen. Smith's order, to Gen. Custer; the signature making it a true copy is mine.

The Judge Advocate then offered the paper in evidence, and read it to the Court:

HD. QRS. DIST. UP. ARK. IN THE FIELD
CAMP NEAR FT. HAYS, KS. *May 3 of '67*

Special Field Orders ⎫
   No. 34   ⎬

Extract

III . . . Brevet Major General *G. A. Custer*, Lieutenant Colonel 7th Cavalry, will march tomorrow with *six (6)* Companies of the 7th Cavalry, provided with *fifteen (15)* days rations, and *five (5) days* grain, to *Fort McPherson, Nebraska.* Full instructions will be given General Custer concerning his march. . . .

By Command Of
Brevet Maj. General *Smith*
/s/ T. B. WEIR
1st Lieut. 7th Cavalry
A true copy   *A.A.A. General*
/s/ T. B. WEIR
1st Lieut. 7th Cav.
A.A.A. General

Q. Examine this paper, and state if you recognize it. (Handing the witness another paper)

A. Yes sir; this is a true copy of a letter given to Gen. Custer to accompany the order just read the Court. This is my signature making it a true copy.

124

The Judge Advocate then offered the paper in evidence and it was read to the Court:

Hᴅ. Qʀs. Dɪsᴛ. Uᴘ. Aʀᴋ. Iɴ Tʜᴇ Fɪᴇʟᴅ
Cᴀᴍᴘ Nᴇᴀʀ Fᴏʀᴛ Hᴀʏs, Ks. May 21, '67

Bvt. Maj. General G. A. Custer
Comg 7th U.S. Cavalry
Gᴇɴᴇʀᴀʟ,

The Brevet Major General commanding directs that you proceed as indicated in S.F.O. No. 34. Ex. 3 C.S. from these Hd. Qrs., in a northerly direction to the Platte, and thence to McPherson, at which point you will find a large supply of rations and forage. As to the length of time you are to stay at Fort McPherson, should you receive no word on your arrival there, you will be governed by circumstances and such information as you may be able to obtain from parties at that place. From Ft. McPherson proceed up the south fork of the Platte to Fort Sedgwick, and thence in the direction of Fort Morgan. If everything is found to be quiet and your presence not required in the vicinity of Forts Morgan or Sedgwick, you may come south to Fort Wallace, at which point you will find further instructions.

The object of the expedition is to hunt out and chastise the Cheyennes and that portion of the Sioux who are their allies between the Smoky Hill and the Platte. It is reported that all friendly Sioux have gone north of the Platte, and may be in the vicinity of Fort Mc-Pherson or Sedgwick. You will, as soon as possible, inform yourself as to the whereabouts of these friendly bands, and avoid a collision with them.

Copies of all letters and telegrams from Department Headquarters concerning the expedition have been furnished you.

I am General
Very Respectfully
Your Obedt Servant
/s/ T. B. Wᴇɪʀ
1st Lieut. 7th Cavalry

A true copy   *A.A.A. General*
/s/ T. B. Wᴇɪʀ
1st Lieut. 7th Cavalry
A.A.A. General

Q. Examine this paper, and state if you recognize it, if so, as what? (Handing the witness another paper.)

A. I do; it is a letter of instructions from Maj. Gen. Hancock, commanding the Dept., to Gen. Smith in reference to the movement of the cavalry, and was referred by Gen. Smith to Gen. Custer. I referred it by Gen. Smith's order, with instructions to comply with the instructions contained in the letter. This is my signature making it a true copy.

Q. Was that letter delivered or sent to the accused?

A. It was.

Q. By whom?

A. It was sent by a messenger from the office to Lieut. Cox of the 7th Cav. who was enroute to Fort Wallace to deliver to Gen. Custer. I had previously informed Lt. Cox I had a message for him, but he started before I knew it, and that was sent to overtake him on the road. I dont remember whether a receipt was returned or not, but I was satisfied at the time that the messenger delivered it to Lt. Cox.

Q. Was that the only letter of instructions you gave to Lt. Cox to deliver to Gen. Custer?

A. I think that was the only dispatch I sent to him.

Q. When was that?

A. I think it was about the middle of July; I dont remember the exact date.

The Judge Advocate then offered the letter in evidence, which was read to the Court, and accepted like the previous two as an exhibit:

Hd. Qrs. Dept of the Mo. in the Field
Camp Near Fort Harker, Kas., July 13, 1867

Bvt. Maj. Genl. F. J. Smith
Comdg. Dist. Upper Arkansas
General:

The Major General Commanding desires you to give instructions to General Custer's Command, which it is understood will arrive at

Fort Wallace about the 17th inst., that until further orders it will operate through Fort Wallace as a base and between the Arkansas and the Platte. He will habitually draw his supplies from Fort Wallace but a sufficient quantity of supplies has been placed at Forts Hays, Larned, Dodge and Lyons in order that, if he should find it necessary to visit those Posts, he will be able to obtain ample supplies. It is not proposed that he shall go south of the Arkansas at present, except in case of hot pursuit.

The Battallion of Volunteer Cavalry will be kept, as a rule, intact and will operate in the general direction of the Arkansas say; from Zarah westward they will be governed by the same rules and orders and will find supplies at any of the posts designated herein and if pursuit leads them to the Smoky Hill at the posts on that route.

The tributaries of the Arkansas will be especially under the supervision of the Volunteer Cavalry.

I wish you would require itineraries from Commanders of every scout in accordance with the reiterated order from these Hd. Qrs. and the General Regulations of the Army. These troops will not belong to any post nor will their Commanders interfere with the Command of any post at which they may be, or through which they may pass, except so far as to draw their regular supplies on proper requisitions.

These troops should move with pack mules, and not wagons; if means of transportation are required for supplies there are sufficient pack saddles at Fort Wallace and directions will be given to send twenty (20) packsaddles to each of the other posts in your districts where Cavalry may be stationed, say, Forts Hays, Larned, Dodge, Lyons, Reynolds and Harker.

You will please determine how much of the 7th Cavalry you propose leaving at Wallace, whether any more than Capt. Keogh's Company or not and give the necessary instructions.

Captain Barnitz' Company should be back at Fort Wallace by the time your orders reach there.

There are some lariats required for the packsaddles at Fort Wallace taken off by General Custer at Fort Hays and used for lariats for his horses; requisitions have been made but you had better see that the rope goes by the first train.

The Cavalry should be kept constantly employed.

> I am General
> Very Respectfully
> Your Obt. Servt.
> /s/ Chauncey McKeever, *Asst. Adjt. Genl.*

A true copy
T. B. Weir
Capt. and A.A.A.G.

> Q. Can you state more definitely as to the time when the letter of July 13th was sent from Headquarters of the District of Upper Arkansas?
> A. I think it was the 17th, from the records.
> Q. Do you think the records show it was the 17th?
> A. Yes sir; the 16th or 17th. The 17th is the day I have in my mind. I remember simply by the records.
> Q. Do you know whether Gen. Custer received these instructions of July 13th?
> A. Yes sir.
> Q. Do you know he did receive them?
> A. Yes sir.
> Q. Do you know where he received them?
> A. No sir; but it was not far from Fort Harker.
> Q. Was it before or after the accused arrived at Fort Harker?
> A. It was before; I know by what Gen. Custer told me.
> Q. Is there any record on the books at Headquarters of the District of Upper Arkansas of any leave of absence for Gen. Custer during the month of July 1867?
> A. There is not.
> Q. Do you know, as Acting Assistant Adjutant General of the District of the Upper Arkansas whether any leave of absence, verbal or written was given?
> A. I do not.
> Q. Do you know when Gen. Custer arrived at Fort Harker, in July?
> A. I do.
> Q. Can you state the date?

The interior of Smoky Hill Station, which was furnished as well as most stations on the overland trail. *Harper's Weekly*, April 21, 1866.

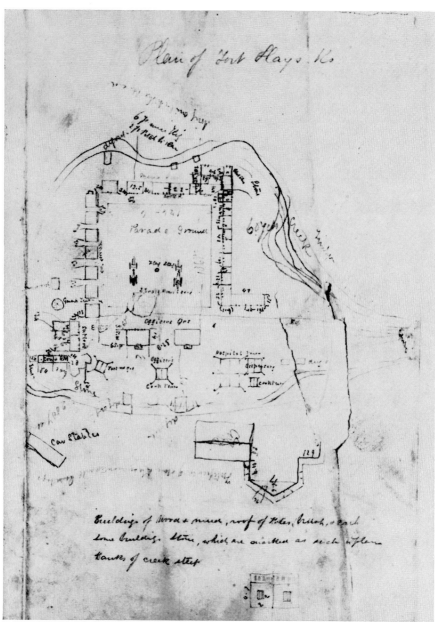

Pencil sketch of Fort Hays, Kansas, found among General Custer's papers.
Author's collection.

A. I think it was the morning of the 19th; it was during the night of the 18th or 19th.

Q. Did he report at District Headquarters?

A. When I first saw him at that time, he was in Gen. Smith's room at his quarters.

Q. Do you know by the records at your Headquarters whether any authority was given to the accused to be present at, or to proceed to, Fort Harker from his command?

A. There is none on record in that office.

Questions By The Accused

Q. Are those orders presented in evidence the only orders Gen. Custer received in the month of July or were furnished from your Headquarters?

A. They are.

Q. Was any other letter of instructions sent to Gen. Custer during that month, but the ones presented in evidence?

A. There was a letter written in reference to that letter of Gen. Hancock's and a copy of that letter also sent by mail.

The accused gave parol notice to the Judge Advocate to present that letter in evidence for the defense.

Q. Where did you get a copy of the communication dated July 13th?

A. In the office.

Q. How did it get in the office?

A. It came in regularly, as other communications came.

Q. What hour on the night of the 18th and 19th did the accused arrive at Fort Harker?

A. About half past two.

Q. At what hour did you first see him?

A. About half past two.

Q. Under what circumstances did you happen to see him?

A. I was sleeping out with an officer in the garrison and some person came and woke me up—it was my impression it was Gen. Smith, and said Gen. Custer is here. I got up and went over to Gen. Smith's room and saw him there.

Q. Was that the only place you saw him?
A. I saw him from that time till he left on the train.
Q. On what train and where for?
A. Fort Riley.
Q. Did you go with him to the train?
A. Yes sir.
Q. For what purpose?
A. Simply socially.
Q. Did you go to show him where the depot was?
A. I dont remember.

The Judge Advocate objected to any further questions in regard to this matter as "it is not a proper cross-examination."

The accused replied: "The purpose of the cross examination is to show that Gen. Smith commanding the Dist. of Upper Arkansas was aware of the departure of Gen. Custer to Fort Riley; that he authorized it by sending for the witness, his Adj. Gen.; that Gen. Smith sent messages to persons at Fort Riley and this can now be shown on cross examination, or, if thought proper, deferred until the opening of the defense."

The Court was cleared for deliberation and upon reopening the doors it was announced that the Court decided that the cross examination must be confined to the matter incited from the questions asked on the direct examination. At 1:20 P.M. the Court adjourned until the following day at 10:00 A.M.

Fort Leavenworth, Kas.
Sept. 23, 1867

The Court opened at 10:00 A.M. with all present save Brevet Major Asbury whose absence was explained by a medical certificate as follows:

HEADQUARTERS DEPARTMENT OF THE MISSOURI
Fort Leavenworth, Kansas, Sept. 23, 1867

I certify that Bvt. Maj. Asbury is suffering from a bilious attack, and is not able to leave his room, or to attend today the Genl. Court Martial of which he is a member.

/s/ I. T. Coates
A.A. Surg., U.S.A.

The above certificate was made by Acting Assistant Surgeon Coates, U.S.A. who attended Maj. Asbury in Leavenworth City. The certificate was made and delivered to the Judge Advocate at Ft. Leavenworth. Surgeon Coates is not stationed at Ft. Leavenworth, but is temporarily present as a witness before the Court.

/s/ R. Chandler
Capt. 13th Infty.
Judge Advocate

Because of the absence of Bvt. Major Asbury, the Court, on motion, adjourned until tomorrow, Sept. 24, 1867 at 10:00 a.m.

Fort Leavenworth, Kansas
10:00 a.m. Sept. 24, 1867

The Court met with all present. Following the reading and approval of proceedings for the past two days, Captain Charles C. Cox of the 10th Cavalry, a witness for the prosecution, was sworn in and questioned by the Judge Advocate:

Q. Were you on duty in this department in the month of July last?
A. Yes sir.
Q. On what duty were you on or about the 17th of July last?
A. I was a Second Lieutenant of the 7th Cavalry commanding the mounted escort of Maj. Gen. Hancock on the return from Ft. Harker to Ft. Wallace.
Q. What time did you return to Ft. Wallace?
A. I left Fort Harker on the night of the 16th of July and proceeded west three miles and halted till the 17th to await the arrival of teams.
Q. On what duty were you on your return to Ft. Wallace?
A. I was returning from escort duty that I had been engaged on from Ft. Wallace to Ft. Harker, and was ordered to escort a train which would meet me at the place I have indicated three miles west of Ft. Harker.
Q. Did you meet the accused on your return from Ft. Harker to Ft. Wallace?
A. I did.

131

Q. At what point?

A. At Bunker Hill, about 30 miles west of Ft. Harker, at nine o'clock at night.

Q. Did you speak to the accused?

A. I did.

Q. At what point. Did you deliver him any message or dispatch?

A. I gave him a dispatch that was sent to me from Gen. Smith's Headquarters by a Sergt. and four men with instructions to give it to the accused when I met him.

Q. On what day did you deliver the dispatch spoken of to Gen. Custer?

A. On the night of the 19th of July.

Q. At what hour?

A. Nine o'clock.

Q. In what direction was the accused traveling when you met him?

A. Eastward.

Q. In what manner was he traveling, on horseback or otherwise?

A. He was in an ambulance.

Q. When did you proceed on your way to Fort Wallace—how long after you met the accused at Bunker Hill?

A. The following morning at two hours before daylight.

Q. On your route from that point to Fort Wallace did you meet any of the troops belonging to the 7th Cavalry?

A. Yes sir.

Q. Did you meet any of the horses belonging to the 7th Cavalry?

A. I met a mounted escort under command of Capt. Hamilton.

Q. On the route to Ft. Wallace did you pass through Fort Hays or Big Creek?

A. Yes sir.

Q. After leaving Big Creek how many and what troops of the 7th Cav. did you meet on the route to Ft. Wallace?

A. On the 21st I took up a man of the 7th Cav. of "M" troop

I think, at Stormy Hollow; on the 22nd I took up one from Downer's; on the 23rd I took up two from Castle Rock and five from Grinnell's Springs. They were at the stations on the road.

Q. Were their horses with them?

A. In a majority of cases they had horses; I don't think there were but two men whose horses were missing.

Q. Do you know the condition of the horses belonging to the men you took up?

A. They were fatigued, worn out, unserviceable for cavalry duty; the men rode in the wagons and led their horses.

Q. Were they not fit for riding?

A. No sir.

Q. About how many horses were in that condition that you took up or saw on the march from Big Creek to Ft. Wallace belonging to the 7th Cavalry?

A. I should say there were seven horses belonging to the troops I picked up and of the seven, five or six were led. Not less than five could not be ridden.

Q. What became of the men and horses you picked up?

A. I transferred them to the Regt. on my arrival at Fort Wallace.

Q. You took them with you to Fort Wallace?

A. Yes sir.

Q. At the time you met the accused at Bunker Hill did you have any conversation with him?

A. Yes sir; I went out to see him.

Q. What conversation did you have?

A. The conversation related principally to the question of Indians. I asked him if he had met any Indians, and I think he asked me if I had met any. The conversation was chiefly on his part, and of that character.

Q. Did the accused speak to you in regard to having lost any of his men on the road?

A. Yes sir; he said he lost two men.

Q. Did he state how?

A. He said they loitered behind the column and were taken by the Indians. That was the impression I gathered from his remarks.

Q. Did he say anything about the rapidity of his march from Fort Wallace?

A. Yes sir; he said he had marched from Fort Wallace to Fort Hays in 55 hours.

Q. During your march from Big Creek to Fort Wallace were there any alarms of Indian attacks?

A. No sir; no alarm directly against the forces under my command. There was a report reached me about 20 miles this side of Monument's by Scout Ezekiel who was passing down the road with a guard that there had been an engagement at Monument's.

Q. Did you deliver any other dispatch to the accused at the time you met him, at Bunker Hill than the one you testified to?

A. No sir.

Q. On what particular duty were those horses and men you picked up on your route?

A. They told me that they belonged to a detachment that was escorting Gen. Custer.

Q. From where?

A. Fort Wallace.

The witness having heard his testimony read over then retired.
Capt. Arthur B. Carpenter, 37th Infantry, a witness on the part of the prosecution, testified to questions by the Judge Advocate.

Q. Where were you stationed in July last?

A. At Downer's Station.

Q. Where was your company stationed?

A. The Headquarters of the company was there; the rest were distributed.

Q. Did you meet the accused at Downer's Station at any time during the month of July?

A. I did sir.

Q. Can you state the date?

A. It was on the 17th of July.

Q. In what direction was he going?

A. Proceeding to Fort Hays.

Q. Who was with the accused at that time?

A. He had a command.

Q. Do you know about the number?

A. I judge from 75 to a 100 men.

Q. What time did that detachment or command arrive at Downer's Station?

A. A little past 11 o'clock in the morning.

Q. What time did it leave there?

A. Near 12 o'clock—half past 12 on.

Q. Do you know anything about an attack of Indians on any part of that command?

A. There was an attack on what I considered the rear guard at that time—about four miles back.

Q. State what you know about that attack.

A. Some time after the command arrived a detachment came in, consisting of a non-commissioned officer and eight men and reported the Indians were near and that they had lost two men. After the command went away I sent out to pick up the bodies of those killed and they brought in one dead man and one wounded man.

Q. To what command did those men belong?

A. The 7th Cavalry.

Q. Were they connected with that command?

A. I don't recollect the troop.

Q. At what time did you send out that detail spoken of?

A. About an hour after the command left—about two o'clock.

Q. Had the accused left at that time?

A. Yes sir.

Q. What were your instructions to the detail sent out by you?

A. To find the bodies and bring them in.

Q. What became of the wounded man thus brought in?

A. He was put in the hospital.

Q. What became of the dead one?

A. He was buried.

Q. Do you know whether any action was taken by the accused to recover the dead or wounded man?

A. I do not.

Q. Did the whole command leave Downer's Station before the dead and wounded men were brought in?

A. Yes sir, except one man who remained there at the Station.

Q. For what reason did that one remain?

A. He reported to the Surgeon and he required his reason for reporting, and he said his horse was not able to go on.

Q. How long did that man remain at Downer's Station?

A. Nearly a week I judge.

Q. Was his horse with him?

A. Yes sir.

Q. In what condition was his horse?

A. He had a sore back, was all I saw.

Q. Could he travel?

A. He could not be ridden.

Q. Did the accused refuse to take any measures to repulse the Indians at that time?

A. No sir.

Q. Or for the defense or relief of the detachment sent out?

A. The detachment fought their own way in—there was no relief from the main command.

Questions By The Accused

Q. Have you not stated, and do you not believe it would not have been judicious for the accused to pursue the Indians that attacked that detachment?

A. It would have been fruitless.

Questions By The Court

Q. What induces you to believe the pursuit of the Indians in question would have been fruitless?

A. I do not think the Indians remained in the vicinity at the time of the attack and any pursuit at that distance would not have resulted in any advantage.

The witness having heard the testimony read over then retired. Sergeant James Connelly, Co. "D", 7th Cavalry, a witness on the part of the prosecution being sworn, testified.

Questions By The Judge Advocate

Q. Were you with the portion of the Regiment on the march from Platte River?

A. Yes sir.

Q. And on the march from Fort Wallace to Big Creek?

A. Yes sir.

Q. State the condition, as far as you know, of the horses of the command when it reached Fort Wallace?

A. The Horses were not in very good condition. They had been a good while without forage and the marches had been severe.

Q. From Fort Wallace to Fort Hays how much of the Regiment was detailed for the march, as near as you can tell?

A. Somewhere over 70 enlisted men—I don't know the exact number.

Q. Under whose command were they?

A. Gen. Custer.

Q. Under whose command was the detachment at the time it left Fort Wallace for Fort Hays?

A. Gen. Custer; he was along in person.

Q. Did Gen. Custer accompany it; if so to what point?

A. He led the column, and Capt. Hamilton was the next officer under him. Gen. Custer came as far as Big Creek Station.

Q. On the march from Fort Wallace to Fort Hays what were your particular duties?

A. I was generally in the rear of the column somewhere. I was sent in some cases back to leave horses behind and pick up stragglers from the rear.

Q. Were you ordered to pick up stragglers and horses?

A. Yes sir; on several occasions by Capt. Hamilton.

Q. On how many occasions during the march did you receive those orders?

A. I could not say.

Q. More than one?

A. Yes sir.

Q. More than twice?

A. Yes sir, but I could not state the exact number of occasions.

Q. Did you at different times pick up stragglers in the rear of the column?

A. Yes sir.

Q. Did you pick up horses?

A. Yes sir; sometimes the men would be along with them. I remember a couple of times I picked up men, after we had been out the second night. The men would fall asleep and would not wake up when the command was given to forward.

Q. On the march from Fort Wallace to Big Creek were any of the horses unable to travel, to your knowledge?

A. Yes sir.

Q. In cases when horses were unable to travel did you receive orders at any time what to do with them?

A. Yes sir; I received orders on two occasions to leave them at stations.

Q. Were any horses left at stations on the route to your knowledge?

A. Yes sir.

Q. State about how many.

A. I disremember how many. I remember on an occasion there were five left at Grinnel's Station, and I know of another that was left at Castle Rock and some at other stations along.

Q. Were any of the horses to your knowledge abandoned or shot on the march?

A. Yes sir.

Q. State how many horses were abandoned and how many were shot.

A. I could not exactly say. I know there were 11 dismounted men at Big Creek Station that were sent to Fort Hays without horses and I expect that was the number of Horses abandoned and shot.

Q. Can you state how many horses were shot?

A. I don't know of any more than three.

Q. Do you know of three?

A. Yes sir.

Q. By whose order were they shot?

A. I think Capt. Hamilton gave the order to Corporal Nizely, who was in charge of the rear guard that day.

Q. When those horses were abandoned that you spoke of what became of them?

A. In every case they were left on the prairie. They could get no further.

Q. What was the cause of their being abandoned or shot as you understood it?

A. I could not say whether it was through sickness or fatigue.

Q. Were they unable to go on?

A. Yes sir.

Q. In all cases where horses were abandoned or shot that came under your knowledge, were they serviceable or unable to proceed?

A. Yes sir; they were unable to proceed any further.

Q. State what you know of an attack by the Indians on that march, giving times and places if possible.

A. On the morning of the 17th we were at Castle Rock Station, and about two miles east of there the command halted for about two hours for the men to get coffee. After the halt was over Gen. Custer told me to take six men and go back after a man named Young, who had his mare—to go back as far as Castle Rock to find him. I did so, and found him there. Gen. Custer gave me a led horse to mount him if his horse was played out.[6] I found him at Castle Rock and his horse was unfit for service and I remounted him. On coming back when near where the encampment had been where I started from, we were attacked by a party of Indians, and they kept it up for three or four miles. One man got killed and one was wounded and we were forced to leave him on the field. I reported to Capt. Hamilton the attack and the nature of it. I struck the command at Downer's Station.

[6] A "led horse" is an extra horse for the purpose mentioned.

Q. About how many Indians did you judge there were?

A. To the best of my opinion there were 50 or 60.

Q. When Gen. Custer directed you to return for that Young man did he give you any other witnesses besides what you have stated?

A. He told me, when I had my detachment of six men out and ready to start, to make no delay and he would move the column on a short distance and wait for me to report.

Q. From the point where you found the man to where you overtook the command, what is the distance?

A. I expect it was about ten miles. I did not overtake the command till I got to Downer's Station.

Q. Where was the attack of Indians—how near Castle Rock?

A. I judge about two or two and one-half miles.

Q. Did you see the wounded man at the time he was wounded?

A. I saw him a short time after. The first time I knew of his being wounded I was within five or six yards of him to his left, and he called out to me that he was wounded; I rode around on his right and asked him where he was wounded. He had his pants inside his boots and the blood was all over his hip. He made no reply but pointed to his hip and I took it for granted that was where he was wounded. I rode to the left again and gave the command to halt to get him tied in the saddle, so as to take him along. At that time two men in front rode on and paid no attention to the command whatever but made their escape and left me with three men. That was about the hottest of the fight and we were forced to leave him on the field. He had not dismounted at that time, and I rode on five or six hundred yards trying to get those men to halt and when I turned back he had fell or dismounted, I could not tell which.

Q. Do you know in what part of the attack the man was killed?

A. He was killed a few minutes before the other man reported to me he was wounded. The man Young was leading Gen. Custer's mare and the Indians were getting close on our right flank and the mare appeared to get excited and turned and took Young about 300 yards to the left of the road. Two Indians from the rear thought to cut him off the detachment, which made some delay, and there were two shots fired at the Indians.

Q. What effect did these shots have?

A. I don't know that they had any effect. The Indians who were trying to cut that man off wheeled to the rear and right flank of the detachment.

Q. Did the Indians fire into the detachment?

A. They had been firing for some time before but seemed to fire tolerably wild. Just as Young was in the act of getting back in the road, I looked to the rear, and saw the man who was killed, and his horse was moving quite slowly and he was very unsteady in his saddle. He was four or five hundred yards in the rear and was surrounded by six or seven Indians, and a few minutes after there was a shot from a pistol I judged and he fell from his saddle. Whether he was wounded before or not I am unable to state.

Q. Was he cut off from the detachment then?

A. He was in the road, and there were no Indians between the detachment and him in the road, but they were nearer to us on the right hand flank than he was to the command at the time I saw him.

Q. After one man was killed and one wounded and two men you say went on without minding your order to halt, what did you then do?

A. I rode four or five hundred yards trying to overtake them, thinking they did not hear me, but I found the horse I was riding was not able to overtake them. I fell back to the rear again and ordered two men whose horses seemed to be better than mine to proceed after those men and if they did not halt when they caught them to shoot them down.

Q. Did the two men obey your orders?

A. Yes sir; so far as to halt the men.

Q. Did you then follow on?

A. Yes sir; at a trot and sometimes a lope. A great many of the

Indians had fallen to the rear when the man was killed and stayed there, which left no more than perhaps 20 on our right flank circling around.

Q. Had the command halted at any point, so far as you could judge between the point you left it to go after Young and Downer's Station?

A. I don't know; I did not find them till I got to Downer's Station.

Q. What was your object in retreating after those two men had been killed?

A. One object was I wanted to join the command as soon as possible, and I did not know how far I would have to go.

Q. Did you expect to join the command sooner than you did?

A. Yes sir; I expected every ravine I passed to see the command while the Indians were in pursuit of us.

Q. After you reported that matter to Capt. Hamilton, what was done by him? Did he report it to Gen. Custer to your knowledge?

A. I don't know. He started over to where Gen. Custer was sitting at Downer's Station, but whether he repeated it to Gen. Custer is more than I can say.

Q. Were those two men—one wounded and one killed—left on the field?

A. Yes sir.

Q. After you reported those facts to Capt. Hamilton were any of the detachments sent out after those men?

A. Not to my knowledge.

Q. Would you have known it if there had been?

A. I would have been very apt to know it if there had been anyone sent out there.

Q. What day of the month and what hour of the day did the detachment leave Fort Wallace for Big Creek?

A. I think it was on the 15th of July, somewhere between six and seven o'clock in the afternoon.

Q. What time did the detachment reach Big Creek?

A. On the morning of the 18th, tolerably early—about day-light, or maybe a little before. My horse gave out the night

before beyond Lookout Station and I got in the ambulance
and fell asleep.

Q. At what point on the march did your horse give out?

A. About five miles west of Lookout Station.

Q. How far is that from Big Creek?

A. I don't know exactly.

Q. Was that march from Fort Wallace to Big Creek continuous?

A. Yes sir.

Q. How long were the halts generally?

A. There were some halts for a short time when the horses
would not be unsaddled and other halts where the men
would have coffee and the horses would be unsaddled and
picketed out to graze.

Q. To the best of your knowledge how many of the detachment
arrived at Big Creek?

A. Somewhere between 45 or 50 mounted men.

Q. What was the condition of the horses of the command when
you arrived at Big Creek?

A. Very fatigued indeed.

Q. Were they serviceable or unserviceable?

A. All the horses except one proceeded a day or two after to
Fort Harker. After a day's rest they made Fort Harker
from Big Creek.

Q. How soon after you returned to Downer's Station after the
attack of the Indians, did the command leave?

A. Somewhere in the neighborhood of 15 or 20 minutes.

Captain Parsons then proceeded with the interrogation:

Q. How far in the rear of the column did you habitually move?

A. Sometimes I was to the right and sometimes to the left, and
at the rear by times.

Q. How many times did you go back or stop to pick up stragglers?

A. I don't remember.

Q. Did you pick up any man who was drunk?

A. No sir; I don't recollect seeing a man drunk on the march.

Q. Did you see 11 horses abandoned or shot?

A. I did not exactly see them; I knew there were 11 men at Big Creek without horses and I knew there were some horses left behind because I left mine behind.

Q. Did you see 11 horses abandoned or did you reason there were that many because 11 men were dismounted?

A. I did not see that many.

Q. Did you see any horses abandoned that were not shot?

A. Yes sir.

Q. Did you notify Capt. Hamilton they were abandoned?

A. I notified him before. The orders would be to go back and try to get them along and if we could not to get the saddles off. First there were orders to shoot them, but that caused delay and they ordered them to be abandoned.

Q. Did Capt. Hamilton know of any horses being abandoned and not shot?

A. I don't know.

Q. Did you report to Capt. Hamilton that you were going to abandon any horses and not shoot them?

A. I had already got the order and I supposed he knew it.

Q. From Capt. Hamilton?

A. Yes sir.

Q. What was the order you speak of?

A. The orders in all cases, I could not exactly say; they were verbal orders.

Q. You speak of a wounded man left after the attack of the Indians; did you not believe when you left the field that he was dead?

A. No sir; I saw him a few minutes before he dismounted, and reported to Capt. Hamilton. I did not believe the Indians saw him dismount.

Q. Did you report that fact to any other person but Capt. Hamilton?

A. I might have said it to enlisted men but not to any officer.

Q. Have you made statements in regard to what you would testify to before being brought on the stand to testify?

A. There are some things I have testified to that I have made statements of.

Q. To whom did you give those statements?

A. The Judge Advocate.

Q. Did you tell him one of the men was wounded?

A. Yes sir.

Q. When did you make that statement to the Judge Advocate?

A. I don't remember the date.

Q. How do you know the man you say you left wounded was not killed?

A. I saw him when I rode out to give the order to halt to have him tied in the saddle and he was not deadly pale as if mortally wounded.

Q. How do you know the first man was killed?

A. I saw him fall from the saddle.

Q. Are all men who fall from their saddles killed?

A. To my best knowledge when five or six Indians are around a man and shots are fired, they are usually killed.

Q. Were there different estimates of the number of Indians by different members of your party?

A. I don't know that there was any different estimates. The first party of Indians we saw were only seven or eight, and we went on some time before we knew the real extent of the attacking party.

Q. Besides the two shots you spoke of being fired were there any other shots fired at the Indians?

A. No sir, not by the detachments.

Q. Was there any information conveyed to the accused that your detachment was in peril till you reported to Capt. Hamilton?

A. None to my knowledge.

Q. How soon after those two advance men got into the station did you get in?

A. I overtook those men in a half mile or so and we went in together.

Q. What did you do then?

A. I moved along the road. The Indians who were left with the killed men commenced flanking us on the right, and we moved along in a trot till we got into Downer's Station.

Q. How far was the accused from Capt. Hamilton when you reported?

A. He might be 40 or 50 yards or so; I don't know exactly. After I reported to Capt. Hamilton as I passed by the station door, I saw him sitting inside the door.

Q. How do you judge how many men arrived at Big Creek; did you call the roll?

A. After starting on the road, I knew how many men were sent to Fort Hays and afterwards I was appointed 1st Sergt. of the detachment.

Q. When you arrived at Big Creek Station did you call the roll of the men?

A. Not when we arrived there.

Questions By The Court

Q. Did the escort or detachment have forage for the horses on the march from Ft. Wallace to Big Creek?

A. Yes sir; we got forage at Monument's Station, or after we started from there, about half a mile or so this side.

Q. How near to Downer's Station did the Indians pursue you?

A. They pursued us to within a mile and a half or so of the station to the right of the road, about the same distance from the detachment after one man was killed, and the other wounded they moved off on our right and continued to move to our right.

Q. How long were you riding from that point to where you reported to Capt. Hamilton?

A. It could not be quite half an hour.

Q. When horses were left at the stations were the men to whom they belonged left with them?

A. In all cases I know of they were.

The witness having heard his testimony read over, then retired.

Chauncey McKeever, Bvt. Brig. Gen. and Assistant Adjutant General, a witness on the part of the prosecution being duly sworn, then testified.

Questions By The Judge Advocate

Q. Do you recognize this paper? (handing the witness a paper)
A. Yes sir; that is a table of distances from Fort Harker to Denver City issued from Department Headquarters. This is my signature making it official. It is issued to govern the payment of transportation accounts. It was made by Lieut. Brown, Chief Engineer of the Department, and so made official by him. The original report of the Chief Engineer was in the office at the time this was printed.

The Judge Advocate then offered the paper in evidence and it was approved and recorded.

TABLE OF DISTANCES BETWEEN FORT HARKER, KANSAS, AND DENVER CITY, C.T. *via Fort Hays and Old Fort Hays*

STATIONS	DISTANCES		DISTANCES BETWEEN POSTS		REMARKS
	Miles	Yards	Miles	Yards	
FORT HARKER to:					
Buffalo Creek,	9	251			Road good, good camp-
Wilson Creek,	10	1,406			ing. Places on the
Bunker Hill,	9	461			Smoky Hill with wood,
Fossil Creek,	10	1,229			water and grass.
Walker Creek,	10	1,361			
"Old" Fort Hays,	4	549	54	1,737	
Fort Hays,	17		17		Plenty wood, water
Lookout Station,	5	880			and grass.
Stormy Hollow,	13				
White Rock,	12	880			
Downer's,	10	880			
Castle Rock,	10	440			
Grinnell Springs,	9	1,320			Good water at stations;
Chalk Bluffs,	13	880			between stations uncer-
Carlyle Hall,	9	880			tain, except during wet
Monument,	9	440			season.
Smoky Hill,	13	1,320			Good grass in bottom,
Russell Springs,	10	880			wood scarce.
Henshaw Springs,	14	1,320			
Fort Wallace,	8	1,320	141	880	

STATIONS	DISTANCES		DISTANCES BETWEEN POSTS		REMARKS
	Miles	Yards	Miles	Yards	
Pond Creek,	2	1,257			Good Water.
Goose Creek,	12	582			" "
Big Timber,	11	776			" "
Cheyenne Wells,	17	1,337			Excellent Water.
Deering's Wells,	15	319			Good "
Big Springs,	12	1,505			Sulphur "
David's Springs	12	847			Good "
Hugo Springs,	13	457			Excellent "
Willow Springs,	12	356			Good "
Lake Station,	13	1,278			Water slightly alkaline
Cedar Point,	11	1,604			" good
Fairmount,	9	782			" "
Benham Springs,	11	383			" "
Bijou,	12	1,146			" "
Kiowa,	12	129			" "
Box Elder,	11	284			" "
Toll Gate,	11	552			" "
DENVER,	9		212	1,341	

OLD FORT HAYS to:

Big Creek Station, 8
Lookout Station, 9   17

DISTANCE FROM FORT HARKER TO DENVER CITY, via OLD FORT HAYS
and BIG CREEK STATION, 420 miles, 1,318 yards.

OFFICIAL:

/s/ C. McKEEVER
Asst. Adj. Genl.

The accused had but one question.

Q. Do you know in what manner Lieut. Brown measured those distances?
A. I do not.

The witness heard his testimony, then retired.
The Court adjourned until 10:00 A.M., Sept. 25, 1867.

FORT LEAVENWORTH, KANSAS
Sept. 25, 1867

The Court reopened promptly at 10:00 A.M. with everyone present. After approval of yesterday's proceedings Bvt. Maj. Gen. Andrew J. Smith took the stand as a witness for the prosecution.

Q. What was your command in May, June and July last?
A. I was commanding the District of the Upper Arkansas.
Q. Was the accused under your command?
A. Part of the time only; that is he was not under my control from the time he reached the Platte till he arrived at Fort Wallace.
Q. Did the accused receive from you any leave of absence or authority to leave his command during the month of July last?
A. No sir.
Q. Did the accused have any authority from you to march from Fort Wallace, Ks. to Fort Hays?
A. He had no orders or authority from me.
Q. So far as you know, was there any urgency or demand of public business for the accused to make such a march?
A. None that I know of.
Q. How far is it from Fort Harker to Fort Riley?
A. I think the distance is called 84 miles as measured for the stage route. What the distance is between the stage route and the railroad I cannot state.
Q. Did the accused have any authority from you to proceed to Fort Riley from Fort Wallace?
A. No sir. He came to the Post and stated that he was going to Fort Riley, and I made no objections to his going. That was at Fort Harker.

Questions By The Accused

Q. When the accused stated he was going to Ft. Riley, did he or not ask you how many days you could give him; and if so what was your reply?
A. I don't recollect that he asked how many days he could have.
Q. Did you or not say to the accused he must hurry back as soon

149

as he possibly could, at the time he stated he was going to Ft. Riley?

A. I might have said so. I know I ordered him back the next morning by telegraph.

Questions By The Court

Q. What induced you to order the accused by telegraph the next morning to return?

A. Gen. Custer came to my quarters between two and three o'clock at night and I don't know that I asked the question how he came down. It was my impression he came by stage. I learned the next morning from my Adj. Gen. Lt. Weir that he came with an escort part of the way, and in an ambulance from Ft. Hays to Ft. Harker, and then I immediately ordered him back to his command. He left for Fort Riley on the three o'clock morning train and from there I ordered him back the next morning after I learned how he came down.

The witness having heard his testimony read over then retired.

1st Lieut. Thomas W. Custer, 7th Cavalry, and brother of the accused, called by the prosecution, testified as follows:

Q. Were you with a portion of the 7th Cavalry on the march between the Platte and Fort Wallace in July last?

A. Yes sir.

Q. On that march who was in command?

A. Gen. Custer.

Q. On that march between the Platte River and Fort Wallace were there any deserters from the command to your knowledge?

A. Yes sir.

Q. At what point on the march were those deserters discovered?

A. About 12 miles south of the Platte.

Q. How far from Fort Sedgwick?

A. About 40 miles west of Fort Sedgwick.

Q. On what day of the month was it?

A. It was on the seventh of July I think.

Q. Were any orders issued in regard to those deserters to you, verbal or written?

A. There were verbal orders.

Q. State what those verbal orders were?

A. To shoot those deserters.

Q. Was that all?

A. Yes sir; to follow them and shoot them.

Q. How many deserters were there?

A. There were 11 or 13, I am not positive which; five of them were mounted and the others were dismounted.

Q. State the exact language of the order as you received it, in regard to shooting those deserters if you can remember it?

A. The accused spoke to me and said "I want you to get on your horse and go after those deserters and shoot them down." That is as near as I can recollect it.

Q. Where were the deserters at the time the order was given?

A. They were about two miles from camp as near as I can judge.

Q. Was the command in camp at the time?

A. Yes sir; they were resting.

Q. Were the supposed deserters in sight?

A. Yes sir; some of them.

Q. How many of them were in sight?

A. About six or seven when we started after them.

Q. Who accompanied you after those deserters?

A. There were three officers went. I was about 200 yards from them.

Q. Was the order given to you separate from any other officer?

A. Yes sir.

Q. State what occurred after you received that order and started in pursuit of the deserters?

A. Major Elliott, Lieut. Cook and myself followed them. Maj. Elliott and Lt. Cook caught up with them before I did; I was about 100 yards from them and could not hear what was said by either Maj. Elliott or Lt. Cook. I saw the men laying down their arms and Maj. Elliott and and Lt. Cook rode toward them. One of the men, I think it was a man named Johnson ran to get his carbine and a man named Atkins, a scout, who was along with the party—I don't know whether he had any orders or not—up to the man and said he would blow his brains out if he attempted to touch his carbine. In the meantime I saw Maj. Elliott and Lt. Cook firing on them. By that time I was with them myself and we fired on them.

Q. State what else occurred.

A. There were three of the deserters wounded.

Q. You say the man Johnson went after his carbine—did he get it?

A. No sir, he did not get his hands on it.

Q. Was he mounted?

A. No sir; he was dismounted.

Q. Did he have his carbine at the time he was fired on?

A. No I don't think he had.

Q. State the name of the men who were wounded by the party sent out after them?

A. I don't remember any names but the man Johnson.

Q. How many of those men were wounded at that time?

A. I think there were three.

Q. Had any of those supposed deserters had any trial that you know of?

A. No sir.

Q. Did you fire on any of those supposed deserters?

A. Yes sir.

Q. Do you know the names of the one or two you fired on?

A member objected to any question that might tend to incriminate the witness.

The Court was cleared for deliberation and when reopening the doors it was announced that the Court had decided to direct the Judge Advocate to explain to the witness his rights and premises and that he might withdraw his answer to the previous question.

After this explanation the witness desired to withdraw his answer to the last question answered, as it might tend to incriminate himself. The Judge Advocate then withdrew the last question.

Q. Were those supposed deserters fired on by order of the accused?

A. Yes sir.

Q. At what point on the march did this occur.

A. About 12 miles south of the Platte.

Q. After those deserters were fired into and wounded as stated what become of them?

A. A wagon was sent out after them and they were brought in.

Q. Where did the wagon come from?

A. It was in the train belonging to the command, I believe.

Q. How far were those supposed deserters from the body of the command when fired into and wounded?

A. They were about two miles or two and one-quarter miles.

Q. How far were they taken in by wagon?

A. I don't know.

Q. Were they taken with the command on the march?

A. Yes sir.

Questions By The Accused

Q. Was the point you have described the only point at which desertions took place on the march?

A. No sir.

Q. Were there any other desertions?

A. There were.

Q. At what other point were there other desertions?

A. Near Riverside Station on the Platte.

Q. How many deserters were there?

A. I don't know how many there were in the Regiment; that night there were ten from my company.

Q. What date was that?

A. It was on or about the night of the sixth of July.

Q. Were there any deserters after the events described in your direct evidence during that march?

A. No sir.

Q. How were you halted when those deserters were discovered. —were you in camp?

A. Yes sir.

Q. Were your tents up?

A. No sir.

Q. How long had you been in camp?

A. About three or four hours.

Q. What do you call being in camp?

A. In camp, unsaddled, and the horses out grazing.

Q. When those deserters were discovered had "boots and saddles" sounded?

A. Yes sir.

Q. Was the command preparing to move?

A. Yes sir.

Q. What hour of the day was it?

A. About three or four o'clock in the afternoon.

Q. At what hour did you return with the deserters?

A. About five o'clock.

Q. How far on the plains could you see from the point where you started when you were ordered out to shoot deserters?

A. Between two and three miles.

Q. You say those deserters were in sight when you were ordered out to shoot them; how long did they remain in sight from the camp?

A. About 10 or 15 minutes I should judge.

Q. How were the deserters you overtook provided?

A. With Spencer carbines and cartridges—boxes full of Spencer carbine ammunition and most of them had haversacks full of rations.

Q. How long did it take you to overtake them?

A. About 20 or 25 minutes I suppose.

Q. Did you pursue them as rapidly as possible during that time?

A. Yes sir.

Q. Were you well mounted?

A. Yes sir.

Q. Did any of the party sent in pursuit of the deserters fire on them after they got them in their possession?

A. Yes sir.

Q. Did you bring in any unhurt?

A. Yes sir.

Q. How many?

A. One was unhurt, and one was hurt by a horse stepping on him slightly.

Q. Did you send in any men unhurt?

A. Yes sir.

Q. How many?

A. I sent in two myself.

Q. You stated you were about 100 yards behind the advance men of the party, when they overtook the deserters?

A. Yes sir.

Q. Could that man Johnson have had his carbine at that time and you not know it?

A. Yes sir; they all had their carbines when Maj. Elliott and Lt. Cook were near them.

Q. Did you overtake any of the mounted deserters?

A. No sir.

Questions Of The Court

Q. Who commanded the party sent out in pursuit of deserters, and how many enlisted men belonged to it?

A. Lieut. Jackson I think commanded it. I don't know how many enlisted men belonged to it; I think there were some six or eight.

Q. You mentioned that as you approached you saw them laying down their arms; had they laid down their arms at the time you saw Maj. Elliott and Lt. Cook firing on them?

A. I believe they had.

Q. Were those three men wounded by reason of carrying out the order of the accused to shoot them?

A. Yes sir.

The witness having heard his testimony read over, then retired. The accused then presented the following communication:

FORT LEAVENWORTH, KANS.
Sept. 25, 1867

Capt. Robt. Chandler
Judge Advocate, G.C.M.

CAPTAIN:

I have the honor to state that I require for the defense in the case of the U.S. vs. Bvt. Maj. Gen. G. A. Custer, 7th Cav., the presence of the following witnesses, viz.: Bvt. Brig. Gen. Patten, Comdg. Fort Sedgwick, Col. and Bvt. Lt. Col. H. G. Litchfield, A.A.A.G. Hd. Qrs., Dept. of the Platte, Omaha, Nebr.

But if for the prosecution you will concede the points to be proven by these witnesses, their attention will not be required. These points are as follows: That certain orders given the accused by Lt. Gen. W. T. Sherman, U.S.A., Comdg. Mil. Div. of the Mo. which will be offered by the accused in evidence were made out and designed to reach the accused at the forks of the Republican. That these orders directing the accused to report to Maj. Gen. Hancock at Ft. Wallace, Ks. where Gen. Hancock should be on his return from Denver City, Col. to Fort Leavenworth, Kas. did not reach the accused in season to prevent the accused, in the execution of previous orders, from proceeding on another scout, thereby he, in obeying all orders then received was prevented from reaching Ft. Wallace before Major Gen. Hancock has passed through that post as contemplated. And the accused will present in evidence before said the Special Order to report, herein named.

The Judge Advocate replied: "On the part of the prosecution I would state there will no harm acrue to the prosecution in admitting this evidence in view of the fact that if we do not admit them the witnesses will have to be sent for and will testify to these facts as I know, and consequently I am willing to admit what the accused wishes to prove by these witnesses as stated: that the order sent by Lt. Gen. Sherman to the accused to report to Gen. Hancock did not reach him in time."

Lieut. W. E. Cook was then recalled for the prosecution.

The accused objected to the examination of the witness as follows: "The accused, in the case of Lt. Cook, a witness for the prosecution, once previously examined for the prosecution, objects to the recall of Lt. Cook as a witness for the prosecution, for that presenting the prosecution is in law, and rightfully supposed to have exhausted all testimony for the prosecution that can be rendered through the witness and there is in existence no precedent whereby a witness, having once been on the stand for either party, can be recalled for the same party, unless to rebut evidence subsequently offered, or to disclose new facts that have been made known since the witness first testified, and neither is now the case.

"And the accused makes this objection not to prevent testimony being rendered by Lt. Cook, for he expects to call him himself, but because the Judge Advocate has erroneously, and since the commencement of this case, made a distinction between certain of the charges and specifications upon which the accused is arraigned, and the Judge Advocate has made this distinction to the prejudice of the accused as will probably be hereafter shown. And if the Court so admit a distinction it will be likewise to the prejudice of the accused, and therefore the accused asks that Lt. Cook be withdrawn as a witness for the prosecution, unless the Judge Advocate can make affidavit that he has been introduced to prove facts made known since he was previously examined, or to rebut new evidence introduced by the defense."

The Judge Advocate said: "Although not fully prepared to answer the objection, this was the design from the commencement of this trial. It was supposed that I would have to take witnesses as I could get them and not pursue the case as I thought it should be pursued; to take the charges and specifications and prove them as I went along, but thus far the witnesses have hereto enabled me to pursue that course. At the suggestion of the Court, or at least as I understood from a portion of the Court, it would be better to pursue the first set of charges first and the second set after, so as to have a full understanding of the case continuously and not take up the specifications of one charge and the specifications of another charge. For that reason I examined all the witnesses on the first charges and Lt. Cook is now recalled to be examined on the additional charges. It has been the custom, as a general thing, to call a witness a second time to prove other charges."

The Court was then cleared for deliberation and upon reopening the doors it was announced that the objection of the accused was not sustained.

The accused then asked that in the case of Lt. Cook, a witness for the prosecution one recalled, and about to be re-examined, that the record read: "Lt. Cook, a witness for the prosecution, being recalled and re-examined for the prosecution testified as follows":

The Judge Advocate said he could not accede that request. The witness is *recalled* and *examined* on new matter.

The accused replied: "The Court cannot originate evidence. If it cannot, then evidence of a witness who has once been introduced and whose examination has once been proceeded with, must, if he has been again introduced, by a re-examination. And the accused concedes that in the case of Lt. Cook the Court may recall the witness and ask any question that may tend to elucidate his previous testimony. But if anything further be introduced it is a re-examination."

The Judge Advocate objected to the word re-examination in the record, as it would seem to imply that it was re-examination on the same subject on which he gave testimony before: "He is now to give testimony on entirely new and separate matter and for that reason I don't think the record should read re-examination. Recalled and examined is sufficient."

The accused replied: "The question is, has the witness once before been examined. If yes, he is about to be again examined. If yes, is not the second examination a re-examination. Since the preface *re* in this case means *again*. And finally, if yes, why should the Court not put upon record what is a fact?"

The Judge Advocate said: "There is nothing in the authorities against this mode of proceeding. The books show when a re-examination takes place it is in regard to matter the witness has testified to before. As a general thing a witness is put upon the stand and examined, then cross-examined, and then re-examined if the Judge Advocate wishes to elucidate anything. That is the only place where a witness is properly re-examined."

The Court was then cleared for deliberation and upon reopening it was announced that the Court had decided not to accede to the request of the accused.

The witness, Lt. W. W. Cook was then examined and testified as follows:

Questions by The Judge Advocate

Q. Were you with a portion of the 7th Cav. on its march from the Platte River in July last?

A. I was.

Q. How many companies of the Regiment were on the march?

A. Six.

Q. On that march were there any deserters?

A. Yes sir; a great many.

Q. What orders were given by whom, in regard to any deserters on that march, written or verbal?

A. I don't know of any orders except on the seventh of July when some men left the command in daylight. That was the only order I heard.

Q. State what orders were given on that occasion.

A. To pursue and shoot them down.

Q. By whom was that order given?

A. Gen. Custer.

Q. Was Gen. Custer in command of the troops?

A. Yes sir.

Q. Did you receive that order from Gen. Custer?

A. Yes sir.

Q. Were any deserters at that time pursued and shot down?

A. There were.

Q. Do you know the names of any who were pursued and shot down?

A. Only from hearsay. I don't know of any of them—I have heard their names mentioned.

Q. Did you know their names at the time?

A. No sir.

Q. How many were shot down?

A. Three men.

Q. Do you know what company they belonged to?

A. Two from "K" troop and one from "D".

Q. Were they wounded?

A. Yes sir.

Q. Were they shot down and wounded in consequence of the order given by Gen. Custer?

A. Not altogether I think.

Q. State what other reasons there were.

A. The men were ordered to halt and surrender and one of them made a motion as if to present his carbine, which I think brought on the shooting.

Q. Who did he make a motion towards?

A. Maj. Elliott of the 7th Cav.

Q. Was he one of the persons sent in pursuit of the deserters?

A. Yes sir.

Q. When those deserters were overtaken did they have arms with them?

A. They had.

Q. All of them?

A. Yes sir; I believe they had—they had three carbines.

Q. In their hands?

A. Yes sir.

Q. Were those three deserters who were wounded mounted or dismounted?

A. Dismounted.

Q. Did more than one offer any resistance by making motions or otherwise?

A. I did not see them.

Q. What became of those three men after they were shot and wounded?

A. Placed in a wagon by Gen. Custer's order and brought in to the command.

Q. How far was it to the command?

A. Two or three miles.

Q. Was the command in camp at the time?

A. The command was saddled and standing by their horses and about to move.

Q. What was done with the deserters when they were brought to the command?

A. As the wagon came up the command moved out to the first

watering place where we camped and the deserters were brought along.

Q. How were they brought?

A. In a wagon.

Q. The wagon they were first put in or another?

A. The same one I think; I don't know.

Q. What kind of a wagon was it?

A. An army wagon.

Q. Do you know whether those three wounded men received medical attention?

A. I do not.

Q. At what particular point did the shooting of the deserters occur?

A. I think it was on the second day from the Platte; it might have been 30 miles south of the Platte; I am not sure about that.

Q. How far was it from Fort Sedgwick?

A. From 60 to 90 miles I should say; that is to go by any practical route.

Q. Did those men who were shot and wounded, to your knowledge, have any previous trial?

A. Not to my knowledge.

Q. Had they any trial, to your knowledge?

A. No sir.

Q. Could the supposed deserters be seen from the camp where the command was?

A. When they were first discovered they could be seen. I lost sight of them before we got half way, going rapidly over the hill.

Q. Do you know whether they intended to desert or not, of your own knowledge?

A. It is my impression they did. In fact they owned they were deserting while we were there.

Q. Did the accused give any orders to others to pursue and shoot those supposed deserters?

A. Yes sir.

Q. To whom?

A. To myself, Maj. Elliott and the officer of the day, I believe.

Q. Who was the officer of the day?

A. Lieut. Jackson, I think.

Q. Was the Regiment at that time on the march?

A. Yes sir.

Q. To what point?

A. To the first water.

Q. Where after that?

A. We were enroute to Ft. Wallace.

Q. Did you see any of those deserters make any resistance yourself?

A. I saw them attempt to make resistance.

Q. In what manner?

A. By raising a carbine as if to present it.

Q. How soon after those deserters were shot did the Regiment go into camp?

A. We marched six or seven miles—not over seven miles.

Q. Did you go into camp then?

A. Yes sir, we went into camp about two hours after that.

Q. Do you know how badly the men were wounded?

A. Not of my own knowledge. I was told by the Doctor it was not of any importance. He seemed to make very light of it. I made no examination at all.

Questions By The Accused

Q. How did you happen to receive order to pursue those deserters?

A. I was standing at the Headquarters of the Regiment and some of the officers reported to Gen. Custer that they were deserters. He called first for the officer of the day and ordered him to pursue them. Then he ordered the officers standing there, Maj. Elliott, Lt. Custer and myself, as the officer of the day was some time in getting out.

Q. Did you or not ask that you be allowed to go after the deserters?

A. I remember to have asked if I should go, or words to that effect.

Q. Were any of the deserters you overtook brought in unharmed?

A. One was pushed over by a horse, but he was not harmed at all.

Q. What was the name of the man who presented or attempted to present his carbine?

A. His name was Johnson, as I afterward learned.

Q. Were there any other wagons but the one containing the deserters immediately with the command when you reached it?

A. No sir; the train had gone on.

Questions By The Court

Q. Were there any ambulances at the camp when the wounded deserters were brought in?

A. I think not. I am unable to say positively. It is my impression there were not.

At 4:00 P.M. the Court adjourned until 10:00 A.M., Sept. 26, 1867.

XI. COURT-MARTIAL
CONTINUED

The post city of "11-Worth" was a jury in itself. Courts-martial were common enough and occurred often enough to provide the main topic of conversation. When a ranking officer was involved, he was fair game for all. Soldier and civilian alike became self-appointed jurymen, judging the case in every bar and home in town. This sport, however, was not restricted to 11-Worth City (so designated by its inhabitants), but was practiced by the members of the garrison, too. Although the testimony was not to be discussed by members of the Court, somehow word got around.

Sides were taken and wagers made. Would they throw the book at Custer? Was he the one selected by the brass to be the goat? Who was being protected and why? Could Custer beat the rap? Was General Grant bucking for president and aiding his political ambitions by placing General Custer on the sacrificial altar so that the blame for the disastrous summer Indian campaign would be taken off the army's ranking general officer? Many thought so. None could be certain.

Custer kept up his correspondence with his friends for many of them were showing their true colors. To Mr. Walker he wrote:

... Slow progress is being made. The Prosecution have examined about half their witnesses, including the most important. I would not hesitate to go to Court on the evidence adduced thus far.

I have obtained evidence that, last spring, when desertions were

164

so numerous, General Hancock telegraphed General Sheridan to shoot deserters down. Genl. Sheridan has been summoned to testify that he ordered me to shoot without trial for the same offence. He himself called my attention to this, and urged me to introduce it in evidence.

He assured me that in any and all circumstances I could count him as my friend, and that, further, the authorities in Washington regard my trial as an attempt by Hancock to cover up the failures of the Indian expedition.

West is drinking himself to death, has delirium tremens, to such an extent the Prosecution will not put him on the witness stand. Parsons is conducting my defense admirably.[1]

On Sept. 26, the Court met at 10:00 A.M. with all members present. After reading and approving yesterday's proceedings, Dr. I. T. Coates, Acting Assistant Surgeon, was called and sworn in as a witness for the prosecution.

Questions By The Judge Advocate

Q. In what command were you in July last?

A. With the 7th Cav.

Q. Were you with the portion of the 7th Cav. on the march between the Platte River and Ft. Wallace in July last?

A. Yes sir.

Q. Who was in command?

A. Gen. Custer.

Q. On that march do you know of any deserters from the command?

A. I know there were deserters from the command. I also know of some men who deserted.

Q. Do you know of any action taken or orders given in regard to deserters on that march?

A. I know of no orders given in relation to deserters.

Q. Do you know of any action taken in regard to deserters?

A. Yes sir.

Q. State what action was taken in regard to deserters at any time during that march?

A. As far as my memory serves me, on the seventh of July a

---

[1] Merington, *The Custer Story*, 211–12.

number of men deserted while the Regiment had halted, and some of those deserters were shot—three of them to my certain knowledge.

Q. Do you know the names of any men who were shot?

A. Johnson was the last name of one of them. Alburger was the name of another, and the other man's name I don't recollect. I believe they called him Barney, and he was a Bugler. I don't recollect his last name though I recollect the man very well.

Q. On what date did this occur?

A. I think on the seventh of July.

Q. Did you see any of those men deserting or attempting to desert?

A. No sir.

Q. When did you first see them?

A. When they had been brought in after they had been shot.

Q. Was the command in camp at the time they were brought in?

A. Yes sir.

Q. In what manner were they brought in?

A. In a wagon.

Q. What kind of a wagon?

A. An ordinary Quarter Master's Wagon—a six mule wagon.

Q. When you first saw them did you give them any medical attention?

A. No sir.

Q. For what reason did you not?

A. When the wagon first came in, I, with a number of others started to it. The men generally of the command started the wagon. As I was going to it I believe Gen. Custer said to me not to go near those men at that time. I stood, of course. I obeyed his orders.

Q. How long were those men in the wagon before you gave them medical attention?

A. I suppose two hours.

Q. What kind of medical attention did you give them?

A. I administered opiates and made them comfortable, just as I should have done on the field of battle.

Q. Did you do anything else besides give them opiates?

A. No sir; in my judgment there was nothing else required. There was a good deal of clothing in the wagon and I am not sure whether any grain sacks or not, but I used everything in the wagon to make them a soft place so they should be comfortable.

Q. How badly were those men wounded—give the particulars about each man?

A. Barney Tolliver, the Bugler, was wounded by one shot, the ball entered his right arm and passed immediately through making a flesh wound, and entered the arm again and passed up making a flesh wound. Alburger had one shot through the shoulder, just above the shoulder blade, making a flesh wound; and another shot in the side between the fifth and sixth or sixth and seventh ribs, running along the ribs for about three inches then coming out again, making a flesh wound, and he was also struck on the middle finger of the left hand, making a flesh wound. He was wounded in three places. Johnson was wounded in two places. He also had a shot in the side, I think the left side, making a flesh wound. He was also wounded in the head, the ball entering the left temple and coming out below, under the jaw, and passing down into his lungs, the same ball entering again at the upper part of the chest.

Q. In your judgement was it the same ball?

A. Yes sir; I am positive of that, the distance from where the ball came out and where it entered again, being very slight and was in a direct line.

Q. Did the appearance of the wound show that the ball entered the left temple?

A. Yes sir, and came out below; there could be no mistake about that.

Q. In what position should you judge he was when he received the wound?

A. The shooter must have been some distance above him, I should judge. The shooter must have been mounted, from the ball having taken that direction.

Q. Did you judge he was standing up, or on the ground?

A. He might have been standing up. From the direction of the ball there is no reason that he must have been on the ground.

Q. How near should you judge him to have been to the person who fired the shot?

A. From the power of the ball he must have been within 25 yards at least, and perhaps much nearer.

Q. Was it a pistol shot or otherwise?

A. It was a pistol shot.

Q. How soon after those men were wounded were their wounds dressed, if dressed at all?

A. I think it was just two days after, as far as I can recollect.

Q. During that time did those men follow the column?

A. Yes sir.

Q. In what manner?

A. In the wagon.

Q. Were there any ambulances with the column?

A. Yes sir.

Q. How many?

A. Two I think.

Q. Why were not the wounded men put in an ambulance as soon as possible.

A. At the time these accidents occurred to the men the ambulances were not there, but in my judgement the men did better in the wagon, going along slow. The ambulances were very poor, the springs were very weak and all the men who had ridden in them complained of their being very uncomfortable, and I found them so myself, having to ride in them.

Q. Did you regard the wagon as easier than the ambulance?

A. I did sir.

Q. How many medical officers were there in the command besides yourself?

A. None but myself.

Q. In your opinion would it not have been better to have dressed their wounds than to have delayed it?

A. It was impossible to dress them on account of not having fresh water. We had no water but in the buffalo wallows and it would have been very hurtful to have dressed the wounds in muddy water. That is the reason I did not dress them. I waited two days until we came to a stream of clear water— the first we came to.

Q. Has it not been usual to dress gunshot wounds as soon as possible with whatever kind of water can be obtained?

A. Sometimes gunshot wounds don't need dressing. Sometimes they do better by allowing the blood to congeal on them. That was the case in these cases. The hemorrhage was arrested by the gluing of their clothes to the wounds and there was no more hemorrhage after the first hour of so. The important thing in gunshot wounds is to arrest the hemorrhage, and that was done in these cases.

Q. How far were the wounded men brought?

A. They were brought to Ft. Wallace.

Q. What was the result of the wound received by Johnson?

A. That wound was fatal—it resulted in his death.

Q. Did he die from the effects of the wound received on the seventh of July?

A. Yes sir.

Q. When and where did he die?

A. At Ft. Wallace. I am not positive when, but I think it was on the 17th of July. I think it was four or five days after we arrived at Ft. Wallace.

Q. You stated that you administered opiates and made the men comfortable as possible; how many times did you administer opiates before their wounds were dressed?

A. That afternoon I think I mentioned I gave them opiates about two hours after they were wounded, and that night I went to see them again and administered opiates and it was my custom after that each morning before they started to give them an opiate, and to see them during the day as the column moved along, and always at night I did that.

Q. Did you examine their wounds at any time between the time they were wounded until their wounds were dressed?

A. Yes sir, I examined their wounds that same afternoon.

Q. How soon after they were wounded?

A. In about two hours I think. I got into the wagon and rode with them some distance. I used to direct the wagon to the right or left of the column to find smooth ground.

Q. Did the wagon keep up?

A. Not immediately. Every night it would come in. Often it would be several miles behind. I ordered the driver to go according to the feelings of the men, and it would be some distance behind, but it would come in every evening.

Q. Did that occur till the command got to Fort Wallace?

A. Yes sir.

Q. Do you know how far it is from the point where those men were wounded to Fort Wallace?

A. I think from Riverside Station to Fort Wallace is about 200 miles, and that was a few hours march after we left the Platte. I should say it was 180 or 190 miles those men were carried after they were wounded.

Questions By The Accused

Q. Did you understand or construe any remark or order given by the accused from the time you first saw the deserters till after they passed out of your charge to be an order not to render them medical attention?

A. No sir.

Q. When you reached camp on the night of the seventh and gave the deserters medical attention, who directed you or instructed you to give them that attendance?

A. Gen. Custer.

Q. In what words or language did he give the order?

A. As far as I recollect now he said to me, "Doctor, my sympathies are not with those men who are wounded, but I want you to give them all necessary attention."

Q. Did he or not direct you to report to him after you made an examination that night?

A. He did.

Q. What was the condition of those men as reported to him?

A. I gave an exact history to him of their wounds and how they were getting along.

Q. Did you have full control of those deserters, and were you allowed authority to attend to them, the same as other patients?

A. Yes sir.

Q. Did or did not the accused frequently inquire after their condition?

A. Yes sir; always at night he inquired and sometimes during the march.

Q. Before dressing the wounds of those deserters did you or did you not state to the accused that the blood drying on the wounds would be the best that could be done for them?

A. I did. I spoke to several officers and tried to explain to them that that was the best I could do for them.

Q. Was or was not the wagon conveying those deserters under your charge during that march?

A. It was entirely. I commanded the wagon.

Q. Did you or did you not ask the accused to keep that wagon for those men, to save the trouble of unloading them, when they would be disturbed?

A. I did.

Q. Did or did not the accused give you permission to return the wagon?

A. He did.

Q. How did the injuries of Johnson compare with the injuries of the other men?

A. His injuries were more severe; the others received simply flesh wounds.

Q. Did you consider any of those men to be mortally wounded at that time?

A. I did not at that time.

Q. Did you or did you not so report to the accused?

A. I did, and I thought they were not and I would explain that Johnson, who afterwards died, was the most cheerful at that time.

Q. State whether in your opinion the man Johnson did or did not die in consequence of any order given by the accused in regard to medical attention?

A. He did not.

Q. In the case of a man wounded more than once, could not one shot have produced all wounds, or could two shots have produced three wounds; that is, was each one of the wounds produced by different shots?

A. In those cases I think each wound, except in the case of Johnson was produced by different shots; that was my opinion at the time.

Q. In regard to the use of the ambulance, did you have occasion to put other patients in a wagon in preference to the ambulance?

A. I have since that.

Questions By The Court

Q. If the person who shot Johnson in the head had been 20 or 25 yards from him at the time, would or would not the shot have went directly through his head without passing down into his lungs?

A. A shot at that distance might have taken the exact course it did. A very slight thing will turn the course of a ball. If you will allow me, it is recorded in medical history of a ball having struck the breast bone, and to have been found lodged in the testicles. I know of one instance of a ball striking what is known as "Adams Apple" and passing clear around the neck and was taken out at the very same place.

Q. Did the wagon in which the wounded men were brought to Ft. Wallace, arrive at that post at the same time with the command?

A. It arrived there at the time or immediately after. We arrived there in the evening and the wagon also arrived there that evening; it was perhaps a mile or two behind the column.

Question by a Member

What did you understand the accused to mean when he directed you not to go near the wagon containing the wounded men when they first came in, and why did you not attend to them immediately when they were brought in?

The question was objected to by the Judge Advocate, as he was apprehensive the answer might not be of any benefit to the prosecution.

The Court was cleared for deliberation and upon reopening the doors, it was announced that the Judge Advocate withdrew his objection.

A. I had at that time an idea the objection was made for effect. There had been a great many deserters—some 30 or 40 the night previous, and the men were crowding around the wagon and I had an idea the General wished to make an impression on the men that they would be dealt with in the severest and harshest manner. I stood back as soon as he gave the order. Soon after the column started and the men were in their proper places, as I said before, I attended to the men.

Q. When you attended to the wounded men two hours after they were brought in, as you have stated, did you do so by order of Gen. Custer or in disobedience of his orders?

A. Soon after I had started to those men, I think just before Gen. Custer moved out with the column, or it might have been immediately after, he told me not to go near them; he said "You can attend to them after a while" or, "It will be time enough to attend to them after a while", or some such expression as that. He said that to me.

Q. Why did you not attend to those wounded men until after the expiration of two hours after they were brought in?

A. It was two hours after they were wounded. At least one hour expired after they were wounded till they got into camp, and about half an hour was expended in getting under way. The order given not to go near those men was about an hour after they were wounded, and it was perhaps half an hour or an hour before I got to see them after that. I waited until after the column moved out.

Q. Did you finally attend to the wounded men of your own accord, or was it by order of the accused?

A. By order of the accused. I received that expression as an order when he said it will be time enough to attend to them after a while, or you can attend to those men after a while, or some such expression. That was the only order I had at that time.

After the witness had heard his testimony read over and retired, the Judge Advocate announced that further and material witnesses for the prosecution were not in attendance although summoned in sufficient time; and asked the Court to adjourn.

At 12:00 P.M. the Court adjourned until 10:00 A.M. Sept. 27, 1867.

At 10:00 A.M., Sept. 27, 1867, the Court convened with all present. The proceedings of yesterday were read and approved.

The Judge Advocate announced that the expected witnesses had not yet arrived, although a telegram was sent day before yesterday to Fort Hays, where it is supposed they were, and it is presumed they are on their way now.

The Judge Advocate then introduced the original official report of the accused, of his march from the Platte to Ft. Wallace, and from Ft. Wallace to Ft. Riley, which was admitted by the accused to be his.

FORT RILEY, KANSAS
Aug. 6, 1867.

Lieut. T. B. Weir
A.A.A.G. Dist. Upper Arkansas

In obedience to the instructions of the Maj. Genl. Comdg. the Dist. I have the honor to submit the following report of my march from the Platte River to Fort Wallace, and from Fort Wallace to Fort Harker. My command left Riverside Station forty-five miles west of Fort Sedgwick on the Platte River at five A.M., this seventh of July and reached Fort Wallace at eight P.M. on the 13th of the same month, having marched (182) one hundred and eighty-two miles in seven days. I am unable to give accurately the march of each day or the location of each camp from the fact that the data for this information is in the possession of Lieut. Jackson, 7th Cav., who I detailed upon this duty and who is now engaged in carefully preparing the accurate map of my entire route. Lt. Jackson was furnished from private sources with an odometer and compass and has kept with great care and accuracy the bearing and distance of each day's march together with the distance between all streams we passed over, and his map when completed will be a very valuable acquisition as it will contain much information regarding a section of country about which little or nothing reliable is known.

No Indians were encountered between the Platte and Smoky Hill Rivers, nor were any trails, except old ones, discovered. The only incident of importance occuring on the march was the finding near Beaver Creek of the bodies of Lieut. Kidder and party of the 2nd Cavalry, but as a special report has been made regarding this lamentable affair it is but necessary to merely refer to it here.

While in the vicinity of the Platte River thirty-five (35) of my men deserted in twenty-four hours. I could not but feel apprehension for the safety of my command as I had before me a long march through a hostile country. When breaking camp about three P.M. on the seventh some thirty miles from the Platte, I caused "Boots and Saddles" to be sounded, when thirteen (13) of my men deliberately shouldered their arms and started for the Platte. This too in open day and in presence of the entire command. As I intended camping out about ten miles from where I then was and not knowing but the remainder of my command or at least a considerable portion of it would leave during the night strictly rendering it impracticable and unsafe for me to make the proposed march with such diminished numbers. I felt that decision and summary measures must be adopted to save what command I still retained. The horses of a few of the officers only were saddled in addition to the guard and picket. I directed Major Elliott, Lieuts. Custer, Cooke, and Jackson with a few of the guard to pursue the deserters who were still visible although more than a mile distant, and to bring the dead bodies of as many as could be taken back to camp. Seven of the deserters being mounted on our best horses and having over two miles start made their escape, six were overtaken, one a dangerous character presented his carbine to Major Elliott, but before he could fire, was brought down by a shot from another of Major Elliott's party. Two others were brought down by pistol shots, the remaining then, by throwing themselves upon the ground and feigning death, escaped being shot. The six were brought back to camp, and from there to Wallace. The wounds received by those referred to above, did not prove serious I regret to say, but the effect upon the command was all that could be desired. Not a single desertion took place from that time so long as I remained with command.

The march from the Platte to Fort Wallace was a forced one, from the fact that although my train contained rations for my command up to the 20th of the month yet when the stores came to be issued they were discovered to be in such a damaged condition that it would be with difficulty they could be made to last until we should reach Fort Wallace. And I take this opportunity to express the belief, a belief in which I am supported by facts as well as by the opinions of the officers associated under me, that the gross neglect and mismanagement exhibited in the Commissary Department through this District has subjected both officers and men to privations for which there was no occasion and which were never contemplated or intended by the Government when my command left Fort Hays for the Platte.

The officers were only able to obtain hard bread and bacon, coffee and sugar for their private messes although it had been known weeks, if not months, before that a large command was expected to arrive at Fort Hays; in the same manner it was known that an expedition was contemplated to the Platte. On my return march to Fort Wallace all hard bread not damaged was required to subsist the enlisted men, while the officers were actually compelled to pick up and collect from that portion of the hard bread which had been condemned and abandoned, a sufficient amount to subsist themselves to Fort Wallace. That this bread was damaged will not appear remarkable when it is known that some of the boxes were marked 1860.

That desertions will occur under the most stringent prohibitary laws I have not a doubt. I am equally well satisfied that to the mismanagement of the Commissary Department is attributable no little of the desertion which has taken place. My march from Fort Wallace to Fort Harker was made without incident except the killing of two men about five miles beyond Downer's Station. A sergeant and six men had been sent back to bring up a man who had halted at the last ranch; when returning, this party was attacked by between forty and

Julius Meyer, interpreter, with Spotted Tail, Iron Bull, and Pawnee Killer, right, who consistently gave Custer a bad time. Photographed (*ca.* 1870) by F. K. Currier.

Custer's scouts, left to right: Will "Medicine Bill" Comstock, chief of scouts; Ed Guerrier, a half-blood Cheyenne; Thomas Adkins, a courier; "California Joe" Moses Embree Milner, scout and Indian fighter (*ca.* 1867–68).

fifty Indians, and two of them killed. Had they offered any defense this would not have occurred, instead however they put spurs to their horses and endeavored to escape by flight.

Respectfully Submitted
/s/ G. A. Custer
Bvt. Maj. Genl.

Court then adjourned until 10:00 A.M. of the following day.

At 10:00 A.M., Sept. 28, 1867, the entire Court met and read and approved the previous day's proceedings.

The Judge Advocate announced that the expected witnesses for the prosecution had not yet arrived, that he telegraphed yesterday to the commanding officers at Fort Hays to find out if the witnesses were there, but the telegraph line is not finished to Fort Hays. The operator sent the telegram as far as the line extends, with directions to have it forwarded to Fort Hays as soon as possible. There has been no answer received to the telegram.

Bvt. Maj. Gen. Grierson stated that from the fact that there were no witnesses present, and that a short adjournment would not probably cause any delay, and on account of sickness in his family, and the interest he took in the organization of his regiment, which he could attend to if a short adjournment took place, he moved the Court adjourn until Wednesday morning next, which motion prevailed.

The Court adjourned until 10:00 A.M. Wednesday, Oct. 2, 1867.

On Wednesday the Court was advised that Custer was unable to attend the "sittings" of the Court as he was suffering from an extremely painful boil on his right thigh, Surgeon David L. Magruder attesting to this in a communication, and declaring that he would be unable to attend for two days.

At the meeting of the Court on Friday, October fourth the Judge Advocate announced that the accused was still too ill to attend the sittings of the Court. That he had visited the accused, and it was expected that his attending physician would furnish a certificate to that effect, but he was not at present to be found in the garrison, but he would furnish such a certificate as soon as found, to be appended in future to the proceedings of the Court.

The Court met the following day with everyone present.

The proceedings of the last three days were read and approved, after which the Judge Advocate then read the certificate of Surgeon Magruder, spoken of in Friday's proceedings.

Major Joel H. Elliott, 7th Cavalry, a witness on the part of the prosecution being duly sworn, testified as follows:

Questions By The Judge Advocate

Q. Were you with your Regiment or a portion thereof on the march from the Platte River to Ft. Wallace in July last?

A. I was.

Q. On that march were there any deserters?

A. There were.

Q. Do you know of any orders having been given in regard to any deserters on that march?

A. I do.

Q. State what orders were given to you, if any, and by whom.

A. There were some men deserted from the 7th Cav. at the place where we had halted, and there were orders given by the commanding officer, Gen. Custer, to go out and bring them in, or arrest them or stop them—I don't recollect the first order. Just as I started the General said to me, "I want you to shoot them", or words to that effect. I was not ordered to go out. I asked Gen. Custer to allow me to go out after those deserters, and I think it was just as I was in the act of mounting horse that I received the order to shoot them.

Q. Did you go after them?

A. I did.

Q. State what occurred at that time, when you went after the deserters.

A. I went a little in advance of the other officers, and a portion of the guard under the officer of the day. We overtook them and three of the deserters were shot and wounded, and the others were sent back without being hurt.

Q. In the pursuit of those deserters state whether any orders were given them or not?

A. When we got within 20 yards of them I ordered them to halt and I think two halted and two did not—there were four in all—and I called to one of them separately the second time, and he halted. I then ordered them to lay down their arms—three men were armed and one was not—two of them obliged, and the other, Johnson of "K" Co., raised his carbine as if to shoot me; that was the appearance his action had. I was riding at a gallop and rode on to him, and whether he threw down his arms before my horse struck him, or just at that time, I could not tell; it was all done so quickly I don't know. I don't know that he intended to shoot me, but his action indicated that, and that was my idea at the time.

Q. How soon after you rode down that deserter was he shot?

A. I can't say exactly.

Q. Was it after?

A. I presume it was after—immediately after—it was all done so quickly, the whole affair not occupying a minute's time, I can't tell which event occurred first.

Q. At the time he was fired on did he have arms in his hands?

A. I think not.

Q. Had the other three deserters surrendered at the time they were fired at?

A. They had; they surrendered at the first order.

Q. Had they thrown their arms down?

A. They halted at the first order to halt, and two threw their arms down at the first order to throw them down.

Q. Who was the man not armed?

A. He was a Bugler of "K" Co.—I don't recollect his name.

Q. Had he any arms at all when you first saw him?

A. I saw none with him.

Q. What was done with those wounded men after they were wounded?

A. There was still another party farther ahead, mounted, and I rode on after them until I saw there was no chance to overtake them, and then I returned to where those men were wounded and sent Bugler Leonard to get a wagon to take those men in and instructed Lt. Jackson, who was officer of the day, to see that they were brought in. I will state that Bugler Leonard reported to me from Gen. Custer, stating that a wagon would be in readiness, and I immediately sent him back after the wagon.

Q. Do you know whether those men were taken in the wagon?

A. I saw them come in where we were halted, in the wagon.

Q. Where was it you halted?

A. At a creek about 15 miles south of Valley Station.

Q. How far was it from where those men were wounded to the place where the command was halted?

A. I think it was about three miles.

Q. Was there any water at the place where the command was halted?

A. There was no surface water. We obtained water sufficient to water the stock and get dinner, by digging in the sand.

Q. What kind of water did you obtain?

A. Passable water; about like all water in that country—strong alkali.

Q. Was it clear?

A. Passably so—not very clear.

Q. Was it fit to drink?

A. It was drank by some of the men, and was used in cooking dinner. I drank coffee made of it.

Q. How much digging did it require to obtain water at that point?

A. I don't remember particularly about that point. We had to dig for water on several occasions.

Q. At what time did the command start on the march from that point towards Ft. Wallace?

A. I don't recollect the hour of the day. We started very soon after the deserters were brought back. It was about three o'clock when we started after them, and I think it was about an hour after that we started on the march.

Q. How far was it from that point to where the command halted that night?

A. It was about ten miles, according to my recollection.

Q. Was there any water in that march of ten miles?

A. None between the creeks that I saw or heard of.

Q. When did this occur?

A. On the seventh of July last.

Q. When the command arrived in camp that night do you know whether the surgeon of the command gave those men any medical attendance or not?

A. I did not see him give them any medical attendance.

Q. Have you any reason to believe he did or did not?

A. I have no reason to believe, except hearsay, anything about it. I don't know anything about it, except what I have been told.

Q. Did you hear the surgeon speak about medical attendance at the time the command was in camp that night?

The accused objected to the question as being hearsay evidence and that not in relationship to the words of the accused, and therefore inadmissable. This rule is so well understood that it is not thought necessary to quote the authorities.

The Judge Advocate stated: "The object in asking the question is to get at the *facts*; to get from the witness the words of the Surgeon and to show he had been ordered not to furnish medical attendance. I don't regard it as hearsay evidence because it is from the Surgeon himself, and is directly bearing on the case."

The accused replied: "In reply to the argument of the Judge Advocate, the accused states that the language used by the Surgeon cannot be employed to give proof of incidents alleged in these specifications for it is known and will still farther be shown, that for purposes of discipline the Surgeon was instructed to conceal from the command the fact that medical attendance was furnished these deserters."

The Judge Advocate replied: "That is all in *futuro*. The only point is whether it would be regarded as hearsay evidence or not. If any remark made to the witness to show that medical attendance was refused these deserters, it is proper to admit it, for the purpose of getting the whole question before the Court."

The accused replied: "The remarks of the Surgeon could only be testified to when the Surgeon was being tried."

The Judge Advocate replied: "That is sometimes the case and sometimes not. In this case it is charged that the accused directed the surgeon not to furnish medical attendance for a certain time, and I want to show by the Surgeon's own language that that is true."

The Court was cleared for deliberation and upon reopening the doors it was announced that the objection of the accused was sustained.

Q. Did you have any conversation with the Surgeon of the command regarding medical attendance for those wounded men at the time the command halted on the night of the seventh of July? If so state what the conversation was.

The accused objected to the question on the same grounds as before and for the same reasons.

The Court was cleared for deliberation and upon reopening the doors it was announced that the objection of the accused was overruled.

A. I had some conversation with the Surgeon after the command was in camp that night. I asked him why he did not dress their wounds; he said he had been ordered not to. We had some further conversation in regard to the nature of their wounds, which I think was all the conversation we had on the subject.

Q. At what time of the day or evening did you have the conversation referred to?

A. About an hour after we went into camp—it was some time after dark. It was dusk when we were going into camp, and it must have been about nine o'clock, I think.

Q. When did the command arrive at Fort Wallace on the march from the Platte?

A. Late in the evening of the 13th of July—an hour or two after dark.

Q. What was the condition of the horses, as far as you know, when the command arrived at Fort Wallace?

A. They were very much exhausted and worn.

Q. Were they fit for service?

A. Not for hard service.

Q. Were they in condition for a march of a hundred or two miles?

A. No sir; they were not.

Q. Had the horses of the command been rested sufficiently to take a march of a hundred or two miles a day or two after that?

A. I think a day or two was not sufficient to put them in condition.

Q. How long did the whole command remain at Fort Wallace?

A. A portion of the command left on the afternoon of the 15th.

Q. For what purpose?

A. They left as an escort for Gen. Custer I believe, who was going east on the road.

Q. How many horses then left Fort Wallace?

A. There were in all 76 enlisted men, all mounted.

Q. Do you know how the men were detailed?

A. I heard the Adjutant give the order to three different company commanders to detail 12 of the best mounted men in their companies. What the order given to the Adjutant was, I don't know.

Q. Did he state for what purpose they were to be detailed?

A. That they were to accompany General Custer.

Q. How many of those men who were so detailed, returned to the command?

A. At the time I left the command 48 had returned.

Q. When Gen. Custer left, who commanded that portion of the Regiment that was left?

A. I commanded it.

Q. Did you have any report, official or otherwise, of the number of men who left with Gen. Custer on their return to Fort Wallace?

A. On their return to Ft. Wallace I required Capt. Hamilton to make a written report, and account for every man by name, which he did. I think it was three days after he returned when I got the report.

Q. Do you remember what the report was in regard to numbers?

A. Yes sir.

Q. State it?

A. There had 46 returned up to that time; two killed and wounded; two remained with Gen. Custer; 20 deserted; and six left back sick.

Q. Did that account for the whole command that left Fort Wallace with Gen. Custer in his way east?

A. It did I believe. I give those figures from memory. Of those six left back sick, two joined the Regiment before I came away, making 48 of the original 76 that had returned.

Q. Did any of those men return to the Regiment, then under your command before the main body returned?

A. There did.

Q. How many in what manner?

A. There were some 12 or 13 returned before Capt. Hamilton returned. They came back two or three at a time, with wagon trains. Some came with Capt. Cox of the 11th Cav.

Q. Did any or all of them have their horses?

A. Some of them did—two or three only—the remainder came back dismounted.

Questions By The Court

Q. Were you second in command with Gen. Custer's expedition?

A. Yes sir.

The witness having heard his testimony read over, then retired.

Lieut. Jackson, a witness on the part of the prosecution, being duly sworn, testified as follows:

Questions By The Judge Advocate

Q. State your name, rank and Regiment.

A. Henry Jackson, 2nd Lt., 7th U.S. Cav.

Q. Were you with the 7th Cav. on the march from the Platte River to Ft. Wallace?

A. I was.

Q. What time was it?

A. On the seventh of July we started from the Platte.
Q. On that march did any desertions occur from the command?
A. Yes sir.
Q. Were there any orders given in regard to deserters on that march?
A. Yes sir.
Q. State what orders were given to you?
A. I was officer of the day on the seventh of July and at the first halting place, on a dry sand creek, the order was given me to take my guard and follow those men and shoot them, and not bring one back alive.
Q. State what you did on receiving that order?
A. I went to the guard house, where the guard was stationed and there were only two or three men present, the rest having gone to their companies. I received further orders to take what men I had, and I started with three men. The deserters were within sight a mile or a mile and a half off. When I got to the ridge, about a mile from the halting place, I saw two men off to my left, and I rode toward them. They halted and laid down their arms and came towards me. I told the corporal to take them to camp, and I saw him do it. I then turned to the ridge to follow the other party, and when I arrived at the crest of the ridge, I saw three men lying on the ground and one running and being shot at.
Q. Did those three men lying on the ground have their arms?
A. No sir; there were no arms near them at all.
Q. Had they been shot at?
A. Two of them were wounded, and I supposed the other was at that time, but I afterwards found out he was not.
Q. Do you know what became of their arms?
A. I found them about 40 or 50 yards from the nearest one. They were nearest to the man Johnson. The arms were lying on the first ridge, and the men were down in a little hollow.
Q. Did you take those arms?
A. I took them and examined them all. One gun was loaded and two were not—there were only three carbines that I found.

Q. What became of those wounded men?

A. When the fourth man had fallen, Maj. Elliott and myself rode on to the next ridge after two or three mounted men which we saw a mile or two ahead of us. The Major said I was to wait there till he sent a wagon and I was to put the men in it and take them to the command, which I did. I waited about three-fourths of an hour, till the wagon came up, when I put the men in it and took them to the command.

Q. What kind of a wagon came for them?

A. A common army wagon.

Q. About what time of day were these men wounded?

A. I should say between two and three o'clock in the afternoon.

Q. On what day of the month?

A. The seventh of July.

Q. Was there anything in the wagon that took those wounded men to camp?

A. Nothing.

Q. Was there no bedding or other articles?

A. No sir, it was perfectly empty when I put them in.

Q. After the wounded men arrived at the command what was done with them?

A. I was ordered to take charge of them in the wagon and march them in the rear of the column.

Q. Were they taken out of the wagon?

A. No sir.

Q. Were they placed under guard under your direction?

A. They were placed under my charge as officer of the day.

Q. What time did the command start?

A. Within 10 or 15 minutes after I arrived with the men in the wagon.

Q. How far did the column march that afternoon after those men were wounded, before you went into camp?

A. About ten or ten and one-half miles from where we halted, and about 12 miles from the ridge.

Q. Were you with the wagon during that march of ten miles?

A. I was sometimes 100 or 150 yards ahead, but most of the time I was right at the wagon with the guard. The wagon stopped very often to shift the position of the men, as they appeared to be in a great deal of pain. I rode this way until within about half a mile of camp where I rode ahead to ask the General where I should put the guard.

Q. Was anything put in the wagon during that march of ten miles?

A. I believe some of the men gave them some overcoats to lie on. I did not see anything else put in.

Q. Did you see the surgeon of the command at any time during that march of ten miles with the wagon?

A. No sir, not at all.

Q. Were you sufficiently near the wagon at all times during the march to know?

A. I was within 150 yards, except within the last half mile. That was the farthest I was from the wagon. I would ride by the side of the wagon and my horse would walk faster than the wagon, and I would get ahead. I would then stop and wait for the wagon. That is the way I marched all the evening, and I never saw the surgeon during the march.

Q. Was there any water at the place where those men were brought into the command wounded?

A. There was water to be obtained by digging in the sand.

Q. What kind of water?

A. The same as when we camped that night; it was tolerable good water—they used it for cooking purposes.

Q. Was it used by the command at that point?

A. I was not with the companies and did not see it used.

Q. Did you use it yourself?

A. Yes sir.

Q. How much digging did it require to get water at that point?

A. From six to eight inches from the surface of the sand.

Q. Was it easily obtainable?

A. The sand was easily moved. I took the scabbard of my sabre and made a little hole and got it.

Q. How long was the command marching from the point where the wounded men were brought into camp that night?

A. About three and one-half hours I think.

Q. How was the water that night at camp?

A. There were one or two little standing places of water, but the water we used we dug for.

Q. During that march of ten and one-half miles did you or not see those wounded men in the wagon all the time?

A. I never looked into the wagon; I saw the guard in there fixing them.

Q. Did you see them after the command got into camp that night?

A. I put them in camp myself. I saw the man Johnson particularly; I looked at him.

Q. What was his appearance?

A. The blood was all over his face, the same as it was when I put him in the wagon.

Q. Did you have any conversation with the Surgeon of the command in regard to medical attendance for those men at the time the command was halted on the night of the seventh of July. If so, state what that conversation was?

The Accused objected to the question on the same grounds that he objected in the case of the previous witness.

The Court was cleared for deliberation and upon reopening the doors it was announced that the objection was over-ruled.

A. I did. I asked the Surgeon if he could not go up and wash the blood off Johnson's face—he was the man I particularly mentioned, and he told me he could not do it because he had orders not to go near them. That was the substance of the conversation.

Q. You stated that when you came up on the ridge, three men were lying on the ground and one was running; do you have the name of the one who was running?

A. Yes sir, his name was Alburger, of Co. "D", 7th Cav.

Q. In what direction was he running?

A. He would run 10 or 15 yards one way, and then would turn and run 10 or 15 yards the other way, on account of the officers pursuing him. When he got near one, he would turn and run away. It lasted about a minute.

Q. Did he have any arms in his hands when he was running?

A. No sir.

Q. How long were those men in your charge, as officer of the day?

A. From the time they were shot till the time we marched the following morning; I think five o'clock.

Questions By The Court

Q. Did those wounded men have medical attendance before you were relieved as officer of the day, so far as you know?

A. I believe they did, during that night, late sometime, but I could not be positive. I think the Doctor was there. Some 10 or 15 minutes after I first asked him to go, he came to my tent and said he was going over, and Capt. West and myself went over with him, and he felt of them to see where they were wounded. I did not see him give them anything and I don't know of my own knowledge that he did give them anything.

Question by a member

Did the Surgeon say by whom he was ordered to give medical attendance to those wounded men?

The accused objected to the question because its only purpose must be to ascertain whether the accused gave that order. If it be shown that he did give the order, then that will be employed as evidence to show that the accused was guilty of one of the allegations contained in these Specifications against him. Thus hearsay evidence, namely the testimony of Lt. Jackson that he heard Dr. Coates say that Gen. Custer, the accused, did deprive the alleged deserters of medical attendance, would be admitted. This, in the judgment of the accused, is violation of the rules of evidence.

The Court was cleared for deliberation, and upon reopening the doors it was announced that the objection of the accused was overruled.

A. He said "by the General."

Q. What were the names of the wounded men, and was Private

Charles Johnson of Co. "K", one of the three men you saw lying on the ground?

A. Their names were Private Tolliver of Co. "K", Alburger of Co. "D", Willis of Co. "K", and Charles Johnson of Co. "K". When I rode on the ridge, three men were lying on the ground, and one was running. Of those three two were wounded and one was not. Johnson was wounded and not able to move. The man running was Pvt. Alburger.

The witness having heard his testimony read over then retired.

The Judge Advocate stated that he had one witness which he proposed to introduce to close the prosecution, but he had concluded not to bring him on the stand, and would announce that the prosecution now rests, reserving the right, of course, to bring in such testimony as will be necessary to rebut any evidence introduced on the part of the defense.

The accused then stated that the first witness whom he proposed to introduce is Lieut. General Sherman; that if the evidence of Gen. Sherman be such as is anticipated, the accused will be relieved from the necessity of introducing any further witnesses upon that point; that Gen. Sherman is expected at the Post next Monday morning, and therefore the accused believes it will save time for this Court to adjourn until Monday morning next.

The accused, through his counsel, further stated: "The accused expected to proceed with the defense immediately upon the close of the prosecution. That expectation was founded upon the confident belief that the principle witness for the defense on the first set of charges, Lt. Gen. Sherman, would be present here today, as indicated by his telegraph to the Judge Advocate. By Monday it will be known whether he will be present or not. If he be not present a new line of defense will be necessitated for the accused. It could not have been anticipated by the accused last Saturday in the assurance he gave the Court. Therefore the accused asks an adjournment until Monday morning next, the seventh instant at 10 o'clock."

Upon this representation of the accused, the Court, on motion, adjourned until 10:30 A.M. Monday, Oct. 7, 1867.

The Court met on Monday at 10:30 A.M. having present the same members as at the last session. Lt. Thomas W. Custer was recalled to testify for the defense and testified as follows:

Questions By The Accused

Q. Were you a member of the mess of the accused during the months of June and July last?

A. I was.

Q. Were you present at a dinner where the accused and Lt. Gen. Sherman, Commanding the Military Division of the Missouri were also present, about the middle of June last?

A. I was.

Q. Did you hear any conversation between Gen. Sherman and the accused, regarding certain orders which Gen. Sherman was going to give the accused?

A. Yes sir.

Q. State what that conversation was.

A. Gen. Sherman told the accused he would receive orders from Gen. Augur, but not to confine himself to those orders, if his judgement led him elsewhere. That if he wished, he could go to Denver City, or he could go to hell if he wanted to. That he could go to any post he wanted to.

Q. Did you accompany the accused on the march from Ft. Wallace to Ft. Hays, as shown in the prosecution?

A. Yes sir.

Q. Did the accused at any time ride in an ambulance between Ft. Wallace and Big Creek?

A. No sir.

Questions By The Judge Advocate

Q. What did that conversation you speak of between Gen. Sherman and the accused, have reference to particularly?

A. It had reference to his going after the Indians.

Q. Was there any other conversation, or were there any other orders given the accused by Gen. Sherman at that time as to the pursuit of the Indians?

A. I don't remember of any being given.

Questions By The Court

Q. Where was the conversation referred to, between Gen. Sherman and the accused?

A. It was near Ft. McPherson.

The witness having heard his testimony read over, then retired.

Lt. William W. Cook was recalled to testify for the defense and testified as follows:

Questions By The Accused

Q. Were you a member of the mess of the accused during the months of June and July last?

A. Yes sir.

Q. Were you present at a dinner where the accused and Lt. Gen. Sherman were also present?

A. Yes sir.

Q. When and where was it?

A. On the Platte, on or about the 16th of June last.

Q. Near what post?

A. Ft. McPherson.

Q. Did you hear any conversation between the accused and Gen. Sherman in regard to orders which would be sent to the accused?

A. Yes sir.

Q. What were those orders to relate to?

A. In reference to his movements on the plains.

Q. What was that conversation between the accused and Gen. Sherman?

A. The general tone of the orders I heard given, was very unlimited.

Q. State as near as you can the exact language employed by Gen. Sherman to the accused?

A. He made the remark that he would receive orders from the Gen. Augur, but not to restrict himself to any orders. He made the remark that he could go to hell if he wanted to.

Q. Did he state that he could go to any special post?

A. He said he could go to any post he chose.

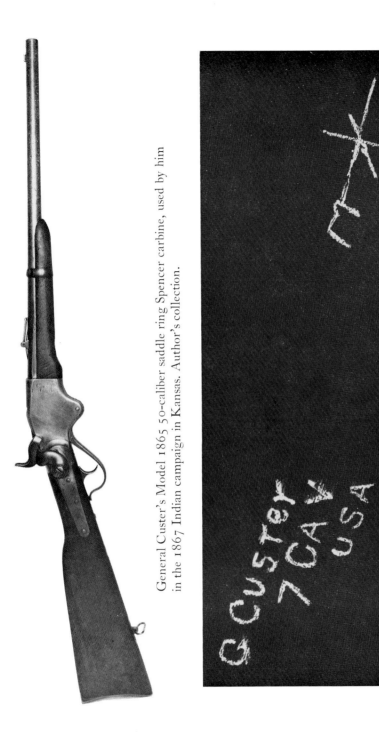

General Custer's Model 1865 50-caliber saddle ring Spencer carbine, used by him in the 1867 Indian campaign in Kansas. Author's collection.

Markings carved on the saddle-ring side of General Custer's carbine butt (markings emphasized with chalk).

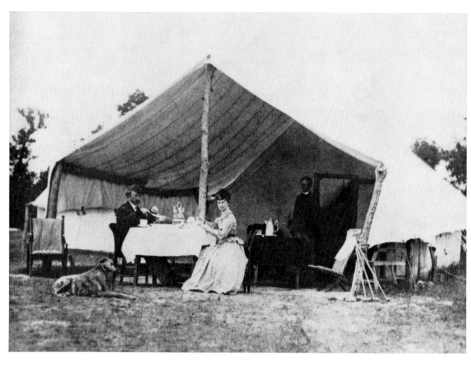

General and Mrs. Custer having breakfast at the Big Creek camp early in
1867, before he began his summer campaign.

Q. Did he name any particular post?
A. No sir, I think not.
Q. Did he say anything about the orders Gen. Augur had received restricting him?
A. Yes sir, he said Gen. Augur would not interfere with him to any extent.
Q. Did he intimate any extreme western post the accused could go to?
A. During the conversation he made the remark that he could go to Denver if he wished.

The witness having heard his testimony read over, then retired.
Capt. Louis M. Hamilton was recalled to testify for the defense and testified as follows:

Questions By The Accused

Q. During the time the accused was with the detachment which you commanded, accompanying him from Ft. Wallace to Big Creek, were there any desertions from the detachment?
A. No sir.
Q. When the accused left you at Big Creek how long did you remain?
A. I remained there about 24 hours.
Q. Where did you then proceed?
A. To Ft. Harker.
Q. How long did you remain there?
A. Two days.
Q. Where did you then proceed?
A. To Ft. Wallace.
Q. On what duty did you then return to Ft. Wallace?
A. Escorting a train.

Questions By The Judge Advocate

Q. Were any desertions on the trip referred to reported by you to anyone, from Ft. Wallace to Ft. Hays?
A. No sir.
Q. Were any desertions reported on the trip?

A. There were some after Gen. Custer left the command—none Between Ft. Wallace and Ft. Hays.

Q. Were any deserters reported by you as having deserted between Ft. Hays and Ft. Harker?

A. Not on the trip in. There were desertions at Fort Harker, but none going in.

Q. How many desertions were there at Ft. Harker?

A. I can't give the exact number.[2]

The witness having heard his testimony read over, then retired.

Mr. S. N. Harper, a witness for the defense, being duly sworn, testified as follows:

Questions By The Accused

Q. State your name and occupation?

A. S. N. Harper, Wagon Master in the Quartermaster's Department both here and at Ft. Harker.

Q. Were you wagon master during the month of July last?

A. Yes sir.

Q. Where were you during that month?

A. In July we were on the Platte.

Q. Whose command were accompanying?

A. Gen. Custer's.

Q. Where were you on the night of the sixth of July?

A. I was on my way to the Platte. I did not arrive there till the morning of the sixth.

Q. Where were you on the night between the sixth and seventh?

A. I was at the Platte.

Q. Did you sleep that night?

A. No sir.

Q. Why not?

A. I was bothered by some men trying to steal the stock and desert.

Q. Who were those men?

A. I only knew one of them; he was horse farrier of Co. "H" 7th Cav. named Starks.

[2] 40 Cong., 2 sess., *House Exec. Doc. 1*, 475: Desertions from October 1, 1866, to September 20, 1867, in the Seventh U.S. Cavalry were 512, with 111 Apprehensions.

Q. Did he make any remarks to you in regard to his object?

A. He said he was going to desert, and that I need not be surprised of it, for there were two-thirds of the command going to desert.

Q. Did he desert that night?

A. Yes sir.

Q. Did he attempt to take any animals?

A. He had hold of the rope of one of the mules when I went out and stopped him.

Q. State all that took place between you and any of the deserters?

A. I went out and there were four other men in among the train. One of my men had come in and told me those men were going to shoot him, and I went out and drove the men out from among the stock.

Q. Did you have any conversation with any others of them?

A. No sir.

Q. What did you tell him?

A. I told him to leave—I recollect that very distinctly.

Q. Did you make any remark about your responsibility?

A. Yes sir, I told him I did not want him to bother the stock, that I was responsible for the stock and Gen. Custer would be getting down on me, or something like that. And I told him he had better not go on the upper side of the train because the Gen. had both officers and men there, and he then went on the lower side of the train.

Q. Did the deserters attempt to get any citizens clothes?

A. They tried to trade for some citizens clothes and the next morning some of the men's clothes were missing.

Q. Did you report all these circumstances to the accused?

A. Not all of them I did not.

Q. Did you make any report to him in the morning?

A. Yes sir. I told him he must look over my not being ready as I was up all night watching the stock.

Q. Did you report to the accused that a portion of the command was going to desert?

A. I did in the morning. I did not go up that night.

Q. What did you tell him in the morning?

A. The words I believe I used to the General was this: I went and reported to him something about not being ready, as I have been bothered the night before and could not get out in time.

Q. Did you tell him why you could not get out?

A. I told him I was bothered by men deserting that night and trying to get my stock.

Questions By The Judge Advocate

Q. How do you know the men you speak of were intending to desert on the night of the sixth?

A. They told me they were going to.

Q. How many of them told you?

A. There were four in one party and the horse farrier of Co. "H" was by himself—there were five I caught trying to take stock. A young man came and reported to me they were going to shoot him and I went out and ordered them out. They did not say anything to me. The horse farrier said so and he did go in a few minutes and I had not time to report it.

The witness having heard his testimony read over, then retired.

Sergt. McMahon, a witness for the defense, being duly sworn, testified as follows:

Questions By The Accused

Q. State your name, rank and Regiment.

A. Peter McMahon, Q.M. Sergt., 7th Cav.

Q. Were you Q.M. Sergt. in July last?

A. Yes sir.

Q. Were you with the companies of the 7th Cav. on the march from the Platte River to Ft. Wallace?

A. Yes sir.

Q. State if you know of any combination among men of that command to desert?

A. It was the general talk among the men that they were going to desert.

Q. Do you know of any of them deserting on the night of the sixth of July?

A. There were so many deserted, I don't know any particular one.

Q. Do you know of any measures being taken for the summary punishment of those attempting to desert on the seventh?

A. Yes sir.

Q. What took place that day?

A. Some men tried to desert and they were shot.

Q. What was the effect of that shooting?

A. It prevented any further desertions.

Q. From your knowledge of the men and their intentions, what would have been the result had that action not been taken?

A. I believe there would have been a number more desert that night.

The witness having heard his testimony read over, then retired.

Dr. I. T. Coates was recalled to testify for the defense and testified as follows:

Questions By The Accused

Q. Did you state in your evidence for the prosecution that between noon halt where those wounded deserters were brought in, and the night camp of the seventh of July, you visited the wagon containing those wounded deserters?

A. Yes sir.

Q. State how soon that was after the column got under way?

A. About half an hour.

Q. Did you administer any opiates to them at that time?

A. Yes sir.

Q. When the accused gave you, after arriving in camp, the order to give those deserters all necessary care, did he give you any other instructions; if so, what?

A. Yes sir; he told me not to say anything about that order he gave me, to the company commanders, because if they knew it, through them the men would get to know it.

Q. What order do you refer to?

A. That I was to give treatment to those wounded men.

Q. State why those instructions were given to you, as far as you know?

A. Because he did not wish the troops generally to know I was treating those men who were shot.

The witness having heard his testimony read over then retired.

The accused then presented the following communication: "The accused desires the Judge Advocate, in presenting this deposition, to state the circumstances under which it was taken and to make that statement a part of the record.

"Last night the Bvt. Maj. Gen. Comd'g. the Dept. asked the accused, through his counsel, to permit Maj. Elliott to return to Ft. Harker, Kansas as he was required at that post on urgent public business. The accused objected to this as he apprehended that the Court would prefer to have Maj. Elliott examined upon those points in open court. But subsequently he yielded to the request of the Bvt. Maj. Gen. upon further consultation with his counsel and the Judge Advocate. But he still desires it to be understood that he wished Maj. Elliott to be placed upon the stand in order that he could be subject to the fullest examination upon these points that might be thought necessary."

The Judge Advocate stated: "Gen. Smith requested of me that Maj. Elliott might be relieved from further attendance upon the Court, so that he might be ordered to Ft. Harker this morning in order to accompany the Peace Commissioners, and he desired him to have command of the detachment. Upon this urgent request, I saw the accused and his counsel, and we concluded to take the deposition of Maj. Elliott, which was done in the presence of the accused and his counsel. The facts set forth in the communication of the accused, so far as I know, are true as I was present during part of the conversation with the Gen. Comdg. referred to."

The accused then offered in evidence the deposition of Maj. Elliott referred to, which follows:

Before the subscriber Judge Advocate of the General Court Martial of which Brevet Major General Hoffman is President appeared Major J. H. Elliott, 7th Cavalry, who having been duly sworn deposed as follows: That when the deponent, as stated in his testimony for the prosecution in case of the United States against Bvt. Maj. Genl. Custer, volunteered to pursue the alleged deserters on the seventh of July, 1867 he, the deponent had heard, and knew fully of, the order to shoot said alleged deserters, and that he volunteered because he was afraid that, owing to the slowness of the guard, the deserters would escape, further, that it was his deponent's opinion that the effect of the order to pursue and shoot the said alleged deserters was good upon the whole command and that had the attempt at desertion been successful, at least one fourth of the command were likely, on that night, to desert. And further, that upon reaching Fort Wallace, Kansas, and not finding Major General Hancock there, the accused stated to the witness that he, the accused, was ordered to report to General Hancock and was disappointed at not finding him there, that owing to the closing of the mail route he, the accused, felt it to be his duty, in the absence of other orders, to follow General Hancock to Fort Harker or the nearest telegraph station to report to him there and ascertain what orders were for him, and that he, the accused, to set out after two days rest at Fort Wallace. And further, at the time when the accused left Fort Wallace, it was the opinion of all of the officers of the command that the command would not be actively engaged, or in condition to be engaged, for three or four weeks after its arrival at Fort Wallace, and that the energies of the deponent were fully employed in recuperating the command and preparing it for the field, and he was unable to get the command ready for the field until nearly a month.

And further, that upon reaching Fort Wallace, the horses of the command were nearly all barefoot—and required shoeing, and that the first horseshoes that reached the post in sufficient quantities for issuing to the command reached the post about the fourth or fifth of August by a train escorted by Captain L. M. Hamilton, 7th Cavalry.

And further, this deponent sayeth not.

Sworn and Subscribed to before me this 6th day of October 1867	/s/ JOEL H. ELLIOTT *Maj. 7th U.S. Cav.*

/s/ R. CHANDLER
Capt. 13 Infty.
Judge Advocate

The accused then stated that the order which he here presents is the order referred to in the point conceded by the Judge Advocate during the course of the prosecution, as not having been received by the accused in time to reach Gen. Hancock as herein ordered at Fort Wallace. The failure to receive being due to the capture and killing of Lieut. Kidder, who bore the order. All of which has been admitted by the Judge Advocate for the prosecution.

The accused then offered in evidence the following certified copy of the order referred to:

HEADQUARTERS MIL. DIV. OF THE MISSOURI
SAINT LOUIS, June 27th, 1867.

Colonel Litchfield
Adjutant General
Omaha, Nebraska

Dispatch to General Nichols received. I don't understand about General Custer being on the Republican awaiting supplies from Fort Wallace. If this be so, and he finds that all the Indians have gone south, convey to him my orders, that he proceed with all his command in search of the Indians towards Fort Wallace and report to General Hancock, who will leave Denver for some place today.

A true copy.

/s/ T. CHANDLER
    Capt. 13 Infty.—Judge Advocate.

The accused then offered in evidence a certified copy of the letter of instructions, sent by Lt. T. B. Weir as follows:

HD. QRS. DIST. UPPER ARK.
FORT HARKER, KAS., July 16, 1867

Brevet Maj. Genl. G. A. Custer
Comdg. 7th U.S. Cavalry
GENERAL,

The Brevet Maj. Genl. Comdg. directs me to forward to you the accompanying communication from Dept. Hd. Qrs. for your information and guidance, and to say that he expects you to keep your command as actively employed as the condition of the animals will admit; you will see by the communication referred to you are not restricted in your movements to the vicinity of Ft. Wallace, but are to operate wherever the presence of movements to Indians may lead you.

> I am, very Respectfully
> Your obedt. Servant
> /s/ T. B. WEIR
> *1st Lieut. 7th Cavalry*
> *A.A.A. General*

A true copy.
/s/ T. B. WEIR
1st Lieut. 7th Cavalry.
A.A.A. General

The accused then offered in evidence certified copies of certain telegrams which read:

Extracts from Telegrams Sent Book

To   HEADQUARTERS, DEPT. OF THE MO.
General W. A. Nichols   FORT LEAVENWORTH, KANSAS
Assistant Adjutant General   January 14th, 1867
Saint Louis, Mo.
GENERAL,

The following dispatch has just been received:

To   Fort Morgan
General C. McKeever,   January 14, 1867

Forty (40) men deserted last night from this post, belonging to Company "L", 7th Cavalry. They left in an organized body, taking their arms and horses. They said they were going to Mexico, but have gone in the direction of Denver. I have only twenty-seven men left, and they cannot be trusted.

> /s/ James Sheridan
> Capt. Comdg.

I request that you will order General Cooke to notify his command at Fort Bridger and elsewhere, in order that these men be captured or killed. It would have a wholesome effect if we should be so fortunate as to overcome them. I have telegraphed to General Carleton to use his most energetic effort to capture them.

/s/ W. S. Hancock
Major General Comdg.

To
General A. J. Smith
Fort Riley, Kansas
General,

Headquarters, Dept. of the Mo.
Fort Leavenworth, Kansas
January 14th, 1867

I send you a dispatch just received:

To
General C. McKeever,

Fort Morgan
January 14th, 1867

Forty (40) men deserted last night, from this post, belonging to Company "L", 7th Cavalry. They left in an organized body, taking their arms and horses. They said they were going to Mexico, but have gone in the direction of Denver, I have only twenty-seven (27) men left, and they cannot be trusted.

/s/ James Sheridan
Capt. Comdg.

I have telegraphed to General Carleton to take measures to kill or capture these deserters if they pass through his command. Have also taken measures to have General Cooke do the same. I believe these men may strike the Republican, and come in that way to the settlements.

You will take such measures as you may think will be likely to intercept them, either your Fort Lyon, or from some point nearer to you.

By command of Major General Hancock
/s/ W. G. Mitchell
Capt. and A.A.A. General

To
Capt. Jas. Sheridan
Fort Morgan

Headquarters, Dept. of the Mo.
Fort Leavenworth, Kansas
January 14th, 1867

Your dispatch received. All possible means have been ordered to kill or capture the deserters. A detachment of recruits is ordered to you up the Platte.

By command of Major General Hancock
/s/ W. G. MITCHELL
Capt. and A.A.A. General

A true copy.
/s/ R. CHANDLER
Capt. 13 Infty.
Judge Advocate

The accused then stated he would now be able to close the testimony for the defense but for the absence of three witnesses, whom the Judge Advocate was notified to produce from the beginning of the trial, and especially so last Saturday. That it is believed he has used diligence in procuring their attendance; that the witnesses have been here, and were allowed to go away and are expected tonight or to-morrow morning.

The Judge Advocate stated: "The witnesses whom the defense desires are Capt. Weir, Lt. Moylan, and Mr. Cattrill, all of whom have been summoned for at least a week, and Mr. Cattrill for at least three weeks. Capt. Weir and Lt. Moylan were ordered to Ft. Harker by the Dept. Commander. I notified the Dept. Commander yesterday that those officers would be required on Monday, if pos-sible, and by Tuesday at least, and he stated he would have them sent for. The accused wished these witnesses, and their absence is not by fault of his."

And the accused thereupon asked for an adjournment until 10:00 A.M. tomorrow when he expects to be able to proceed.

The Court thereupon adjourned until 10:00 A.M., Oct. 8, 1867.

On the following day the Court met and called W. H. Cattrill, a witness for the defense, who being duly sworn, testified as follows:

Questions By The Accused

Q. State your name and occupation.
A. W. H. Cattrill, Supt. of what is called the Denver division of the U.S. Express Co.

Q. Where do the stages of that company run?

A. From the terminus of the U.P.R.R.E.D. to Denver City, Colorado.

Q. What was the condition of the mail route in July last?

A. It was in very bad condition; the mails were not transported with much regularity.

Q. Between what dates in July did this irregularity take place?

A. The irregularities in the through mails occurred about the tenth of June, and continued from that time until the first of August.

Q. During the month of July did the mails reach Fort Wallace with regularity?

A. No sir. It was impossible to run out to Monuments more than twice a week, and the stock was all gone above Monuments, and we did not get a mail through to Fort Wallace and Denver more than once in seven or eight days. I don't recollect the precise time.

Questions By The Judge Advocate

Q. During the month of July did the mails run at least once in seven or eight days?

A. I think they might possibly have got through once in seven or eight days in July, that is the through mails for Denver. About the first of June the cars ran to Salina, and about the tenth of June, in consequence of the flood, there was a suspension of traffic between Junction City and Salina, and we did not get a mail for eleven days, and did not carry out any mails, and then the railroad brought up about seven or eight tons of mail matter. I run it out on coaches as far as Monuments. Then it run eight days longer without any mail when we got seven or eight tons more, and I ran that out to Monuments. We were very short of stock above there. After about the first of July the mails came regularly and I ran to Monuments three times a week and from there to Denver once in seven or eight days. We did not get all of this mail to Denver until the second of September. The mail that reached Monuments first was the last to get through, and mail matter might have been delayed there for a month or more.

The witness having heard his testimony read over, then retired.
Lieut. Thomas W. Custer, was recalled by the defense and testified as follows:

Questions By The Accused

Q. Were any precautions taken on the night of the sixth of July to prevent desertions from the detachment of cavalry with which you were serving?

A. Yes sir.

Q. Were any unusual precautions taken?

A. Yes sir.

Q. What especial orders did you receive?

A. I received orders to place six men on stable guard and two of my best non-commissioned officers.

Q. What was the usual number?

A. Three men and a non-commissioned officer.

Q. What was the result of the precautions taken?

A. Ten men deserted from the company I was in command of that night.

Q. What was the conduct of the guard?

A. Some of the stable guard deserted, I don't remember how many.

Q. Did either of the non-commissioned officers desert?

A. Not that night.

Q. Did they the next day or soon after?

A. One of them deserted the next afternoon.

Q. Were any of the officers of the Regiment placed on guard that night to your knowledge?

A. On the night of the seventh there were two officers on guard most of the night, and while there were not two there was one.

Q. Do you remember any occasion when all the officers were placed on guard for the whole night?

A. On the night of the seventh they were all on by reliefs, not all at the same time.

The witness having heard his testimony read over, then retired.
Capt. Louis M. Hamilton, was recalled by the defense, and testified as follows:

Questions By The Accused

Q. Do you know of any precautions being taken on the night of the sixth of July against having desertions in the command with which you were serving?
A. I don't know the date, but the night we were on the Platte the guard was doubled.
Q. Did you receive any orders in regard to it?
A. Yes sir.
Q. What was it?
A. To double the stable guard.
Q. What was the result?
A. I lost eight or nine men that night.
Q. Do you remember any occasion when deserters broke through the guard?
A. Yes sir, on several occasions.
Q. Where was it?
A. Near Fort Hays.
Q. Do you remember when you pursued any deserters?
A. I did on one occasion.
Q. State the circumstances.
A. The alarm was given about the middle of the night by the firing of the sentinel, and I came out of my tent, and caused my squadron to be saddled and sent Mr. Hill in one direction and went the other direction myself.
Q. Did you overtake any of the deserters?
A. No sir.

Questions By The Judge Advocate

Q. What is the letter of your Company?

A. "A".

Q. Who were the officers of your Company on the sixth of July?

A. I was the only officer serving with the Company.

Q. Was Lt. Custer attached to your Company on the sixth of July?

A. There was no other officer serving with the Company at that time.

The witness, having heard his testimony read over, then retired.

Lieut. William W. Cook was recalled by the defense and testified as follows:

Questions By The Accused

Q. Did the accused, during the trip from Fort Wallace to Big Creek, overhaul any stages carrying the mail?

A. Yes sir.

Q. Did he search the mails?

A. Yes sir.

Q. For what object?

A. To obtain any orders there might be in reference to his movements. We had had no mail for about a month.

Q. Did he make any inquiries of any trains he met?

A. Yes sir.

The witness, having heard his testimony read over, then retired.

The accused asked that the following witnesses be called:

Capt. Cox, 10th Cav. to prove that Maj. Gen. Hancock, Commanding the Department, rode from Ft. Wallace to Ft. Harker in an ambulance many trips, made in the month of July last, and while the witness was in command of the detachment escorting Gen. Hancock on that trip;

Bvt. Maj. Gen. John W. Davidson, to prove that during the month of July, 1867, it was the custom in this Dept. for officers to ride in ambulances in making trips upon the plains, and no orders against this custom were enforced;

Capt. Bradley, Assistant Quarter Master, to prove that Bvt. Maj.

Gen. Smith, Commanding District of Upper Arkansas had, during the month of July last, an ambulance or Government spring wagon, for his own use, and did make use of it for himself whenever he wished to;

Capt. Belcher, Assistant Quarter Master, to prove the ambulances or spring wagons, the property of the Government were kept, during the month of July last, at Fort Leavenworth, for the private use of the Major General Commanding the Department and all other officers of the post and their families;

Lieut. Moylan, Regimental Adjutant, 7th Cavalry, to prove that the accused, before proceeding to act summarily against deserters, as shown, on the seventh of July, did take the following measures of a less severe nature, to prevent desertions from the command, viz.,

By pursuing and attempting to over take deserters;

By preferring charges against all deserters and bringing them to trial as promptly as practicable;

By attending to the strict execution of all sentences upon deserters;

By doubling all the guards whenever indications of desertions were observable;

By charging all officers of the command to exercise the utmost vigilance to detect indications of desertions and to prevent the same being realized;

By frequently giving orders to the officers of the day and of the guard to keep their own horses and those of the guard saddled, and themselves under arms all night to check desertions;

By frequently detailing the 1st Sergeants and other most reliable non-commissioned officers to report, armed and equipped, to the officer of the day, for duty all night.

And that the accused had, with Lt. Gen. Sherman the same conversation, in the same language, and to the same effect, as shown by Lieuts. Custer and Cook.

The Judge Advocate admitted that the witnesses asked for, would, if present, swear to the facts as alleged by the accused in his request.

The accused then offered in evidence a telegram from Gen. Augur, the genuiness of which is admitted by the Judge Advocate:

Telegram

From FORT LEAVENWORTH, June 25

To   Recd. June 25, 1867, P.M.

Gen. Custer
Care Major Elliott
Sedgwick

Your dispatch of 22nd received. I answer here on the 23rd. I infer from a dispatch recd. from Gen. Sherman that he will order you again to Smoky Hill route. If not, proceed to carry out such instructions as you have already recd. from him concerning your present scout, and having completed it, return to Sedgwick. Gen. Myers is purchasing a hundred and fifty horses for you, how rapidly I cannot say. I think it very important to get Pawnee-Killer and all other Indians who desire to be friendly, out of the Republican country, and wish you to do all you can to accomplish it. If your instructions from Gen. Sherman will allow it, pitch into the Cheyenne Villages by all means. Unquestionably the Cheyennes are the depredators along the Platte and I hope you will be able to punish them. I leave here in a few days for Fort Sanders, and shall be somewhere along the telegraph line for a month or more. Your despatches to Sedgwick will reach me. If you do not meanwhile receive orders from Gen. Sherman, I will have none for you on your arrival at Sedgwick. Meantime scout the country well. Pawnees are all engaged.

/s/   C. C. AUGUR
B.M.G.

A true copy.
/s/   R. CHANDLER
Capt. 13 Infty. Judge Advocate

The accused then offered in evidence an order signed by Gen. Sheridan, the signature to which the Judge Advocate admitted was genuine, which read as follows:

HEADQUARTERS MIDDLE MILITARY DIVISION
January 5th, 1865

Orders,

Private Charles King, Company "S" 3rd New Jersey Cavalry,

and private Henry Righ, Co. "S" 3rd New Jersey Cavalry having been arrested in attempting to desert and having given information to one of my Staff Officers of the location of my troops, and all changes of troops with great accuracy supposing the Staff Officer to be Rebel, and afterwards exchanging their own United States uniform for that of the Rebel uniform are hereby sentenced to be shot to death by musketry at twelve o'clock noon, Friday, January Sixth, Eighteen hundred and Sixty-five, under direction of the Division Commander, and in presence of the Brigade to which they belong.

/s/ P. H. SHERIDAN
Major General Commanding

A true copy.
/s/ R. CHANDLER
Capt. 13th Infty.
Judge Advocate

The accused then offered in evidence a tabular statement taken from the record books of the Regt. showing the desertions from the 7th Cav., the correctness of which is admitted by the Judge Advocate:

DESERTIONS FROM COMPANIES A, D, E, H, and M, 7th CAVALRY
From July 1st To July 13th, 1867, Inclusive

Cos.	Average Enlisted Men Present	South Fork Republican River	Bob Tail Deer Creek	Black Tail Deer Creek	Chief Creek	Platte River 40 Miles West of Sedgwick		Camp on Dry Creek 20 Miles from Platte Riv.	Total
Non comd. staff	5	"	"	"	"	"	"	"	"
A	56	"	"	"	"	"	"	7	7
D	53	"	"	"	"	"	"	"	"
E	56	"	"	"	"	"	"	6	6
H	50	"	"	"	"	"	"	10	10
K	63	"	"	"	"	"	"	8	8
M	47	"	"	"	"	"	"	3	3
	330	"	"	"	"	"	"	34	34

Week Ending July 7th:

Cos.	Average Enlisted Men Present	Camp on Sand Hill 49 Miles From Platte R.	Chief Creek	North Fork of Republican Riv.	Thickwood and Brand Creek	Short Nose Creek	Near Fort Wallace	Total
Non comd. staff	5	"	"	"	"	"	"	"
A	49	"	"	"	"	"	"	"
D	53	"	"	"	"	"	"	"
E	50	"	"	"	"	"	"	"
H	40	"	"	"	"	"	"	"
K	55	"	"	"	"	"	"	"
M	44	"	"	"	"	"	"	"
	296	"	"	"	"	"	"	"

Six Days Ending July 13, 1867

RECAPITULATION

	Number of Companies	Average Enlisted Men Present	Deserted
Week end April 25th	8	546	11
Five (5) days ending April 30th	8	523	11
Week ending May 7th	8	537	8
" " " 14th	8	584	5
" " " 21st	8	563	24
Ten (10) days ending May 31st	8	536	31
Week ending June 7th	6	346	9
" " " 14th	6	344	2
" " " 21st	6	334	21
" " " 30th	6	325	0
" " July 7th	6	321	34
Five (5) days ending July 13th, 1867	6	296	0

Total deserted from April 19th to July 13th, 1867, inclusive. 156

DISTANCES MARCHED FROM JUNE 1st, 1867, TO JULY 13th, INCLUSIVE
DISTANCES MARCHED

DATE			CAMPED	DISTANCE MARCHED FROM FORT HAYS KANSAS		MILES	REMARKS
June	1	-67	North branch Big Creek	15	miles		
"	2	"	Saline River	16	"	31	
"	3	"	Solomon River	26	"	57	
"	4	"	Bow Creek	19	"	76	
"	5	"	North branch Beaver Creek	22½	"	98½	
"	6	"	Republican River	35	"	133½	
"	7	"	Medicine Lake Creek	18	"	151½	
"	8	"	" " "	18	"	169½	
"	9	"	Platte River	25	"	194½	
"	10	"	Near Ft. McPherson	35	"	229½	
"	11	"	" " "	"	"	"	
"	12	"	" " "	"	"	"	
"	13	"	" " "	"	"	"	
"	14	"	" "	"	"	"	
"	15	"	12 miles west of McPherson	12	"	241½	
"	16	"	12 miles west of McPherson	"	"	"	
"	17	"	12 miles west of McPherson	"	"	"	
"	18	"	Medicine Lake Creek	32	"	273½	
"	19	"	Blackwood "	30½	"	304	
"	20	"	Palader "	19	"	323	
"	21	"	Republican River	26	"	349	
"	22	"	Republican River near North Fork	11	"	360	June 22—Co.
"	23	"	Republican River near North Fork	"	"	"	"D" left camp
"	24	"	Republican River near North Fork	"	"	"	for Wallace for subsistance
"	25	"	Republican River near North Fork	"	"	"	stores distance about 90 miles

DATE	CAMPED	DISTANCE MARCHED FROM FORT HAYS KANSAS		MILES	REMARKS
" 26 "	Republican River near North Fork	"	"	"	returning June 28/67.
" 27 "	Republican River near North Fork	"	"	"	Co. "K" left same day
" 28 "	Republican River near North Fork	"	"	"	scouting on Beaver Creek
" 29 "	Republican River near North Fork	"	"	"	and vicinity returning with
" 30 "	Republican River near North Fork	28	"	288	Company "D".
July 1 "	Republican River South Fork C T	25	"	413	
" 2 "	Bob Tail Deer Creek C T	15½	"	428½	
" 3 "	Black Tail Deer Creek	21½	"	450	
" 4 "	Chief Creek	6	"	456	
" 5 "	Platte River 40 miles W of Sedgwick	59½	"	515½	
" 6 "	Platte River 40 miles W of Sedgwick	"	"	"	
" 7 "	Dry Creek 24 miles from Platte	24	"	539½	
" 8 "	Sand Hill Dry Camp	25	"	564½	
" 9 "	Chief Creek	21	"	585½	
" 10 "	North Fork of Republican River	26	"	611½	
" 11 "	Between Thickwood and Beaver Creeks	27	"	638½	
" 12 "	Short Nose Hole	25	"	663½	
" 13 "	Near Fort Wallace, Kans.	33	"	696½	
	Total	696½	"		

Number of enlisted men present in Companies A, D, E, H, K, and M:

June 1st/67 357
July 13/67 296

213

The accused explained that as the abstract terminates on the 13th of July, it is proper to state that the accused wrote to Lt. Moylan, Regimental Adjutant for a transcript showing the desertions from the Regt. up to the time it reached Fort Wallace. The Regt. reached Ft. Wallace on the 13th of July and the transcript was accordingly made to terminate then. It was the intention of the accused to embrace the remaining days he was in command of the Regt. and if there was still time, those would be sent for.

On account of the absence of Capt. Weir, a material witness for the defense, the Court adjourned until 10:00 A.M. the following day, Oct. 9, 1867.

At 10:00 A.M. on Oct. 9, 1867, Capt. Thomas B. Weir, 7th Cav. was recalled to testify for the defense, and testified as follows:

Questions By The Accused

Q. To the best of your recollection who awakened you on the morning of the 19th of July last?

A. I think Gen. Smith did.

Q. Did you go to his quarters and meet the accused there?

A. I did.

Q. What conversation occurred between you and the accused in presence of Gen. Smith in regard to going to the depot?

A. I don't recollect the conversation. I had scarcely entered the room and shaken hands when Gen. Custer made the remark that we had to hurry up or we would be too late for the train. I don't remember any other conversation but the ordinary greetings.

Q. Did Gen. Smith accompany you as far as the door or farther?

A. I think he did.

Q. Did he send any messages to persons at Fort Riley by the accused?

A. Yes sir; just as we went out of the door, he said "Give my respects to the ladies" or something to that respect.

Q. To the best of your knowledge and belief did the accused go to the depot to start to Ft. Riley with the knowledge of Gen. Smith?

A. I should judge he did.

Q. Did any conversation take place between you and the accused in regard to Gen. Smith having given him permission to be absent?

A. I don't remember what the conversation was. I think I asked him—I know I was anxious to know, and I know there was some conversation. Either I asked Gen. Custer what Gen. Smith said or something of that kind. There was some conversation of that nature, but I don't know what it was.

Q. What was the reply of the accused, if any?

A. I don't remember what his reply was; it was such that I supposed he had talked with the General on the subject. That was my impression.

Questions By the Judge Advocate

Q. What time in that day or night did this conversation you allude to occur?

A. I have no means of knowing, except from the time the train starts. The train starts at three o'clock; and it was nearly train time. I supposed it was between half past two and three o'clock in the morning, before daylight.

Q. How long did the accused remain at Fort Harker?

A. I have no means of knowing.

Q. How long did he remain from the time you saw him until he left?

A. I just entered the room, and we started almost immediately for the depot and I think we had to hurry to get to the train. We drove rapidly from the post to the depot.

The witness having heard his testimony read over, then retired.

The accused announced the testimony for the defense closed and asked until Friday morning, the 11th inst. To prepare his written defense.

The Judge Advocate stated that he would also have his reply in readiness at that time, so there should be no delay.

The Court then adjourned until 10:00 o'clock A.M. Friday, Oct. 11, 1867.

215

At 10:00 A.M. on Friday, Oct. 11, 1867 the Court met pursuant to adjournment. Present:

Bvt. Maj. Gen. W. Hoffman.
Bvt. Maj. Gen. B. H. Grierson.
Bvt. Brig. Gen. P. Morrison.
Bvt. Brig. Gen. M. R. Morgan.
Bvt. Brig. Gen. F. D. Callender.
Bvt. Lt. Col. T. C. English.
Bvt. Major Henry Asbury.
Bvt. Major S. C. Lyford.
Captain R. Chandler, Judge Advocate.

The proceedings of the last session were read and approved, then the accused was asked to present his written defense. His counsel, Captain Parson, proceeded to read this defense:

May it please the Court.

Upon the close of the testimony in this case it devolves upon me to present my written defense.

To this I invite your earnest and most patient attention. I have sought to compress it within the smallest possible compass and if it still seems long, it is because fewer words could not be employed to express what I believe to be a fair and temperate review of the evidence now before you.

While I rely confidently upon your sense of justice and impartiality, gentlemen, I do not flatter you, or myself, with the notion that every circumstances entitled to be regarded in my favor has become apparent to you at once, or will become so mild placed in that order which governed me throughout the entire course of conduct included within the range of testimony here adduced. On the contrary, I know that as the evidence for the Prosecution has gradually been developed, every mind has opened and being so well satisfied as to reach a conclusion, yet as the Defense has opened and continued, every mind has been compelled to retrace its steps of reasoning to attain again that position of independent judgment where it can deliberate maturely and determine justly the cause now in hearing.

Here, gentlemen of the Court, I wish to meet you, and here I trust to receive your favorable finding. Yet it is but due to myself to say that I do not regard it as essential to a finding of entire acquittal upon every charge and specification upon which I am arraigned, that I should bring your individual judgments to approve of the course dictated by my own, under all the circumstances herein recited.

The mind of man is so diversely constituted that individuals governed by the same honorable motives, and laboring for the same generous ends, may differ upon the means they shall employ and the methods they shall pursue; such points of difference may be even antagonistic without prejudice to the sincerity, or good faith of those who are concerned. By the degree of good faith and sincere desire to discharge well and faithfully the responsible duties devolving upon me, which I hope to be able to make evident to your mind, I claim to be judged.

Moreover to indulge in another explanation which may properly preface this defense, it may be remarked that it is easy to see after the blow is struck. And so after the facts in this case have fully taken place, when instead of incurring, as I expected, and still believe I had sufficient cause to expect, an unqualified approbation of my superior officers for the course I have pursued, I am arraigned before a General Courtmartial; it is easy for me to see that had I done otherwise than I did, these results might not have ensued. Here in the same view as before, I claim to be judged not entirely by what is now known but in the light of that information which was afforded me when the events contemplated in the first set of these charges transpired.

When I look at the voluminous record of this court, I find, as you will doubtless find, a large mass of testimony perhaps, I may say, the larger mass out of all the testimony which has no direct or practical bearing upon these charges and specifications. This I desire to dismiss as briefly as possible.

To proceed to that which is of consequence I have first to take up these allegations in the order in which has been adopted by the prosecution.

I am charged first with absence without leave from my command. In this that I left my command at Fort Wallace, Kas. on the 15th of July, 1867, without proper authority and proceeded to Fort Riley,

Kansas, a distance of two hundred and seventy-five miles (275) and this at a time when my command was expected to be actively engaged against hostile Indians.

There are two stages of the journey which I alleged to have accomplished that must be considered separately. The first from Fort Wallace to Fort Harker a distance of 212 miles, occupying a little more than three days, viz.: from six o'clock in the evening of the 15th, to two o'clock in the morning of July 19th, and that from Fort Harker to Fort Riley, a distance of about eighty miles occupying less than three hours.

Of the first stage of that journey, viz.: from Fort Wallace to Fort Harker, I have to say that I accomplished it on account of what I believed to be, and had just cause to believe to be, urgent public business. And of the second I have to say that I went to Fort Riley with the full knowledge and consent of Bvt. Maj. Gen. Smith, my immediate commanding officer. In support of the first proposition the following account of the operation of my command is submitted. The Court will see that it is certified by the evidence on the record.

In the month of June last I found myself with the six companies of the 7th Cavalry which formed my command, upon the Platte River in pursuance of the orders of Bvt. Maj. Gen. Smith. (May 21, 1867) At this time I came under the immediate command of Lieut. Gen. Sherman, commanding this military division. On the 17th of June I left the vicinity of Fort McPherson in pursuance of Genl. Sherman's orders—these are the only orders under which I acted from the time I left Genl. Smith's district, until I reported to that officer again on the 19th of July, which are not on file among these proceedings.

I have not been able to produce these orders because they were first given me by Gen. Sherman verbally and subsequently the General accompanied me about twelve miles on the march repeating his instructions. The exact order, not including however the more general instructions, but so much as indicated the directions I should take and the points I should strike on my scout, was given me in a written form just after General Sherman left me and as I was then in the saddle and afterwards continued on the march the order was lost and I cannot therefore have recourse to it now. This however is almost immaterial because I completed the scout as directed and then received

218

other orders which are here in evidence. The conversation which took place in regards to these orders is very important for this was the last personal interview I had with anyone of the several commanding officers under whom I served until I reported to Genl. Smith on the 19th of July and therefore the last information I received in regard to what was expected of me in connection with the general movement against Indians on the Plains. The details of that conversation which took place at that time as testified by Lieuts. Custer and Cook and as would have been by Lieut. Moylan had he been present were much more ample than I have been able to show in evidence.

The instructions given me left my movements almost discretionary with myself. I was told that I could go to any post that I thought best and that I could go to Denver was especially impressed upon my mind because General Hancock was then enroute for that city and the purpose of communication directly with him upon reaching the Smoky Hill route was the only object that could have taken me to Denver. How, in the face of this direct, explicit and unmistakable authority for me to go to a city more than 200 miles away from the scene of Indian hostilities, or to any other post I should choose, can I be found guilty of absence without leave, or even of the slightest irregularity, for reporting to my commanding officer at Fort Harker, a military post, the base of my supplies and within eight or ten miles of which I was likely at any time to go in pursuit of Indians. Here, gentlemen, if the theory of the Prosecution be adopted, it is an absurdity that must be ridden bareback to arrive at any conclusion unfavorable to myself.

Leaving the vicinity of Fort McPherson as I have said, on the 17th of June, I set out upon a scout to the Republican which after striking I was to follow to its forks and thence pursuing the South fork I intended to strike the Platte again about fifty miles west of Fort Sedgwick—several swollen streams which were supposed to be fordable but before which I was obliged to pause until bridges could be built (the season you will remember had been an unusually rainy one) delayed me so that when I reached the forks of the Republican on the 22nd of June my supplies were nearly exhausted. Halting here, therefore, I sent my train across to Fort Wallace, the nearest practicable depot, and meantime dispatched Maj. Elliott, Second in command, across to Fort Sedgwick for such orders as General Augur might have for me.

In this case I pursued the rule I have usually adopted, of remaining myself with my command and sending the next most responsible officer to report to or consult with those under whose orders I am serving. Maj. Elliott returned with the telegraphic dispatch. (June 25, 1867) In this you will observe Gen. Augur leaves almost everything to my discretion and states that "after I have reached Fort Sedgwick if Genl. Sherman has no orders for me, I will have none." That is, as you can plainly see, "continue to carry out the orders and instructions you have already received. I do not interfere with you," thus leaving me still subject to the instructions I had received during my last interview with General Sherman.

You will notice also that he refers to Gen. Sherman's probable intention of sending me back to the Smoky Hill, and at once the idea suggested itself that I was expected next to confer with Gen. Hancock, whom I supposed to be in the vicinity of Denver. Here it may be remarked, that immediately upon Maj. Elliott's arrival at Sedgwick information of my situation was conveyed to Gen. Sherman who answers in the order (dated June 27, 1867). I ask you, gentlemen, to read that order carefully. "I don't understand about Gen. Custer's being on the Republican awaiting supplies from Fort Wallace." This, although I feel authorized to say, implies no censure, refers, you will bear in mind, to the fact that I was then expected to be nearer the Platte as I should have been but for the swollen stream I have before mentioned. "If this be so," continues the order, "and he finds that all the Indians have gone south convey to him my orders that he proceed with all his command in the search of the Indians towards Fort Wallace and report to General Hancock, who will leave Denver for the same place today." But of this I may say I was sent to Fort Sedgwick after Maj. Elliott had left with Gen. Augur's orders, if they may be called such. The former therefore was committed to the care of Lieut. Kidder, who with an escort of 10 men set out to overtake me, with instructions if he did not find me at the forks of the Republican to follow my trail. Meantime, upon the return of Maj. Elliott I set out in obedience to my previous orders confirmed by General Augur's dispatch to continue my scout up the South fork of the Rupublican to the Platte.

Lt. Kidder, arriving, as it is since surmised, at the forks at night took up the trail of my train toward Fort Wallace and arriving within forty miles of that post was attacked by a party of Indians and, with his whole escort, slain. I found and buried the remains upon my return. I reached the Platte at Riverside station on the fifth of July and at once telegraphed to the Commanding officer at Fort Sedgwick in accordance with appendix to learn if there were any orders for me. In reply came an inquiry if Lieut. Kidder had not overtaken me and also the order of General Sherman which I have quoted. Acting upon this order I set out in an instant for Fort Wallace in order, if possible, to meet General Hancock if there. The unhappy fate of Lt. Kidder, which I already feared to have taken place, had I apprehended, delayed me considerably but I still hoped to be in time to obtain some method of consulting with Gen. Hancock before he should get out of the Indian country. Pressing through without a moments unnecessary delay I reached Fort Wallace on the 13th of July, only to find that General Hancock had passed through that post a week earlier.

Now Gentlemen, it is proper to come to judgment. My orders were before me. I was directed to report to Gen. Hancock. Fort Wallace was the point named where it was expected, it seems, to meet him, under the supposition that I would receive my orders a week earlier than I did. But even, as if to provide for an unforseen failure, Fort Wallace was not named as the point where I should report to him. On the contrary I was ordered to proceed with all my command in search of Indians towards Fort Wallace and report to General Hancock. Couple this with the instructions I had received as shown in evidence, to go to Denver, when it was supposed that Gen. Hancock was there, or to any other post I might find necessary, and what do you make of the spirit, or the letter of my order? Plainly this, that, departing from one Department into another, from one theatre of action into another, parting from one Department into another, from one commander, from whom I had received no definite orders, to another who expected to make out for me a clear line for the remaining summer's campaign—plainly this, that under each and all of these circumstances I was to obey my order so clearly expressed and report to Gen. Hancock.

Whether he were at Wallace or Denver or Harker, at one of which, or between two of which, he was then. There it is gentlemen, fairly stated, and if there were room for doubt at that time in the premises you can see the conclusion which I had just cause to arrive at, and which I did arrive at, stated in Maj. Elliott's deposition; to this effect. "That upon reaching Fort Wallace and not finding Gen. Hancock there, the accused stated to witness, that the accused was ordered to report to Gen. Hancock and was disappointed in not finding him there, that owing to the closing of the mail route, he, the accused, felt it to be his duty in the absence of other orders to follow Gen. Hancock to Fort Harker or the nearest telegraph station to report to him and ascertain what orders were for him."

You have then, gentlemen, the expression of the sense of duty under which I was acting and with the light which was then afforded me, with the direct order given, and the verbal instructions which were the last I received from the General officer giving that order. What else could have been expected of me except the very course I had determined upon? Without fear of contradiction I assert that had I failed to report at Fort Harker or the nearest point of direct communication, and had General Hancock been there awaiting me, as I then supposed he was, and had any unfortunate result in the campaign ensued, had this been the case, I assert without fear of contradiction, that I would have been court-martialed for disobedience of orders.

And yet, for obeying those orders, which, it seems to me, could not be mistaken, I am being court-martialed today.

There are other ways of reporting than in person. How was this at that time and place and under those circumstances?

First, there was indisputably no reliable means of mail communication. I can state this confidently upon the evidence of Mr. Cattrill, who says once in seven or eight days possibly a coach got through. When I reached Wallace there was no indication of even that average irregularity, and certainly I had no right to look to that when I knew I could get through in three days myself.

But still another method suggested itself—that of sending dispatches through by an officer.

The untimely fate of Lt. Kidder, the unexpected delay to which I had been subjected, through the death of that officer, convinced me that this was a most hazardous and in all respects unsatisfactory method of opening communication.

Finally it seemed to me clearly right and certainly best that I should go myself. It was I who was ordered to report. I knew as shown by Maj. Elliott's evidence that the command could not move in a greater number of days than would be required for the round trip—it did not move until just a month after I left—therefore I judged and with sufficient cause, that I should myself set out to report to Gen. Hancock at the nearest possible point. Even then I sought with utmost diligence on the way to discover if orders had been made ready for me and to this end, as shown in the evidence of Lt. Cook, searched every mail bag that we met and inquired of every train. At Monuments, forty-five miles from Wallace, you will have seen from the evidence, I found the first mail—See Mr. Cattrill—and searched it—See Lt. Cook.

Now it may be asked why I did not turn back upon receiving the orders (Fort Harker, July 13, 1867) delivered to me by Capt. Cox at Bunker Hill, twenty-eight miles from Harker. To this I reply that upon reading the endorsement, I found it to state that "Instructions in compliance with this letter have been forwarded." Now where were those instructions? Certainly not on the right way to me because I had intercepted every mail bag, train, or possible bearer of dispatches between Wallace and Bunker Hill. As I was within twenty-eight miles of Harker and as I had already completed one hundred and eighty miles of my trip I concluded at once that it was best for me to proceed to that post and learn where those instructions were, and what they were, more especially, as this realized fully my original intentions and enabled me to confer, as I needed to, personally with Gen. Smith. Here I will remark a feature of Capt. Cox' testimony. He was given that order, he said, and told "to give it to Gen. Custer when he should meet him." Now could anyone show more clearly that I was expected to be met coming in from Wallace for orders? To me, it was supposed, in the order itself, that I would not have reached Wallace until the 17th, and that therefore Capt. Cox would not probably find me far from that post, but this was a calculation founded only on dates and, in reality, had I waited until Capt. Cox reached Wallace how long would I have been there? I arrived there on the 13th. Capt. Cox after two days march was twenty-eight miles from Harker. At this rate of travel and even at a more rapid rate, and this he scarcely could have accomplished, for he was escorting a train, Capt. Cox would have reached Wallace not sooner than fourteen or fifteen days. As he left Harker on the night of the 16th, moving out only three miles, he actually left that post on the 17th. Upon this calculation he would have reached Wallace on the 31st of July. Let me say Capt. Cox says he met me on the night of the 19th. If it were the 19th the calculation would be still more striking for he would have been three days, viz.; the 17th, 18th, and 19th making twenty-eight miles. But to return. Suppose I had waited from the 13th to the 31st of July for orders at Fort Wallace. Can you tell me, gentlemen, what would have been thought of me, or said of me at the Head Quarters of the Department? If nothing would have been said, how does this long period of absence, during which I would have had no orders, correspond with the language of the Specification "this at a time when he was expected to be actively engaged against hostile Indians?" Now gentlemen, the Prosecution may choose either horn of the dilemma; either they did not expect me to be actively engaged against the Indians as here specified, or they expected me to be so engaged under the orders of Gen. Sherman, which orders I obeyed in reporting at Fort Harker. One more, and I trust the last, allusion to that order. I have said that I tried to obey it in the letter and the spirit. In the letter I certainly did, in the spirit I feel also I answered the expectations entertained of me.

The plain intention for me to confer personally with Gen. Hancock upon reaching the Smoky Hill route was expressed not in the language of Gen. Sherman to me in the conversation spoken of, when he told me I could go to Denver if I chose, but likewise in the terms of this very order—"towards Fort Wallace and report to Gen. Hancock who will leave Denver." Now the last phrase was without doubt especially inserted in order that, to meet Gen. Hancock, I should not diverge to Denver as had been originally contemplated.

Clearly, gentlemen, every instruction was given me to show that I was expected to meet Gen. Hancock and less than that, I was not at liberty to suppose.

I have shown, I trust to your satisfaction, that I left Fort Wallace and repaired to Fort Harker in all good faith to place myself in immediate communication with my Commanding officers.

Does anything remain which showed me in the slightest degree culpable under the first Specification of the first charge?

I did, it is true, leave the greater part of my command at Wallace, but for this act of manifest good judgment I do not expect the slightest censure. A large portion of my command was worn out and the rest which would be afforded during my absence was what they required. Fort Wallace, I intended to recommend—and with entire confidence that my recommendation would be approved—should be the basis of my future operations against the Indians until winter should close in. It was therefore fitting that I should leave at Fort Wallace all of my command except what I thought it judicious to take with me. In the latter respect I was governed by two considerations. First, the very slight one relating to my own personal escort. So far as this was concerned I felt confident of being able to go through to Harker with fifteen men at farthest. But in addition to this I expected to apply for Quarter Masters' supplies that were actually required, the most important of which are alluded to in Maj. Elliott's deposition, and besides, I needed a large number of fresh animals. The latter I had cause to expect from General Augur's telegram, and the supply being purchased for my use I concluded would be sent down to me from Omaha and through to the Smoky Hill, or otherwise substituted, be furnished me from the stables at Leavenworth. It was well known and conceded that I required these animals and therefore I supposed that they would be ready for me. After careful consultation and calculation I concluded that seventy-five men would answer every purpose that was required of me—to furnish my own escort say fifteen—to escort the fifty, already required for, say forty-five. Now of the selections I made for this number it may be said, as shown in evidence, that I took picked details so that the horses should answer all that was required of them.

In that way, gentlemen, I left Fort Wallace on the evening of the 18th and reached Fort Harker on the morning of the 19th of July. And if ever an officer acted more thoroughly in accordance with the orders given him, or consistently with the conscientious sense of duty, with which, without arrogance, I claim ever to be animated I do not know who he is, or under what circumstances he could possibly be placed.

I proceed now to the second stage of that trip, viz., from Fort Harker to Fort Riley. I give you, gentlemen, a plain statement of what took place at Harker upon my arrival there, and I leave it to you to determine, in view of all the facts within your knowledge, how truthful it is.

I reached Harker about two o'clock in the morning of July 19th. Crossing the track of the Rail Road, I learned for the first time that the cars were running to that post and that a train was to leave for Fort Riley an hour afterwards, and then conceived the idea of asking permission of Genl. Smith to visit my family at Fort Riley, returning at the very moment he desired. You will understand that twenty-eight miles back I had learned from the order given me that Gen. Hancock was not at Harker and that the report and the recommendations I had to make must be telegraphed to him at Jefferson Barracks and a reply awaited.

Upon reaching Gen. Smith's quarters in the garrison I found a light there but the General was asleep. I awakened him, sat down beside him, told him why I was there (that I was ordered to report to Gen. Hancock but of course it would do as well to report to him), gave a general report of my marches from the time I had left his district, mentioning every detail that occurred to me (Gen. Smith taking notes of what was said, saying I will telegraph this to Hancock in the morning). Made my recommendations for the remaining campaign, stated all, in fact, that I thought would be of interest to him, or to Gen. Hancock. He expressed himself as most gratified to meet me. Let me pause to say that if there was anything wrong in my coming, why did he not say so? He states in his evidence that he supposed that I came by stagecoach. Does it make any difference in a case of absence without leave whether the offending officer came in a stagecoach, or by any other conveyance? No, this was an afterthought and has no bearing upon my case. When I had completed my report, to which he listened attentively, he said, "Well here is Weir's bed, lie down and take some sleep." I replied to him "No General, I would like to go down to Riley and see my family—how long can you give me?" He answered, "Hurry back, we shall want you," and then he said "wait a moment, I will go over and get Weir and he will show you over to the depot." He arose at once and went after Capt. Weir and the moment that Capt. Weir entered the quarters, after exchanging greetings I said to him "well we must get off at once in order to catch the train." Gen. Smith accompanied us out of the door and in recognition of what I had said told me to remember him to my family at Riley. I left him and took the cars in the firm confidence, which to this moment is undisturbed, that I was going with his knowledge and consent. Does a Commanding Officer allow his subordinate to go off in this manner without knowing why and wherefore? If I went with his knowledge, and he admits in his testimony, for he says he made no objection, did I not go with his consent? For of whom else could I ask permission, since he was the Commanding Officer of that district and the senior officer for within more than five hundred miles. Gentlemen, you have the probabilities, as well as the facts, to weigh and when you know that I met officially that night no one but Gen. Smith, of whom could I have obtained leave but from him? No—it was he who gave me that leave and when the next day I received a dispatch directing me to return to Harker at once, I was as much surprised as Gen. Smith probably was himself when he sent it. I did return and when a sufficient time had elapsed I was placed in arrest for absence without leave. Absence without leave from what? From Wallace to Harker where I traveled under plain, and uncontrovertable orders; or from Harker to Riley where I traveled with the fullest knowledge, and, I venture to add with the consent, of my immediate Commanding Officer?

In every theory, gentlemen, there must be something probable, something reasonable, and that of my guilt in these premises is wholly destitute of either element. It is neither probable, nor reasonable, that if I had come to Harker without leave and under circumstances which justified my arrest and prosecution, Gen. Smith would have allowed me to go off to Riley without making some objection. And now in support of what I have said, witness the testimony. It is admitted by Gen. Smith that he knew of my going and made no objection. It is known by Capt. Weir that Gen. Smith went over to awaken him, that almost the instant he came in I said "we had to hurry over or we would be too late for the train." Showing plainly that I had expected him to go to the depot with me and that, not on account of any conversation that had passed between Capt. Weir and myself. With whom, then, had the understanding been entered into but with Genl. Smith? It is further shown by Capt. Weir that Gen. Smith accompanied us as far as the door and sent messages to persons at Fort Riley and finally in reply to this question "did any conversation take place between yourself and the accused in regard to Gen. Smith having given him permission to be absent," Capt. Weir states, "I don't remember the conversation. I think I asked him. I know I was anxious to know and there was some conversation, etc., etc.," and in reply to the next question "I don't remember what his reply was. It was such that I supposed he had talked with the General on the subject, etc., etc."

It may be asked why I did not bring Gen. Smith upon the stand to testify in regard to all these particulars and I will answer that it was because I could not fail to see from Gen. Smith's testimony for the Prosecution that his recollection of what transpired that night was most indistinct, and wholly unavailable for evidence. The lateness of the hour, the fact that Gen. Smith was awakened from a profound sleep at that hour and that a brooding pestilence hanging over Harker at that time probably caused him deep anxiety, all this contributed to direct his attention from what passed between us and that which is most important to me is now apparently forgotten.

Here, gentlemen, I leave the first specification of the first charge.

Passing to the second I have to say that the very gist of this lies in the one single phrase that is not so much as referred to by the Prosecution in evidence viz.: "the said march being upon private business, etc., etc." Now it is only necessary, I remember, that the substance of a Specification be proven, but here is the very substance not proven. If I did not go on private business I expect that I am not likely to be court-martialed or even censured for making a rapid march upon public business; more especially as I had been instructed during the whole season to march as fast as I thought best. If that phrase relating to private business be stricken out, the entire remaining portion of the Specification is of no account and should also be stricken out because there is not one particle of evidence which is even professed to be introduced to sustain it.

One other allegation of this Specification is not proven, viz.: "and when the horses belonging thereto had not been rested." They had been rested two days—longer than they had before been rested for weeks—but were they unfit for service? Speaking generally of the whole Command they were; of those selected especially—and inspected to accompany me, I assert they were not. Major Elliott, speaking generally of the whole Command, thinks they were not fit for service. But Capt. Hamilton, who commanded the detachment, speaking of the horses of the detachment, says positively, as I myself knew, "They were fit for service but not in high condition." That some were expected to give out is evident. They do that in every march and the men are dismounted and, if necessary, placed in wagons. Anticipating that these horses would give out, I gave orders to leave those horses, with their riders, at the mail stations enroute. Capt. Hamilton says two horses were shot by his order and also says that he did not think I knew of it. Sergt. Connolly has stories of three horses shot and others abandoned but no one but Sergt. Connolly knew of that. Had it been reported to me I would have provided a remedy either in longer halts, if these were necessary, or by detailing a proper guard to take care of failing horses. I do not think it could have taken place because it was beyond my knowledge and that of Capt. Hamilton.

Now in regard to the rate of march it is shown that it was slow but continuous. It was such as seemed perfectly judicious to me and that it did so to Capt. Hamilton I infer, from the fact that he never asked any delay except at Downer's and then only on account of the presence of Indians. I cannot dwell on this because here is a great deal of superfluous testimony. What has the fact of twenty deserters, if there were twenty, to do with this? Capt. Hamilton swears that no one deserted while I was with the detachment. What took place subsequently ought not to be introduced in this trial. When I reached Big Creek I left Capt. Hamilton there and his horses were not then so worn out but that after a rest of one or two days he could move on to Harker.

One more reference to this Specification. Gen. Smith was asked if there was any urgency of public business that required me at Harker. That was not an admissable question—that is the very issue the Court is directed to try, or, not that only, but whether I had cause to believe that I was required at Harker, or whether in going there I was exceeding the bounds of my orders. Gen. Smith's reply to that question is not evidence. It has not even a bearing, and if I have shown that I was going to Harker in pursuance of orders received before reporting to Gen. Smith, the question might just as well have remained unasked.

What else concerns this Specification has been fully discussed in canvassing the previous one.

The second specification of the second Charge I judge will be abandoned by the Prosecution: first, because it has not been shown that I was executing an unauthorized journey upon private business; secondly, because it has not been shown that I procured two ambulances and eight mules at Fort Hayes. And third, because it was universally the custom in this Department in the month of July last to make use of ambulances for the service of officers and I expect I had used them as little as any one who has been upon the plains this summer.

The third Specification of the second Charge refers to the alleged incidents of an attack upon a small party of my command eight miles from Downer's Station. It is alleged that I failed to take proper measures for the repulse of said Indians or the defense or relief of said detachment.

Now gentlemen, the incidence shows you that I knew nothing of that attack until Sergt. Connolly came and reported that it had taken place. Now then, could I have taken any measures to repel Indians of whose presence I had no knowledge, or for defending or relieving a detachment when I did not know it was in peril?

I ask your careful attention to that, gentlemen, because the Specification directly alleges that it was in my power to do all these things when it is well known to you that, as I have stated, I knew nothing of the affair until it had fully taken place. But, continuing, the Specification charges me with having neglected, after receiving the report that two of the detachment had been killed, to take any measures to pursue such party of Indians, or recover or bury the bodies of those of my command who had been so killed. The latter part you will have observed is incorrect for the fact of the supposed killing of the two men was reported to Capt. Carpenter, Commanding Officer of Downer's, who sent out and buried the one actually found dead and brought in the one found alive. This was the best arrangement that possibly could have been effected, as I think will be admitted. In regard to pursuing the Indians Capt. Carpenter himself states that he thinks it would not have been good policy for me to have pursued the Indians, and every one agreed that in the conversation that took place when the report came in.

That report as made to me was that Sergt. Connolly had been attacked about eight miles back by a party of forty or fifty Indians. I well knew, and so did everyone else who knows of Indian warfare, that any party I might send back, by the time it reached the scene of attack, would find no trace of the Indians. The latter would not even leave a trail to follow and it would have been the measure of absurdity to have undertaken such an errand. That I was not averse to meet the Indians at that time with my force, if there be any doubt on the subject, may be inferred from the fact as testified to by Capt. Hamilton that when he recommended a delay on account of the excitement among the men and the probable presence of Indians in the vicinity, I declined to accede to his suggestion, and mounting my command at once set out upon the march.

I do not know what is left of this Specification but I wish to make two remarks concerning it. First, it is singular that the Prosecution should in one Specification charge me with going off with horses unfit for service and directly afterwards imply an offense because I did not use these to pursue Indians who were, no one knows where. And second, Sergt. Connolly is mistaken when he says he reported to Capt. Hamilton that only one of his men was killed, or else Capt. Hamilton is mistaken in this testimony that the Sergt. reported that two men were killed, for thus he distinctly swears. He says some man spoke of only one man being killed but it seemed of so little account that he was satisfied that both were killed. However it may have been, Capt. Hamilton of course reported to me that both were killed, and until after I was here arraigned I supposed that such was the case. I infer that Capt. Hamilton was right in regard to the report of the Sergeant, not only from my confidence in him, but also because the alleged offence would have been vastly aggravated had one of the men been wounded instead of killed and had the fact been within the knowledge of the Prosecution I don't imagine they would have spared anything on my account.

I have reviewed carefully and I think candidly the first set of charges.

As I come to the second, I cannot fail to speak of them—of the spirit which animated them and of the manner in which they are framed in terms of strongest denunciation. In so doing I do not expect to affect your judgment thereby. But I know when a deep wrong, that does not arise from an honest difference of opinion, is done by me and I place here on record the expression of my indignation that anyone should have been found in the service to propose these charges, to defeat the purposes of discipline, and to set facts that received the unanimous approval of all my officers and right-minded enlisted men, so far as I have learned, when they transpired, in such array, against me as to excite the apprehension in the minds of many that I was not only arbitrary, but even inhuman.

Here are facts for you which at most should have been embodied in but two specifications viz.: That I gave certain orders as the result of which three men named, were shot down or wounded; second, that I refused medical attendance to these men, the result of which was that one man—named—deceased.

And yet, contrary to law, which forbids more than one specification upon the same alleged fact and forbids the accumulation of charges and specifications which may be imbraced in me—these two alleged offenses are so dissevered, distorted, and twisted as to comprise four specifications and with this specimen of cunning handiwork.

The scene of the second Specification is laid in different terms than that of the first, with no other apparent intention than to induce the belief that they were two separate occurrences.

When I have stated what is the sense of wrong in connection with these "additional charges" under which I labor I have nothing further to do except under a solemn sense of responsibility for the action taken to say, what of these charges is true and why that should have been so.

The first Specification of the Charge called "Additional Charges, etc." is true with this exception—I did not order the whole party sent in pursuit of the deserters "to bring none alive". I only gave that additional order to Lieut. Jackson and not to either Maj. Elliott or Lts. Custer or Cook as you will see from the evidence. I make this statement because it has this to do with the circumstances. When those deserters were pointed out to me escaping over the hill, the attention of nearly the whole command was directed toward me to see what I would do. It was well known, as shown in the evidence of Mr. Harper, of Q.M. Sergt. McMahon and of Maj. Elliott, that there existed a combination for a general escapade from my command before we should leave the vicinity of the Platte. It was also well known that I would take prompt measures to suppress the first development of that conspiracy; that I had stated.

When these men in the face of the whole command were pointed out to me, I called Lieut. Jackson, the officer of the day, to me and gave that order. He understood well what it meant and that it was done for necessary effect upon the men and that it did not contemplate anything inhuman, for in the execution of that order, he first came upon two men, as he testifies, who lay down in the grass and pretended to be dead. He took these men and sent them back to camp under charge of a corporal and suitable guard. Now if he had understood that order literally, he would either have shot those men when he came upon them or he would have offered some explanation for not obeying the order. Nothing of the kind took place. And again, if I had intended that order to be obeyed literally, or if I had meant more than to have a desirable and necessary effect upon the command, I would have had those men shot when they were brought in and I would have held Lt. Jackson responsible for disobeying my order. Nothing of this kind took place.

Now the horses of Lt. Jackson and the guard were not saddled when the order was given. Those of several officers near me were. They, appreciating the necessities of the case, came up to me and asked if they had not better set out after the deserters and to Maj. Elliott and Lt. Cook. So voluntarily I gave the authority to go, repeating the same order I had given Lt. Jackson save that, as none heard me save themselves, I did not tell them to bring none in alive. They went at once in pursuit and as a consequence three men were wounded and brought in, none dead, you will observe, and three were brought in alive and unharmed, except one who was accidentally ridden over by a horse.

The circumstances under which the three wounded men were shot can only be learned from the evidence. The Prosecution asked Lt. Cook, one of the witnesses, whether they were shot in consequence of my order, to which he replied, "not altogether, I think." Then questioned again "As to what other reasons there were," he replied, "The men were ordered to halt and surrender and one of them made a motion as if to present his carbine which I think brought on the shooting." This man Johnson, the wounded man who afterwards deceased, is variously shown to have taken such attitude with his carbine as to threaten the pursuing officers and thus he was shot. Whether he or the other two received the wounds given before or immediately after they threw down their arms I do not know. If afterwards, the circumstance of shooting was not an unnatural one for all was in the confusion of a hasty pursuit and as Maj. Elliott testifies, the whole transaction hardly occupied a moment. Two men were wounded when Lt. Jackson got up and Alburger was still running. He afterwards was shot and then Maj. Elliott and Lt. Jackson rising the crest of the hill found that the mounted fugitives had so gained upon them that further pursuit was useless. So they brought the wounded men back to camp, Lt. Jackson convoying the wagon.

Now if this shooting, gentlemen, were the result of this order which I certainly gave, and which—I say it calmly and not in any spirit of defiance—I should feel compelled to give were it all to be done over again, there is this for you to take into consideration.

From all the trustworthy information which had been given me there was manifest in my command a determination to desert which assumed the full proportions of a mutiny. Nothing more insubordinate could have been imagined than the disposition of those men who left the noon camp before the eyes of everyone and undertook to escape. Deeply conscious of what I was taking upon myself and, on the other hand, of what I owed to the service and to the men who were well disposed, I did that which under the same circumstances it seemed to me an officer in my position was expected to do. What, it is becoming in me to inquire, would have been the result had I not taken those summary steps? Let the evidence of Maj. Elliott and of Sergt. McMahon and let your own judgment answer. The evidence given in this regard might have been accumulated to my extent had I thought it necessary. In regard to this summary action I have added to the record two appendices viz.:

First is the series of telegrams from Maj. Gen. Hancock relating to the means for pursuing and punishing certain deserters of last winter. "Capture or kill" is the phrase once and "kill or capture" is employed in another dispatch. You can read that and see if it were not the same in spirit as my own order of the seventh of July. A second appendix is the order of Gen. Sheridan given me in the Shenandoah Valley for summary shooting under the most deliberate method of procedure. That was, it is true, in time of war, but even in time of war it is held in law that deserters shall be tried and the fact that an emergency then may authorize summary steps, can be safely referred to for the purpose of showing that the steps may be again resorted to in a similar emergency. And when could that emergency have been more pressing than in the country of hostile Indians when I was likely to be abandoned by a large part of my command? I summoned Gen. Sheridan here as a witness to show that he authorized and endorsed similar proceedings under another emergency after the close of the war but as his attendence could not be procured I have not the opportunity to cite these cases.

The second Specification I dismiss as being a repetition of the first with the names of the wounded men inserted and the scene of the allegation merely laid to deceive the Court.

The third Specification, regarding the alleged refusal of medical attendance will require brief attention. It is shown by the only witness who can testify to the facts—the Surgeon of the command—that I not only did not "neglect and positively and persistently refuse to allow the said soldiers to receive any treatment or attention from the Acting Assistant Surgeon, or any other medical or surgical attendance whatever", as alleged but that I directly ordered Dr. Coates to give them all the attention that was necessary—that I required him to report their condition to me and that I repeatedly inquired after them. Moreover, it is shown that they were conveyed in a wagon upon the express request of the surgeon and that he had full control of that wagon. The testimony of other witnesses show that they were not hauled eighteen miles that day and again Dr. Coates that the Surgeon employed every facility for treating the wounded men that I could afford them.

If the Court, as I trust is the case, have so far comprehended the spirit and intention of my orders, it will have seen why I preserve injunctions of strict confidence in regard to the attention which those men received. I will only remark that I excluded the officers of the command from the confidence, not because I was distrustful of them, but because situated as we were, enlisted men could hear almost all the conversation among officers, and in this way I apprehended the fact which I wished withheld from them, would become known. There is some testimony in regard to the condition of the water at the camp of July seventh from Lt. Jackson which I suppose is intended to rebut Dr. Coates' views in regard to the propriety of dressing those men's wounds. I do not know anything about this. I am not on trial for malpractice, nor am I to be held responsible for Dr. Coates' professional views, although I will aver that from long observation I have the highest confidence in them. Hence it is sufficient to know that I did not stand in the way of the dressing of those wounds.

The fourth Specification is composed of gleanings from the other three and therefore I need say nothing farther of this.

And I conclude here also the review of this case.

Contrary to the conjectures which have been expressed in places regarding my defense I have not sought to relieve myself of these Charges and Specifications by reference to any record which I might have made the basis of an appeal were I forlorn object of compassion. Had I resorted to such a line of defense, however, it would under any circumstances, have been only to show that, through six years which I have tried honestly and faithfully to devote to my country and to all, in my judgment, that was honorable and useful in my profession. I have never been once absent from my command without leave as here charged. I have never wearied or in any way made use of my men for the advancement of my private wishes or interests—as here charged, or severely tasked any living creature as here charged, except under a sense of duty.

I have never made use of any government conveyance, as here charged, except such as was universally conceded to be the right of an officer. I have never turned away from our enemy, as here charged, or failed to relieve an imperiled friend, as here charged, or left unburied or without having provided for the burial, of a single fallen man under my command, as here charged. Or took upon myself the responsibility of a single summary action that did not seem to be demanded by the occasion, as here charged. Or finally, ever saw a man in any strait suffer when by my authority I could relieve him, as here charged.

So if I felt guilty of all or one of the Charges or Specifications, it is an era of my life of which I am not conscious.

Without any intention to repeat habitual expressions, I thank you, gentlemen of the Court, for your attention and I desire to place upon record my obligations to the Judge Advocate of this Court for his uniform courtesy.

I ask at your hands, gentlemen, in the name of justice, a finding of acquital upon all of these Charges and Specifications save those of "Additional Charges" so called in which, of the first Specification I ask a finding of guilty "But attach no criminality thereto" and of the remaining Specifications a full finding of acquital.

/s/ G. A. CUSTER
Bt. Maj. Genl., U.S.A.

After Captain Parsons had retired to his seat, Colonel Hoffman gave the floor to Captain Chandler who, as Judge Advocate, read his reply:

May it please the Court.

In reviewing the evidence in this case it is not my intention to *reply* to the address of the accused, but to endeavor to recapitulate and methodize the import of the evidence, applying it distinctly to the facts of the charge, and to give a synopsis of the testimony in as brief manner as the time allotted will allow. In adopting this method it is hoped the evidence will be presented in a consolidated form as applicable to each Specification, and of service to the Court by way of reference.

Upon the first Charge and its Specification the prosecution has shown by the testimony of General Smith that the accused was under his command at the time he arrived at Fort Wallace in July; that the accused received no leave of absence or authority or order from General Smith to leave his command, and march from Fort Wallace to Fort Hays or Fort Riley; that there was no urgency or demand of public business for such a march as far as General Smith knows; that the accused came to Fort Harker between two and three o'clock at night and stated to General Smith that he was going to Fort Riley, and no objection was interposed.

General Smith does not recollect what the accused said to him in reference to his going to Fort Riley, but the next morning as soon as it was discovered how the accused came to Harker he was ordered back by telegraph, to his command, by General Smith.

The records of the Office of the Assistant Adjutant General District Upper Arkansas, show no leave of absence granted to the accused as appears from the evidence of Captain Weir.

The time when the accused left Fort Wallace without authority, is shown by Captain Hamilton, and is the same as alleged in the Specification.

The distance from Fort Wallace to Fort Harker is shown to be 192 miles, by the table of distances introduced in evidence and from Fort Harker to Fort Riley. The Documentary evidence contained in the letters of Instruction and orders from Generals Hancock and Smith, to the accused, shows that the command was expected to be actively engaged against hostile Indians—especial reference is had to the letter of July 16th from General Smith, introduced *by the accused* as evidence.

The evidence for the defense upon the Specification of the first Charge is that of Lieutenants Custer and Cook who testified they were present at a dinner conversation which occurred near Fort Mc-Pherson between General Sherman and the accused regarding certain orders which General Sherman was going to give the accused to the effect that the accused would receive orders from General Augur, but not to restrict himself to them, that if the accused wished he could go to Denver or any post or place he desired; that this conversation has reference particularly to going after the Indians, and to movements on the plains which was elicited by the cross examination. It was admitted also that Lieutenant Moylan would testify to the same facts were he here.

This is all the testimony bearing upon the first Charge and Specification offered by the accused.

At this point I would remark to the Court that, not having heretofore perused or heard the written defense of the accused, it cannot be expected that I will reply to the argument contained therein, nor do I intend to do so. But I desire here to state that the argument of the accused upon the first Charge and its Specification, is based entirely on *assumed* facts and testimony. *Nowhere* in the Record is it shown that the accused *received* the order of General Sherman to report to General Hancock at or near Ft. Wallace. On the contrary it has been shown in evidence, and admitted by accused that *that* order (St. Louis, June 27, 1867) was sent by Lieut. Kidder, who was killed when conveying it, and that it was not received.

But admitting that the accused did receive the said order, by the express language of the same he would thereby have no authority *to leave* the vicinity of Ft. Wallace in search of Gen. Hancock.

The Court will excuse me for this digression from the course I intended to pursue in this review, but I could not let it pass without calling your attention to the fact that the defense, on this point, is founded entirely on a statement of *assumed* facts and evidence.

Upon the first Specification to the second Charge, the Official Report of the accused concerning his march from the Platte to Wallace, which is in evidence, shows that "the command had marched 182 miles in seven days" to reach Fort Wallace and that this march was "a forced one." The testimony of Captain Hamilton shows that the horses of the command "were in a very bad condition" upon their arrival at Wallace. Major Elliott testifies that the horses were very much "exhausted and worn" not fit for service and "not in condition for a march of a hundred or two hundred miles; that a day or two's rest was not sufficient to put them in condition."

Captain Hamilton testifies that the accused ordered a detail of three officers 72 men from the command at Fort Wallace, to accompany him to Fort Hays; that a portion of this detail was *selected* on account of good horses; that this detachment set out from Wallace on the 15th of July for Hays or Big Creek under his (Captain Hamilton's) command; that it escorted the accused who accompanied it as far as Big Creek, about nine miles south of Hays; that it arrived at Big Creek about daylight on the 18th July; that the march was continuous, and about five hours were consumed in resting during said march; that the distance was between 140 and 150 miles; that the horses were in bad condition when they reached Fort Hays; that two (2) horses were shot, and some abandoned on said march, because they could not keep up with the command; that the horses were in worse condition when they reached Fort Hays than when they left Fort Wallace.

Lieutenant Cook testifies that the escort left Fort Wallace about five or six o'clock in the morning and arrived at Big Creek in about 57 hours.

Captain Cox testifies that on his way to Wallace escorting a train he took up several men and horses belonging to the escort which had accompanied the accused to Fort Hays and that nearly all of the horses were entirely used up and had to be led.

Captain Carpenter testifies that one man belonging to the escort stopped at Downer's Station because his horse could not be ridden.

Sergeant Connolly testifies that the horses of the command were not in good condition when they reached Fort Wallace; that he was generally in the rear of the column on the march from Wallace to Hays, and was on several occasions sent back to pick up stragglers and horses; that on two occasions he was ordered to leave horses at stations when they were unable to travel; that several were left at stations on the route; that several horses were abandoned and left on the prairie, and that *three* were shot, because they could not go no further, and that between 45 and 50 mounted men only of the escort arrived at Big Creek.

Major Elliott testifies that he heard the order given to *three* company commanders to detail 12 of the best mounted men in their companies, for the escort going east with General Custer.

The only testimony offered by the accused bearing upon the first Specification of the second Charge is the conversation heretofore referred to which occurred between General Sherman and the accused near Fort McPherson, as testified to by Lieutenants Custer and Cook. This testimony is undoubtedly intended to refer to that portion of the Specification which alleges that the accused executed a march from Wallace to Hays without proper authority or any urgency or demand of public business. No testimony had been offered by the accused touching the other allegations contained in this Specification.

The only testimony produced by the prosecution upon the second Specification of the second Charge is that of Lieutenant Cook, who testifies that four mules belonging to the Government were obtained from the Quartermaster at Fort Hays to use in an ambulance for the conveyance of the accused and part of the escort to Fort Harker.

The accused has shown by admitted and ample testimony that it was the custom for officers in the Department to ride in ambulances in making trips on the plains, and at all other times when they desired, and that no orders against this custom had been enforced.

The prosecution having discovered too late that this Specification was defective in the allegation regarding the procuring of ambulances at Fort Hays for the use of the accused, no further testimony was offered than that concerning the obtaining of four mules at Fort Hays.

Upon the third Specification, second Charge, the prosecution has shown by the testimony of Sergeant Connolly that a party of Indians had attacked a small party detached from the escort which accompanied the accused near Downer's Station, and that one man of said party was killed and one wounded; that after the return of said detachment to the command, a report of said attack and the nature of it was made by the Sergeant to Captain Hamilton, commanding the escort. Captain Hamilton testifies that Sergeant Connolly reported to him at Downer's Station that the Indians had succeeded in killing two of his men about four or five miles back, and that the accused made no answer as remembered by Captain Hamilton; that no action was taken for the pursuit of the Indians and that no measures were taken by the accused to recover the bodies of the men reported wounded and dead as known to the accused.

Sergeant Connolly testifies that the two men (one killed and the other wounded) were left on the field; and that no measures were taken by the accused to recover them to his knowledge.

Captain Carpenter 37th Infantry, testifies that he sent out a detachment from Downer's Station to recover the bodies of those killed, that said detachment found and brought in one dead man and one wounded man belonging to the 7th Cavalry; that this detachment was sent out *after* General Custer and his command had left Downer's; that this occurred on the 17th of July while the accused was at Downer's Station with his command.

Sergeant Connolly testifies that the Indians pursued his detachment to within a mile and a half or so of Downer's Station to the right of the road.

The accused introduced *no defense* or testimony upon the third Specification of the second Charge.

Upon the first Specification of the Additional Charge, the testimony of Lieutenants Custer, Cook and Jackson, and Major Elliott, and the official report of the accused in regard to his march from the Platte to Fort Wallace shows conclusively that the accused ordered a party of three or four commissioned officers of his Command in pursuit of supposed deserters who were then in view leaving camp, and that he did also order said party to shoot them down, and bring none in alive. The time and place is also shown by these witnesses to be the same as set forth in the Specification. No denial as to these facts being made by the accused except a general justification which will be hereafter considered it is not deemed necessary to recount the testimony of the witnesses in this point.

Upon the second Specification of the first Charge it is shown by the same witnesses or by a portion of them, that by said orders of the accused, Bugler Toliver, Privates Johnson and Alburger were shot down as supposed deserters, but without trial, and that they were severely wounded is shown by the testimony of Dr. Coates. The time and place are also shown. The accused likewise offers no evidence upon this Specification except a general justification.

Upon the third Specication of the Additional Charge, Lieutenant Cook testifies that the three men, after they were wounded were placed in an army wagon by General Custer's order, and brought two or three miles in to the Command, and as the wagon came up, the Command moved out to the first watering place, and the deserters were brought along in the same wagon; that the Command marched six or seven miles and went into camp about two hours afterward.

Doctor Coates testifies that the three men named in the Specification were shot and wounded. Tolliver was wounded by one shot, a flesh wound; Alburger was wounded in three places, all flesh wounds; Johnson was wounded in three places, one was in the head, the ball entering the left temple and coming out below under the jaw and passing into his lungs, and again entering the chest, and the other two wounds flesh wounds; that these men were brought into camp in a six mule wagon; that when the wagon first came in with the wounded men and when the witness was going to it, General Custer *said to him not to go near those men at that time*, and the witness stopped just where he stood and obeyed the order of the accused; that in about two hours after the men had been in the wagon, the witness administered opiates and made them comfortable just as he should have done on the field of battle; that he did nothing else but give them opiates, as in his judgement there was nothing else required; that there was a good deal of clothing in the wagon and he used it to make the men comfortable; that their wounds were dressed just two days after they were wounded, and during that time the men followed the column in the wagon; that there were two ambulances with the command, but in bad condition; that the witness regarded the wagon as easier than the ambulance; that there was no other Medical Officer with the command; that it was impossible to dress the wounds of these men on account of not having fresh water; that there was nothing but buffalo wallows, which would have been hurtful; and that this was the reason why the witness did not dress them; that the witness examined the wounds about two hours after the men were wounded and got into the wagon and rode with them.

Major Elliott testifies that the distance from the point where these men were wounded to the halting place, was about three miles; that there was passable clear water to be obtained at the place the men were brought in wounded by digging in the sand; that it was drank and used for cooking dinner and watering the stock; that the command started about four o'clock P.M. from the halting place on the seventh of July, and halted that night after a march of about ten miles; that the witness had a conversation that night with the Surgeon of the Command after they arrived in camp, about nine o'clock, in which witness asked him why he did not dress the wounds of those wounded men, and that the Surgeon replied he had been ordered not to.

Lieutenant Jackson testifies that at the time these men were wounded, Major Elliott directed him to remain with them until a wagon could be sent for them; that he, witness, waited about three-fourths of an hour when the wagon came up and the men were put in and taken to the Command; this was between two and three P.M. of the seventh of July; that there was no bedding or anything else in the wagon, perfectly empty; that witness took the men to the Command, etc., etc.

Upon the fourth Specification of the Additional Charge it is shown by the testimony of Doctor Coates that Private Charles Johnson died from the effects of the wound received on the seventh of July.

The defence offers no testimony on this Specification.

The theory of the defence relative to the Additional Charge in this case, as appears from the *evidence* produced, is a general justification of the acts of the accused in shooting deserters, under the circumstances in which he was placed. No evidence had been introduced by the defence, applying *particularly* to any of the Specifications of the Additional Charges, except to the third Specification in regard to medical attendance. The evidence upon the Specification has been briefly referred to.

The defence has shown by the evidence of Captain Hamilton that during the time the accused was with the detachment which went from Wallace to Big Creek there were no deserters from the Command, but that there were desertions at Fort Harker from this detachment, adduced by cross examination. Major Elliott testifies that the shooting of deserters had a beneficial influence on the whole Command, and that had the attempt on desertion (on the seventh) been successful at least one-fourth of the Command were likely, on that night, to desert.

Quartermaster Sergeant McMahon testifies that it was the general talk among the men on the march that they were going to desert; that there were a great many desertions on the night of the sixth of July; that on the seventh of July some men tried to desert and were shot, which action prevented any further desertion; that had not these men been shot there would have been a number more deserted that night.

The documentary evidence offered by the accused, and admitted in evidence offered by the accused, and admitted in evidence, relating to a band of deserters from Fort Morgan, belonging to Captain Sheridan's Company, showed that General Hancock directed that these deserters be captured or killed if they could be found.

The order issued by General Sheridan in January 1865, shows that two men had been arrested for desertion, that they had been given information of the location of the troops of General Sheridan's Command and that they had exchanged their United States Uniforms for Rebel Uniforms, for which crimes they were ordered to be shot in the presence of the Brigade to which they belonged.

The testimony of Captain Hamilton and Lieutenant Custer, shows that notwithstanding all the precautions taken to prevent desertions, several desertions occurred in their respective companies.

The admitted evidence of Lieutenant Moylan shows that the accused used stringent measures to prevent desertions from his command, before resorting to shooting.

The Tabular Statement of Deserters, admitted in evidence, shows that there were 156 desertions from April 18th to July 13th, 1867, from the 7th Cavalry.

Having thus briefly and imperfectly referred to the testimony bearing upon this case and having carefully abstained from an expression of opinion as to the guilt or innocence of the accused, I respectfully submit it to the Court with full confidence that upon the judgment and conscience of the members, the weighing of the evidence rests, and that by deliberate caution and patient investigation a verdict will be obtained on the side of truth and justice.

/s/ R. CHANDLER
Capt. 13, Infty.
Judge Advocate

The Court was then cleared for deliberation, and after considering the evidence adduced found the accused, Bvt. Maj. Gen. G. A. Custer, Lieut. Col. 7th U.S. Cavalry, as follows:

Of the first Specification first Charge—Guilty of the Specification, substituting the words, "Ft. Harker" for the words "Ft. Riley"; omitting the words "two ambulances and," and substituting the word "four" for the word "eight," and omitting the words "ambulances and," and attach no criminality thereto.

Of the third Specification of the Additional Charge—Guilty.

Of the second Specification of the Additional Charge—Guilty of the Specification omitting the words "the following named and designated soldiers of his Regiment, viz.: Bugler Barney Tolliver,

Co. K, Private Charles Johnson, Co. K., Private Alburger, Co. D. and other," and substituting the word "three" in place of the words "the said."

Of the third Specification of the Additional Charge the Court finds the facts as stated in the specification except the words "and did then and there neglect and positively and persistantly refuse to allow the said soldiers to receive any treatment or attention from the acting assistant Surgeon with his command, or any other medical or surgical attendance whatever," and attach no criminality thereto.

Of the fourth Specification of the Additional Charge—Guilty.

Of the Additional Charge—Guilty.

In consequence the Court sentenced Brevet Major General G. A. Custer, Lieutenant Colonel, 7th U.S. Cavalry, to be suspended from rank and command for one year, and forfeit his pay for the same time.

XII. FROM LABOR
TO REFRESHMENT

Aᴌᴛʜᴏᴜɢʜ Cᴏʟᴏɴᴇʟ Cᴜsᴛᴇʀ had received the verdict and was adjudged "Guilty" by the Court-martial, there was hope that the reviewing officer would see the proceedings differently. On the fourteenth of October a transcript of the entire proceedings was transmitted to the Adjutant General. Time would tell.

On November 18 Lieutenant General Sherman issued a statement that the "proceedings, findings and sentence in the case of Brevet Major General Custer are approved by General Grant . . . in which the levity of the sentence, considering the nature of the offenses of Bvt. Major General Custer if found guilty, is to be remarked on."[1]

The reviewing officer, according to Assistant Adjutant General E. D. Townsend, "is convinced that the Court, in awarding so lenient a sentence for the offenses of which the accused is found guilty, must have taken into consideration his previous record."[2] Thus ended a review of justice.

Libbie, ever the faithful wife, had written to her friend Rebecca Richmond that "the trial had developed into nothing but a plan of persecution for Autie."[3] She added that she couldn't write much since

---

[1] J. Holt, *Review of the Trial of Gen. G. A. Custer for Shooting Deserters Without Trial; and of Leaving His Command Without Orders.*

[2] *Daily Conservative* (Leavenworth), January 19, 1868.

[3] Merington, *The Custer Story*, 213–14.

she had copied fifty pages of foolscap for the defense—"a labor of love, of course."

Thinking back over the events of the summer, Libbie had much to be thankful for. In her *Tenting On The Plains*[4] she tells us how Autie had been overwhelmed with the discouragements that he met when he first reached Fort Wallace; the wretched food, the men dying of cholera for lack of proper medical supplies, the poor communication. To add to his misery was the fear that she had succumbed to cholera, since he had received no letters from her for a considerable period of time. She, in turn, had been deeply concerned as to whether he had survived both the cholera and the Indian campaign. And when they met at Fort Riley, "There was in that summer of 1867 one long, perfect day."

The Special Artist for *Harper's Weekly* had been quite happy to see Fort Harker at the end of the grueling 700-mile horseback ride with Custer. He, Davis, had arrived at some conclusions which he did not hesitate to express. In an article prepared for *Harper's Monthly* it was his opinion that:

> A peace had lately been made with the Indians. This they will keep through the winter. If, when the grass is come again, they are not out on the warpath it will be contrary to the teachings of all previous experience.
>
> The Indians feel that they are rich when at war and poor while at peace; naturally they prefer war; that is, when they have it, as they invariably do, entirely in their own way. . . .
>
> There are many old chiefs who prefer peace, but the young men are invariably for war . . . .
>
> I have yet to meet the frontiersman who does not prefer peace with the Indians to war; and it is due these hardy men to say that few can realize the outrages they suffer at the hands of the redskins before they reach the trusty rifle that hangs in the antlers over the mud fireplace of the ranch, which is their home only so long as they are suffered by the Indians to occupy it.[5]

[4] Pages 700–702.

[5] Davis, "A Summer on the Plains," *loc. cit.*, 307; James W. Dixon, "Across the Plains With General Hancock," *Journal of the Military Service Institution* (June, 1886), 196.

The mounting public pressure on Congress resulted in the appointment of a Peace Commission in the latter part of July, 1867, aiming "to establish peace with certain hostile Indians."[6] It was authorized to confer with the various hostile chiefs in order to determine the cause of their hostility and, if feasible, to make treaties with them for the express purpose of: removing the cause of war; securing the frontier settlements and the safe building of the railroads; and developing some plan to civilize the Indians.

Shortly after the adjournment of Custer's court-martial on October 11, the Peace Commissioners convened, meeting at Medicine Lodge, Kansas, October 17. The better part of a month was utilized in listening to the various speakers and taking the testimony of witnesses. The commission consisted of: N. G. Taylor (Commissioner of Indian Affairs), President; Lieut. General W. T. Sherman; Major General William S. Harney; Senator J. B. Henderson; General John B. Sanborn; Major General Alfred H. Terry; Colonel S. F. Tappan; and Major General C. C. Augur.[7] Over five thousand Indians of the Kiowa, Arapaho, Cheyenne, Apache, and Comanche tribes, and their agents, were present.[8]

As the conference proceeded it became evident that this was not a case of reasonable men carefully weighing each other's views with the purpose of arriving at a just and acceptable conclusion. The four principal contestants soon formed alliances because of similarity of thinking. Civil officials representing the settlers and the railroads, along with the military, thought in common. The Indians and the representatives of the Bureau of Indian Affairs joined hands in their similar convictions. Thus, two sides formed and attempted to dominate the conference.

Governor Crawford, who was one of the witnesses, observed that the Indians believed that the more murders they committed and property they destroyed, the more presents they got from the Government; that capturing and selling women and children to the Government was more profitable than stealing horses.[9]

[6] Manypenny, *Our Indian Wards*, 194.
[7] *Ibid.*; *Report, Commissioner of Indian Affairs* for 1867, 2–4; Crawford, *Kansas*, 265.
[8] Stanley, *Early Travels*, I, 229; Crawford, *Kansas*, 272.
[9] Crawford, *Kansas*, 271.

On October 5 Crawford submitted a prepared statement to the president of the Peace Commission, Indian Commissioner N. G. Taylor. Primarily a report of the Indian depredations and atrocities committed in Kansas during 1865, 1866, and 1867, it concluded with an attack on the activities of J. H. Leavenworth, Indian agent for the Comanches and Kiowas. Crawford charged him with using his traders to supply the Indians with "everything necessary . . . to prosecute the war against our people," and ended the lengthy communication with the recommendation that Leavenworth be replaced by a reliable agent, since he was considered to be "directly responsible for many of the outrages committed by Indians."[10]

Commissioner Taylor had a different idea about the cause of the unrest. Believing that war springs from a sense of injustice, he thought war could be avoided by performing no unjust act. And that, "When we learn that the same rule holds with Indians, the chief difficulty is removed."[11]

In the conclusions offered to the President, the Peace Commission was emphatic in stating that they were not censuring General Hancock for having organized the expedition that summer, since "he had just come to the department, and circumstances were ingeniously woven to deceive him." And that, "if he erred, he can very well roll a part of the responsibility on others . . . ."[12]

Former Indian Commissioner George Manypenny took a dim view of any attempt to apologize for Hancock's conduct. Drawing attention to several military colleagues of Hancock on the Commission he offered that: "to thinking people, with the facts before them, no valid excuse can be given. . . . It was not his or General Custer's fault that only six Indians were killed in the campaign."[13]

It took the full capacity of the eloquent Sherman to gloss over the military inadequacy of the past summer. In his annual report to the House of Representatives he stated that Commissioner Buford was in error in tracing the cause of the spring outbreak to Hancock's burning of the Indian camp on Pawnee Fork in April. It was his belief there

[10] *Ibid.*, 265–72.

[11] *Report, Commissioner of Indian Affairs* for 1868, 502.

[12] *Ibid.*, 499; Manypenny, *Our Indian Wards*, 172.

[13] Manypenny, *Our Indian Wards*, 172–73.

was every evidence of a combined operation against all roads by the Sioux of the north and the Cheyennes, Arapahos and Kiowas of the south as soon as the grass grew. "General Hancock has made to me a full and satisfactory report . . . and I believe his movements so early in the spring prevented a combination that might otherwise have been vastly more destructive than it has been. To talk of those people [the Indians] desiring to live at peace with us, is to all men on the plains absurd. . . ."[14]

News correspondent Stanley had sympathized with the military, feeling that it was a thankless job fighting Indians, and gave the Peace Commission credit for changing the Indian feelings from wanting war to a desire for peace.[15]

At about this same time, the solution to one of the great mysteries of the year was about to unfold. The reader will recall the events leading up to the massacre of Lieutenant Lyman Kidder, his ten-soldier escort, and a Sioux Indian guide while he was carrying Sherman's message to Custer from Fort Sedgwick. Kidder was expected to meet Custer's command at the fork of the Republican River but, arriving too late, had followed the trail toward Fort Wallace, missing the fresh trail Custer had taken to the west.

Young Kidder had served during the struggle between the North and South as an officer and, subsequently, had refused to follow his father's footsteps in the practice of law, preferring the more exciting course of the army.[16] On the twenty-ninth of June his commandant, Lieutenant Colonel J. H. Potter, ordered him to carry very important dispatches to Custer.[17] He was instructed that: "Should General Custer have left that [the fork of the Republican River] point, you will take his trail and overtake him. After delivering your dispatches you will return to this post. Until you reach General Custer you will travel as rapidly as possible."[18]

[14] 40 Cong., 2 sess., *House Exec. Doc. 1*, 66.

[15] Stanley, *Early Travels*, I, 289–90.

[16] Brininstool, "The Kidder Massacre," *loc. cit.*, 12.

[17] Communication sent from Fort Sedgwick, C.T., July 25, 1867, by Lieutenant Colonel J. H. Potter to the Adjutant General. Record group No. 94, AGO-468-P-1867.

[18] Brininstool, "The Kidder Massacre," *loc. cit.*, 12.

The country through which they were to travel was swarming with hostile Indians. Why young Kidder (he was but twenty-five years old, with no previous experience against Indians) was selected for this important detail, accompanied by youngsters, only one of which was over his age, is a part of the mystery.[19] A seasoned scout would have balked at such hazardous duty.

Missing Custer's trail was his undoing—he had followed the larger trail created by the wagon train headed for Fort Wallace and supplies, thinking this was Custer's main cavalry column. Custer's remaining column had turned west. Kidder had no means of determining which of the columns Custer would remain with. From that point on his fate was sealed.

Once Lieutenant Kidder's father, Judge J. P. Kidder of Vermillion, Dakota, had received Colonel Custer's full and detailed account of his tragic death, the judge gave evidence that he was determined to obtain the remains of his son and remove them to St. Paul where other relatives had been buried. It was Custer's painful task to inform the grieving father that there was no possible chance of recognizing his son's body. He related their interview at Fort Leavenworth in his *Life on the Plains*:[20]

"Was there not the faintest mark or fragment of his uniform by which he might be known?" inquired the anxious parent. "Not one," was the reluctant reply. "And yet, since I now recall the appearance of the mangled and disfigured remains, there was a mere trifle which attracted my attention, but it could not have been your son who wore it." "What was it?" eagerly inquired the father. "It was simply the collar band of one of those ordinary check overshirts so commonly worn on the plains, the color being black and white; the remainder of the garment, as well as all other articles of dress, having been torn or burned from the body." Mr. Kidder then requested me to repeat the description of the collar and material of which it was made; happily I had some cloth of very similar appearance, and upon exhibiting this to Mr. Kidder, to show the kind I meant, he declared

[19] *Ibid.*, 12–13. Brininstool wrote that: "half of them were under five feet in height. Four were 19 years of age, three were 23, one was 22, one was 21, and one 36."

[20] Pages 100–101.

that the body I referred to could be none other than that of his murdered son."

Judge Kidder was greatly excited as he related how his wife had made two shirts, of a similar material, for her son. Mr. Kidder had been to Fort Sedgwick on the Platte River, and there determined that his son had worn a checkered shirt when leaving the post on his ill-fated mission.

Judge Kidder advised Custer by letter that it was his desire to disinter his son. In a letter addressed in late October he told him he could not start after his son's

... remains until about the middle of December next in consequence of my courts which come on between now and then. Where do you expect to be at that time? Where will Sergeant Connolly who prepared the graves be then? Some one who knows where the grave is should go with me, or I might not find it. Could I be furnished with transportation from Fort Hays by the government to the place where the bodies are for myself and to return with the remains? I want to know how this is, for, altho I should not hesitate in relation to the expense if within all I posses on earth if it should come out of me, yet I prefer to know just how it is before I start, that I may be prepared before I start.

Were the skeletons of the men separated at the joints? or were they whole? If separated, I might need a surgeon to find all the parts, even if I could identify the *head*, or any other part of the body.[21]

Custer replied in detail and ended by saying: "The skeletons of one perhaps two of the men were separated at the joints. That however which I now believe to have been that of your lamented son was not so separated, but was entire in all its parts."[22]

Lieutenant Henry Jackson, who was present at the burial and had received a similar inquiry from Judge Kidder, answered that:

The arms were on the body. The scalp was taken off with nearly all the hair it had only a little left near the neck at the back of the head. The skull was smashed in. There was a strip of the shirt left

[21] Letter from Judge J. P. Kidder to General Custer, dated October 22, 1867, Vermillion, Dakota. Original in author's collection.
[22] Letter from G. A. Custer to Hon. J. P. Kidder, Fort Leavenworth, Kansas, November 2, 1867. Copy in Dr. R. Burnside collection.

around the neck about three or four inches broad the rest was torn off. I cannot remember about the legs. I think they were off. The bodies had been so mutilated and dragged about by wolves. The bodies are buried on the trail from Fort Wallace to the Forks of the Republican on the north side of the creek—about 30 or 40 yards from the creek. . . . Sergeant Connolly is positive he can recognize the body of your son.[23]

The judge arrived at Fort Wallace in bitterly cold weather. Upon being furnished an escort he started out for the scene of the massacre. The graves were located after two days of searching and young Kidder was exhumed. His identification was complete once the black-and-white-checked collarband was found on his body. By this remarkable bit of evidence a devoted mother and father were able to identify and reclaim their son and give him proper burial.[24] On this tiny shred of evidence Judge Kidder had proceeded four hundred miles to Fort Wallace where, in the dead of the winter, with the aid of a military escort, he visited the grave of the massacred men. Thus was the manifest love of a mother for her son the means by which his body was recognized and claimed.[25]

Phil Sheridan was in New York when Custer's court-martial ended. On November 19 he wrote Autie, "I presume the court made everything right for you from what I have heard from some of the members—If not I feel certain that General Grant will."[26] It would appear that some of the members of the Court were "polishing the apple," for Major General Sheridan was the superior of every member of the Court. Custer was his favorite, and it wouldn't do to appear in Sheridan's eyes as one who went out of the way to prosecute his protégé.

Libbie managed to keep her closest friends informed. On the twentieth of November she advised Rebecca Richmond that Autie had received official notice and that "the sentence is as unjust as possible.

[23] Letter from Lieutenant Henry Jackson to J. P. Kidder, Fort Harker, Kansas, November 5, 1867. Copy in Dr. R. Burnside collection.
[24] Brininstool, "The Kidder Massacre," *loc. cit.*, 18; *Chicago Westerners Brand Book* (1962–63), 41–42.
[25] G. A. Custer, *My Life*, 101.
[26] Communication from Maj. Gen. P. H. Sheridan to Gen. Custer, New York, November 19, 1867. Original in author's collection.

Autie merits acquittal." The suspension of rank and pay proper did not bother them, she said, since their emoluments amounted to more than the $95 a month pay they would lose. On this they could live well enough. And they could be together for a year and a half.[27]

Autie, too, had more time to correspond. To Mr. Walker he wrote that he was beginning to write his memoirs, having completed fifty pages. About the trial he said:

> . . . All with whom I have conversed deem the verdict not sustained by the evidence, as I have been adjudged guilty on some specification on which the Judge Advocate declined to take testimony. I will go into particulars when I meet you.
>
> I have written General Sheridan to make no effort to obtain a remission of any portion of my sentence. I would not accept it.[28]

[27] Merington, *The Custer Story*, 214.
[28] *Ibid.*

XIII. JUSTIFICATION

December found Colonel Custer in a singular position. Following the promulgation of Custer's sentence, General Sheridan had been ordered to Fort Leavenworth, where he was to take over General Hancock's command.[1] Finding Custer without rank or quarters, he promptly offered Custer and his wife the use of his suite of apartments as long as they desired them. This offer they accepted, occupying the quarters till early summer. This impressive display of friendship, and the many others shown them by the officers of the Seventh Cavalry, made that winter a most enjoyable one for the Custers.[2]

Phil Sheridan wrote to Custer on December 12th from Somerset, Ohio:

> . . . I did not intend to occupy the large house so your occupation is alright. I will be at Leavenworth about the first week in January unless there is some change I have no reason to believe will take place. . . . I will be in Washington the 20th of this month. I hope to be able to look into your case a little more—even against your will—I had no reason to suppose any such punishment would be awarded when I wrote from New York.[3]

The newspapers across the country had carried various accounts of

[1] 40 Cong., 2 sess., *House Exec. Doc. No. 1*, 26–27.
[2] Merington, *The Custer Story*, 211.
[3] From the original in author's collection.

Custer's courtmartial, but perhaps none brought a more interesting reaction than one from his adopted state, Michigan. It all began in an editorial published in the Adrian, Michigan, *Times and Expositor* on December 9, 1867. Taking issue with an article in the Grand Rapids, Michigan, *Daily Eagle* under the heading "*Gen. Custars* [*sic*] *Case*"[4] in which the opinion was offered that Custer should have been shielded from "so petty a prosecution" and that "it is hoped that the gratitude of the country may yet be shown by the remission of the sentence," the editorial criticized Custer "for truckling to Andy Johnson," thereby securing his present command. It objected to any attempt on the part of the General or his friends "to cover his present short comings by an appeal to the past," particularly since they believed that the charge made of "cruelty to his men" carried more weight with the Court and with General Grant than that of "absence without leave." It was concluded that "when General Grant deems Custer guilty, there must be good and sufficient reasons for such a conclusion. . . ."

This article seemed to have started a minor chain reaction, for on December 28, 1867, the Detroit, Michigan, *Advertiser and Tribune* headed an article GENERAL CUSTER DEFENDS HIMSELF. It drew attention to a long letter written by Custer and published that same day in the Sandusky, Ohio, *Daily Register*. Mention was made of the charges of cruelty to his men and Custer's reply, and then the article indicated that "Gen. Custer complains of the composition of the Court that tried him, four members being his inferior in rank and one member a commissary who had been censured by him for corruption in issuing rations."

The Sandusky *Daily Register* of December twenty-eighth contained not only the lengthy letter of Custer's, but also an interesting editorial relating to it as follows:

> *General Custer*—Recently General GEORGE A. CUSTER, whose name during the war, was a household word, and a synonym for all that is dashing, brave, and successful, has been tried by courtmartial on charges preferred by General HANCOCK, convicted of some technical offences, and sentenced to be suspended from command for

[4] December 5, 1867. In the *Daily Eagle* Custer's name was spelled correctly.

one year. This misfortune of a gallant soldier has been taken advantage of by his enemies, personal and military, to put in circulation statements and reports as cruel as they are slanderous. A few days since we found in the Detroit *Tribune* an article taken from the Adrian (Michigan) *Times*, which pretended to give an authentic account of CUSTER's offences, and the leading statement was that "while making a long, forced march on the plains, a portion of General CUSTER's men and horses became exhausted, as in the case on all hard marches, and lagged behind; that CUSTER became enraged at this unavoidable straggling and sent back an officer with orders to *shoot* the tired and belated soldiers; that this order was literally obeyed, several men being shot, and that General CUSTER then refused to permit the wounded soldiers to ride in ambulances, of which there were several, but put them into jolting army wagons instead." Had the publication of this statement been confined to the obscure sheet with which it originated, no one would have noticed it, but after being copied without comment by the Detroit journals, published near CUSTER's home, we observed that it was circulating very generally through our exchanges in other parts of the country. Having served under General CUSTER's command during the better part of his singularly brilliant career, and still feeling a lively interest in the good name of a comrade whose temporary political error could not blind us to his great qualities as a soldier, or dim his well-earned fame, we inclosed him the statement referred to, expressing the belief that said statement was "either wholly false or grossly exaggerated." General CUSTER's reply will be found elsewhere. It is long, but fully repays a reading; and as it is the first word that has been published in his defense, and this not of his own motion, we trust that its substance will be as widely copied as have been the untruthful statements that called it forth. If the letter we publish is not a full vindication of its author's acts, it is at least such a palliation as will leave his record substantially without a stain. Without discussing the merits of the case, we close by remarking that the course which General CUSTER adopted to prevent the destruction of his command by desertion was obviously the only one suited to the emergency, and will commend itself to every reasonable man.

Custer's letter of December twenty-first followed. In general, it reviewed the entire proceedings of the court-martial, with an explanation of the various charges. He prefaced his statement with the remark that he would endeavor "to be wholly impartial and just," then went on to say "that while I desire to possess and retain the good opinion of all men, I particularly desire the confidence and esteem of those who shared with me the trials and dangers of a soldier's life during the war of the rebellion."[5]

Asserting that the alleged facts in the Adrian *Times* were totally untrue, Custer went into some detail to show that the charge of cruelty had been disproven in the testimony of his surgeon, Dr. Coates, and that the finding of the Court was regarded as equivalent to acquital since it had added to the finding, "and attaches no criminality thereto."

The editor of the Adrian *Times* had printed as factual:

> It is asserted that on one occasion, when on a scout, when horses and men had become fatigued some soldiers dropped to the rear as is the case in all long marches. Custer claimed that these soldiers intended to desert, and sent back an officer with instructions to shoot the tired men.

In reply to this allegation Custer quoted from the Court record the circumstances of mid-day desertion in the midst of the Indian country. He indicated that his summary measures were effective, since there were no further attempts at desertion while he remained in command.

Dwelling upon the charge of "absence without leave," Custer had no doubt that the testimony of several officers clearly proved he had not absented himself without authority. It had been his belief before the trial began that his problem would not be "in the character of the charges and specifications . . . but in the composition of the Court." Quoting the 75th Article of War and various other authorities to show that "No officer shall be tried . . . by officers of an inferior rank if it can be avoided," nor should an inferior officer, particularly without command experience, be permitted to sit in judgment upon a superior who has held a command, he indicated that of the eight officers detailed for the trial, four were his inferiors in rank, two being majors and two being captains.[6]

[5] The publisher of the Sandusky *Daily Register*, A. B. Nettleton, had served with Custer during the Civil War, having been breveted a brigadier general—see F. B. Heitman's *Historical Register, and Dictionary of the United States Army*.

[6] Major Michael R. Morgan, Major Thomas C. English, Captain Stephen C. Lyford and Captain Henry Asbury.

To add to his discomfiture "three of the officers composing the Court belonged to the General Staff, or Staff Corps of the army and, as such, are never called upon to exercise command of troops in the field . . ." nor had they ever commanded a company of troops. On this point he concluded that "Among the members of the Court, including therein the Judge Advocate, were three officers of General Hancock's staff,[7] one of whom is now his secretary."[8] His reason for not objecting to the several members of the Court referred to was the advice of counsel that "a failure to have the objectionable members removed would only serve to irritate them and prejudice my own interests."

Reference was made to General Hancock's statement offered to an officer immediately after the last set of charges was preferred by Captain West in which he was "sorry the last set of charges had been preferred against Custer, as he had not intended to notice his conduct disapprovingly in regard to his course with deserters . . . but . . . to suppress or pass unnoticed the second would have appeared inconsistent."

The letter ended in a categorical denial of all of the charges placed against him and the hope that he was able to "disabuse your mind of any unjust or undeserved impressions which might be derived from the slanderous statements put forth against me . . . ." And so ended his newspaper trial in the Midwest.

[7] Colonel Pitcairn Morrison, Major Michael R. Morgan and Captain Robert Chandler. Lieutenant Colonel John W. Davidson, who was removed from the Court as a result of Custer's objections, was a member of Hancock's Department staff. See *Returns for August, 1867*, Department of the Missouri, commanded by Maj. Gen. W. S. Hancock, among the records of the Adjutant General's Office, National Archives.

[8] Captain Robert Chandler became General Hancock's acting assistant adjutant general on November 29, 1867, when Hancock assumed command of the Fifth Military District at New Orleans. On January 25, 1868, Chandler was Hancock's assistant secretary of civil affairs. See 40 Cong., 3 sess., *House Exec. Doc. 1*, 202–203, 210.

XIV. RETURN
TO COMMAND

THE END OF 1867 did not mean that Custer's troubles were at an end. Hangovers on New Year's Day were not uncommon then and, even though a total abstainer, Custer was to have his for several weeks running. On January 4, 1868, the Leavenworth, Kansas, *Daily Conservative* published the following:

> A warrant was yesterday issued for Justice Adams' court, in this city, for the arrest of Gen. Geo. A. Custar [*sic*], U.S.A., and Lieut. W. W. Cook, of the 7th U.S. Cavalry, on a charge of murdering one Johnson, a soldier, who, it is claimed, was shot by Cook, under orders from Custar, in Colorado Territory, near Fort Sedgwick, Nebraska, on the 7th of July last. Constable Kirkham and Deputy Stillwell served the warrant, and the prisoners came down from the Fort last evening and gave bonds in the sum of $1,000 each for their appearance for examination on Wednesday, the 8th inst., before Justice Adams. Gen. A. J. Smith and Surgeon M. Madison Mills are their bondsmen.

Defended by W. P. Gambell and E. N. O. Clough, Custer and Cook's case commenced before Judge Adams on Wednesday, January 8. On a motion by the defense counsel to dismiss the case on the grounds of informalities, and a question of the jurisdiction of Justice Adams in this case, the motion was granted and the prisoners discharged.

A warrant was issued after a new complaint was filed, and by 2:00 P.M. Custer and Cook had been re-arrested and a new examination had begun.

Captain Robert M. West was the first to testify, giving the Court a description of the episode of July 7 that had ended in the death of one of his company, Charles Johnson.[1] He told of his lack of confidence in the attending surgeon of the command, and how he had requested the assistant surgeon at Fort Wallace, Assistant Surgeon Turner, to examine Johnson, and how he had done so. He completed his testimony by telling of the burial of Johnson by the men of his company, and that he had read the Episcopal service over his grave.

On cross-examination, he recalled seeing six men leave camp, although he had not known who they were. After a roll call, he had reported the absence of the men to Custer and had included Johnson's name among those missing. Then he remembered telling Colonel Custer that Johnson was a desperate man and would not be brought back without a fight. He recalled that two armed parties were sent in pursuit; the first under Major J. H. Elliott, and the second commanded by Lieutenant Henry Jackson.

Lieutenant Henry Jackson then gave testimony on January 9 that he had been given an order by Colonel Custer to take his guard and pursue the deserters; to shoot them; and to bring none back alive. He related how he had overtaken two men and sent them back to camp, and then started after the other men who had gone over the hill. When he came up on the hill he had seen Johnson lying on the ground wounded, but had seen none of the shooting. He had been left in charge of the wounded men, waiting with them until the wagons came, and then accompanied them back to camp.

Clement Willis, one of the deserters from Company K, testified that he was ten steps from Johnson when he saw Lieutenant Cook shoot him with a revolver. He told of being in a ravine, when they

[1] Merington, *The Custer Story*, 211: Letter from Custer to Mr. Walker, September, 1867, "West is drinking himself to death, has *delirium tremens*, to such an extent the Prosecution will not put him on the witness stand." Although it has no direct bearing except in judgment of character, it is interesting to know that West was placed under arrest the following month on charges of drunkenness while on duty several times, of which the Court found him guilty in part. See JAGO files, Records group No. 153 for December 23, 1867.

received a command to halt and give up their arms. This, he said, they had complied with, and then were told to leave. He said they began to run, and Major Elliott, Lieutenants Custer, Cook, and their men began to fire. Johnson, when shot in the arm, fell to his knees begging not to be killed. He stated that Lieutenant Cook then shot him in the head. After that Johnson asked him to kill him; to finish him off. He then related how he visited Johnson each day until his death on July 16.

Lieutenant Myles Moylan then testified that about an hour after the men had gone in pursuit of the deserters a bugler had returned from Major Elliott with a request to Colonel Custer for wagons for the wounded. Custer had immediately ordered one of the wagons unloaded and sent out. It returned in about an hour loaded with the three wounded men. He believed that Custer had not denied proper medical attention. He then concluded that the affair took place nine and a half days from Fort Wallace.

On January 19, the Leavenworth *Daily Conservative* printed the following:

MAJ. GEN. CUSTAR.—Gen. Geo. A. Custar [*sic*] was yesterday discharged from arrest upon the charge of murder, upon which he has been for several days undergoing examination. The charge, the Judge finds, was not sustained by evidence.

It is not in our heart to kick a falling man, and we have, therefore, abstained from all comment touching his offenses against military law, and his trial, conviction and sentence by a court martial.

Even after he had been so unwise as to appeal to the public through the press, for vindication against the mercy-tempered judgment of the court; which compelled Gen. Grant, as reviewing officer, to say that "the court in awarding so lenient a sentence for the offences of which the accused is found guilty, must have taken into consideration his previous services." Even after this, we say, we should not have called public attention to the matter had not Gen. Custar presented us with a copy of his newspaper defense, with the remark, "use it as you see fit."

It is a letter to Col. Nettleton, editor of the Sandusky, Ohio, Register, and occupies nearly four columns of that paper, under the head of "A Complete Defense." The gist of the whole article is this: That the conviction did not rest upon the charges and specifications upon which he was arraigned, but upon the composition of the court, which he more than intimates was a packed one, at the instance of Gen. Hancock, who was his accuser. He says: "Among the members of the court, including therein the Judge Advocate, were three officers of Gen. Hancock's staff, one of whom is now his private secretary. One of these staff officers *at least* had a biased opinion against me and had prejudged me before the trial."

We object to this wholesale charge of perjury against the members of the court martial. It is not reasonable that Gen. Custar could not secure an impartial court. That he had such an one is clear to us by the unfair means used to prove it otherwise. The General speaks of the Judge Advocate as a member of the court, which any one conversant with the composition of such bodies knows is not the case. One of the other staff officers he objected of, so there was but one of Gen. Hancock's staff instead of three in the court.

The gentleman receiving this threat, as Judge Advocate, was Capt. Robert Chandler, a man *we know* to be utterly incapable of crowding a hair's breadth upon his oath or the strictest rules of justice. He is a man of method, not of passion. He entered the service from civil life, and has to-day a reputation less broad, but quite as solid as that of Gen. Custar.

Gen. Custar illustrates the danger of putting upon a man more honor and responsibility than he can carry. He was fortunately surrounded with political influences that kept his promotions far ahead of his earnings all through the service. He had a great deal of "dash," that gave him popularity, because officers less in rank, and men equal in valor, generously paid the penalty of his rashness, and redeemed his mistakes with the dogged valor of true soldiers.

Yet he attained high distinction, and we profoundly regret that he has not had the wisdom to retain his laurels, whether earned or not. We regretted his becoming a political prostitute in the harem of Andrew Johnson. We regret his military disgrace, and would not have aided its publicity had he not forced himself upon the press.

In answer to all the criticism heaped upon Custer when he chose to accompany and support President Johnson on a political tour just the year before (1866), he had answered General R. A. Alger's query about it with:

The personal spleen which may be indulged in by those who are only familiar with paper-bullets will have but little effect upon one who has been exposed to bullets of a more deadly character. As I have survived the latter, I certainly need not fear the former.[2]

He retained the same equilibrium when writing of his experience in his *My Life On The Plains*, by refusing to introduce the details of the court-martial or its postludes. The matter was disposed of in the statement, "It will suffice to say that I was placed in temporary retirement from active duty, and this result seemed satisfactory to those parties most intimately concerned in the matter."[3]

Whittaker wrote that it hardly could be said Custer did penance for his misdeeds in leaving Fort Wallace, for he had quite an agreeable time with his comrades at Fort Leavenworth, meanwhile availing himself of General Sheridan's proffered apartment there.[4]

The arrival of spring brought a change of feeling to Custer. To indulge in the comradery that winter brings to the barracks is one thing; to see his comrades-in-arms prepare for the summer campaigns was another. In June, Custer and Libbie left for Monroe, Michigan.

In this beautiful little town on the shore of Lake Erie, he was able to hunt, fish, and boat with many of his old friends and companions. It was here that he wrote a major part of the memoirs that were to be published later. Detroit was only thirty-five miles away; Toledo, twenty. Yet, in spite of the pleasantness of his surroundings and his companions, he constantly longed for his comrades in the far west, even though he knew their efforts were unsuccessful.[5]

Reports had been coming through that the campaign General Sully had been conducting as a reprisal against the raiding Indians was unsuccessful. General Sully had been defeated that summer when he had led the Seventh Cavalry and some infantry against the combined forces of the Cheyennes, Kiowas, and Arapahos, near Camp Supply. General Sandy Forsyth and a company of men were nearly wiped out by the Sioux.[6]

[2] Communication from Custer to Gen. R. A. Alger, Monroe, Mich., October 3, 1866, published in the Monroe *Commercial*, October 11, 1866.

[3] Page 124.

[4] *A Life of Gen. Custer*, 413.

[5] G. A. Custer, *My Life*, 124.

[6] Battle of Beechers Island, Colorado, September 17, 18, 1868.

One wonders what Custer thought when he picked up the Monroe *Commercial* on August 27, 1868, and read the following:

> THE INDIAN OUTRAGES IN KANSAS—Dispatches from Gen. Sheridan confirm the press dispatches about the Indian outrages. Gen. Sheridan says the outrages are too horrible to detail. Gen. Sherman orders Gen. Sheridan to continue the pursuit and drive the savages from that section of the country, and when captured to give them summary punishment. The Secretary of War communicated the intelligence to the president, who acquiesced in the stringent measures which the Secretary of War and Gen. Sherman are taking in the matter.
>
> Gen. Sheridan has issued an order that the Indians committing the outrages (Cheyennes and Arapahoes), be forcibly driven to their reservation south of Kansas, and that they be compelled to deliver up the perpetrators of the acts.

Then it happened: Custer was dining at the home of a friend in Monroe on the evening of September 24, when a telegram was delivered to him:

> HEADQUARTERS DEPARTMENT OF THE MISSOURI,
> IN THE FIELD, FORT HAYS, KANSAS, September 24, 1868
> *To General G. A. Custer, Monroe, Michigan*
> Generals Sherman, Sully, and myself, and nearly all the officers of your regiment, have asked for you, and I hope the applications will be successful. Can you come at once? Eleven companies of your regiment will move about the first of October against the hostile Indians, from Medicine Lodge Creek toward the Wichita mountains.
>
> (signed) P. H. SHERIDAN[7]
Major General Commanding

The depth of his gratification would have been difficult to fathom. His first reaction was to telegraph General Sheridan that he would leave on the next train to join him. It was his firm belief that the application of Generals Sherman and Sheridan, as well as the other officers, would bring a favorable response from Washington authorities. He wrote:

[7] G. A. Custer, *My Life*, 125.

The following day found me on a railway train hastening to the plains as fast as the iron horse could carry me. The expected order from Washington overtook me that day in shape of an official telegram from the Adjutant General of the Army, directing me to proceed at once and report for duty to General Sheridan.[8]

Custer arrived at Fort Hays on the morning of September 30 and reported immediately to General Sheridan. At the time, his regiment was near the Arkansas River southeast of Fort Dodge. On October 4 he wrote to Libbie from Fort Hays:

> I breakfasted with Genl. Sheridan and staff. He said, "Custer, I rely on you in everything, and shall send you on this expedition without orders, leaving you to act entirely on your own judgment."[9]

No more than arriving at the Seventh Cavalry camp several days later he was welcomed with an Indian attack upon the camp by a band of warriors. The Washita campaign had begun.

[8] *Ibid.*
[9] Merington, *The Custer Story*, 217.

BIBLIOGRAPHY

Books

Athearn, Robert G. *William Tecumseh Sherman and the Settlement of the West.* Norman, 1956.

Bates, Charles Francis. *Custer's Indian Battles.* Bronxville, 1936.

Bell, William A. *New Tracks In North America.* 2 vols. London, 1869.

Benét, S. V. *A Treatise on Military Law and the Practice of Courts-Martial.* New York, 1866.

Berthrong, Donald J. *The Southern Cheyennes.* Norman, 1963.

Billington, Ray Allen. *Soldier & Brave.* New York, 1863.

Brown, Dee. *Fort Phil Kearny–An American Saga.* New York, 1962.

Browning, Orville. *The Diary of Orville Hickman Browning.* 2 vols. Springfield, Ill., 1933.

Cameron, Simon. *Revised United States Army Regulations of 1861.* Washington, 1863.

Carrington, Henry B. *Ab-Sa-Ra-Ka.* Philadelphia, 1879.

———. *Some Phases of the Indian Question.* Boston, 1909.

———. *The Indian Question.* Boston, 1884.

Chandler, Melbourne C. *Of Garryowen and Glory.* Washington, 1960.

Craig, Reginal S. *The Fighting Parson.* Los Angeles, 1959.

Crawford, Samuel J. *Kansas In the Sixties.* Chicago, 1911.

Crofutt, Geo. A. *Great Trans-Continental Tourist's Guide*. New York, 1870.

Custer, Elizabeth B. *Tenting on the Plains*. New York, 1887.

Custer, George A. *My Life on the Plains*. New York, 1874.

Dellenbaugh, Frederick S. *George Armstrong Custer*. New York, 1917.

Dodge, Richard I. *The Black Hills*. New York, 1876.

——. *The Hunting Grounds of the Great West*. London, 1878.

Everett, Robinson O. *Military Justice in the Armed Forces of the U.S.* Harrisburg, Pa., 1956.

Gard, Wayne. *The Great Buffalo Hunt*. New York, 1960.

Grinnell, George Bird. *The Fighting Cheyennes*. New York, 1915.

Hart, Herbert M. *Old Forts of the Northwest*. Seattle, 1963.

Hassrick, Royal B. *The Sioux*. Norman, 1964.

Hodge, Frederick W. *Handbook of American Indians*. 2 vols. New York, 1959.

Holmes, Louis A. *Fort McPherson*. Lincoln, Nebr., 1963.

Hunt, Elvid. *History of Fort Leavenworth*. Fort Leavenworth, Kans., 1926.

Leckie, William H. *The Military Conquest of the Southern Plains*. Norman, 1963.

Long, Margaret. *The Smoky Hill Trail*. Denver, 1947.

Manypenny, George W. *Our Indian Wards*. Cincinnati, 1880.

Merington, Marguerite. *The Custer Story*. New York, 1950.

Monaghan, Jay. *The Life of General George Armstrong Custer*. Boston, 1959.

Parker, W. Thornton. *Personal Experiences Among Our North American Indians*. Northampton, 1913.

Perkins, J. R. *Trails, Rails and War*. Indianapolis, 1929.

Pride, W. F. *The History of Fort Riley*. n.p. 1926.

Rister, Carl Coke. *Border Captives*. Norman, 1940.

Rodenbaugh, Theo. F. *From Everglade to Canon with the Second Dragoons*. New York, 1875.

Roenigk, Adolph. *Pioneer History of Kansas*. Denver, 1933.

Root, F. A. and Connelley, W. E. *The Overland Stage to California*. Columbus, Ohio, 1950.

Rosa, Joseph G. *They Called Him Wild Bill*. Norman, Okla., 1964.

Russell, Don. *The Lives and Legends of Buffalo Bill*. Norman, 1960.

Ruth, Kent. *Great Day in the West*. Norman, 1963.

Stanley, Henry M. *My Early Travels and Adventures*. 2 vols. London, 1895.

Ware, Eugene F. *The Indian War of 1864*. Topeka, 1911.

Welles, Gideon. *The Diary of Gideon Welles*. 3 vols. New York, 1911.

Whitman, S. E. *The Troopers*. New York, 1962.

Whittaker, Frederick. *A Complete Life of Gen. George A. Custer*. New York, 1876.

Wilder, D. W. *Annals of Kansas 1541–1885*. Topeka, 1886.

Wyman, Walker D. *The Wild Horse of the West*. Caldwell, Idaho, 1946.

Printed Documents

Army Register. 1866, 1867, 1868.

Barracks and Hospitals Circular No. 4. Washington, 1870.

Carrington, Henry B. *Indian Operations on the Plains*. 50th Cong., 1 sess., *Senate Exec. Doc. No. 33*.

Condition of the Indian Tribes. Report, Joint Special Committee, Washington, 1867.

Difficulties with the Indian Tribes. 41st Cong., 2 sess., *H. R. Exec. Doc. No. 240*.

Drill Regulations for the Cavalry, United States Army. Washington, 1896.

Heitman, Francis B. *Historical Register and Dictionary of the United States Army*. 2 vols. Washington, 1896.

House Report. 38 Cong., 2 sess.

———. 41 Cong., 2 sess., *Exec. Doc. No. 240*.

Kappler, Charles J. *Indian Affairs; Laws and Treaties*. 3 vols. Washington, 1913.

Manual for Courts-Martial, United States. Exec. Order No. 10214, Washington, 1951.

Military Posts Division of the Missouri. Washington, 1876.

Report, Commissioner of Indian Affairs. Washington, 1866.

———. Washington, 1867.

———. Washington, 1868.

Report, Indians Taxed and Not Taxed in the U.S. 11th Census. Washington, 1894.

Report, Secretary of War. 40th Cong., 3 sess., *H.R. Exec. Doc. No. 1.*
———. 40th Cong., 2 sess.

Revised United States Army Regulations of 1861. Washington, 1863.

Manuscripts

Alterations and Returns of the Seventh U.S. Cavalry for July 1867. Records Group No. 94.

Court of Claims, Indian Depredations; Wells, Fargo Co. VS United States–1867. Topeka.

General Court Martial of Captain Robert M. West at Fort Leavenworth, Kansas, December 23, 1867. Records Group No. 153, Office of the Judge Advocate General.

Holt, J. *Review of the Trial of Gen. G. A. Custer for Shooting Deserters Without Trial, and of Leaving His Command Without Orders.* Bureau of Military Justice, November 8, 1867.

Jackson, Lt. Henry. *Itinerary of the March of the United States Seventh Cavalry–1867.*

National Archives, Washington:
Fort Hays, Kansas, Special Orders.
Letters Received, Miscellaneous Branch, Adjutant General's Files, 1867.
  1. Capt. Robert Chandler
  2. Lt. Col. G. A. Custer
  3. Maj. Gen. W. S. Hancock
  4. Lt. Lyman B. Kidder
  5. Maj. Gen. P. H. Sheridan
  6. Lt. Gen. W. T. Sherman
  7. Col. A. J. Smith
Record Group No. 94–1867.
List of Re-interments, Fort Wallace, Kansas.
Post Returns, Fort Wallace, Kansas, July 1867.
Records of Deceased Citizens, Fort Wallace, Kansas.
Records of Deceased Soldiers, Fort Wallace, Kansas.

Proceedings of a General Court Martial at Fort Leavenworth, Kan-

sas for the Trial of Brevet Major-General G. A. Custer, September 15, 1867.

Periodicals

Blackburn, Forrest R. "The 18th Kansas Cavalry and the Indian War," *The Trail Guide* (Kansas City) (March, 1964).

Brininstool, E. A. "The Kidder Massacre," *Hunter-Trader-Trapper*, Vol. LXV, No. 6 (December, 1932).

Davis, Theo. R. "A Summer on the Plains," *Harper's Monthly Magazine*, Vol. XXXVI (February, 1868).

Dixon, James W. "Across the Plains with General Hancock," *Journal of the Military Service Institution* (June, 1886).

Gray, John S. "The Kidder Massacre," *The Westerners Brand Book* (Chicago), Vol. XIX, No. 6 (August, 1962).

———. "Will Comstock–The Natty Bumppo of Kansas," *The Westerners Brand Book* (Chicago), Vol. XVIII, No. 12 (February, 1962).

Harper's Weekly (1867).

Inman, Mrs. Henry. "Memories of Old Fort Harker," *True West Magazine*, Vol. 11, No. 4 (March–April, 1964).

Kansas Historical Collection. Topeka, 1926–28.

Kansas Historical Quarterly (Topeka), Vol. XXIII (1957).

Mattison, Ray H. "The Army Post on the Northern Plains," *Nebraska History Magazine*, Vol. XXXV, No. 1 (March, 1954).

Montgomery, Mrs. Frank. "Fort Wallace and its Relation to the Frontier," *Kansas Historical Collections*, Vol. XVII (1928).

Nye, Col. E. L. "Marching With Custer," *Veterinary Bulletin* (April, 1941).

Unrau, William E. "The Story of Fort Larned," *Kansas Historical Quarterly*, Vol. XXIII, No. 3 (August, 1957).

Newspapers

Advertiser and Tribune, Detroit, Michigan, 1867.

Commercial, Monroe, Michigan, 1866, 1867, 1868.

Daily Conservative, Leavenworth, Kansas, 1868.

Daily Eagle, Grand Rapids, Michigan, 1867.

Register, Sandusky, Ohio, 1867.

Times and Expositor, Adrian, Michigan, 1867.

INDEX

273

107, 109, 114, 117–18, 120–23, 127,
132, 134–35, 137–38, 146, 149–50,
174, 176–77, 191, 193–94, 206, 230,
237, 239–41, 253, 266; *see also*
"Old" Fort Hays
Fort Laramie, Wyoming Territory: 6,
46
Fort Larned, Kansas: 9, 16–17, 28–29,
31, 81 n., 127
Fort Leavenworth, Kansas: 29n., 31,
51, 54, 86, 88–89, 92 & n., 96, 104,
114–16, 125, 130–31, 149, 156, 201–
202, 208–209, 225, 252, 256, 265
Fort Lyon, Colorado Territory: 127
Fort McPherson, Nebraska: 6, 37, 42,
44–47, 49, 54, 60, 105, 124–25, 192,
218–19, 238, 240
Fort Morgan, Colorado Territory: 125,
202, 244
Fort Phil Kearny, Dakota Territory:
6–7, 44
Fort Reynolds, Colorado Territory: 127
Fort Riley, Kansas: 5, 7, 13, 51, 81n.,
85–86, 89, 93 & n., 119, 130, 149–
50, 174, 214, 217–18, 226–28, 237–
38, 245, 248
Fort Sanders, Wyoming Territory: 209
Fort Sedgwick, Nebraska: 34, 37, 41,
46–48 & n., 49, 52–54, 65n., 67, 69,
75–76, 85, 101–102, 104n., 105, 125,
156, 161, 174, 209, 219, 221, 251,
253, 261
Fort Union, New Mexico: 54
Fort Wallace, Kansas: 20, 34, 37, 47,
49, 51–54, 57, 59–60, 64n., 69, 74,
76–78, 80–81 & n., 83, 86–89, 91,
93, 99, 100–102, 104–107, 109–111,
114, 117–18, 121–23, 127, 131–34,
137–38, 142–43, 146, 149, 156, 162,
165, 169, 170, 172, 174, 176, 178,
180–81, 183–84, 191, 193–94, 196,
199–200, 204, 207, 214, 217–25,
227, 237–40, 242, 244, 248, 251–52,
254, 262–63, 265
Fossil Creek Station, Kansas: 25
Fourth United States Artillery: 16, 42
Fourth United States Infantry: 48

Gambell, W. P.: 261
Grand Rapids, Michigan: 257
Grant, Lieutenant General Ulysses S.: 6,
10–11, 86, 96, 164, 247, 254, 257,
263
"Great American Desert": 4
Grierson, Colonel Benjamin H.: 96–97,
177, 216
Grinnell's Springs, Kansas (stage sta-
tion): 133, 138
Guerrier, Edmond (interpreter): 17, 19

Hale, First Lieutenant Owen: 91
Hamilton, Alexander: 104n.
Hamilton, Captain Louis M.: 57–60,
81, 85–86, 91, 93, 100, 104 & n.,
132, 137–38, 142, 144–46, 183–84,
193, 199, 206, 229, 231, 238, 240–
41, 253
Hancock, Major General Winfield
Scott: spring campaign in 1867, 7,
11, 46; restricts sales of firearms, 8;
mobilizes troops, 12–13; conference
with Indians, 16–19, 22, 27–28; destruction of Indian village, 21, 23–
26; campaign, 31; at Fort Wallace,
34, 49, 51, 80, 156, 199–200, 221–
24, 226, 244, 250–51; replaced by
Major General Philip H. Sheridan,
87, 260n.; Hancock expedition, 33,
35n., 36, 41, 53, 85, 87–88, 219–
20, 234, 238–39, 256, 258, 260, 264;
charges against Custer, 89 & n.
Harney, Brigadier General William S.:
249
Harper, S. N.: 194, 232
Harris, Corporal: 80
Hays City, Kansas: 105n.
Henderson, United States Senator J. B.
(of Missouri): 87, 249
Henshaw (stage station): 117
Hide hunters: 31n.
Hill, Mr.: 206
Hoffman, Colonel William: 96, 198,
216, 237
Hunt, Governor (of Colorado): 41
Hunt, Major Lewis C.: 48

277